To John Garv...
Friend and colleague
With gratitude
Carl A. Anderson

PRAISE FOR
THESE LIBERTIES WE HOLD SACRED

"... the key to resolving America's most corrosive social issues."

In this collection of essays, Carl Anderson shows why the Knights of Columbus have flourished under his leadership for two decades. He reminds us that the things we cherish most—liberty, love, life—are God's gifts. That article of faith is not a pious observation, but the key to resolving America's most corrosive social issues.

—JOHN GARVEY, President,
The Catholic University of America

"[Offers] clarity in analyzing concrete problems and putting forward solutions."

We are facing several challenges that could turn lethal: hatred for life, radical Islam, and the growing gap between communities in modern countries. For us to meet them, some virtues are called for. An intellectual one: clarity in analyzing concrete problems and putting forward solutions. One halfway between the intellectual and the moral: the ability to put one's finger where it hurts and call a spade a spade. And a moral one, verging on the theological: love of one's enemies and readiness to forgive. Carl Anderson's book is a case for those virtues and an example of them.

—REMI BRAGUE, Emeritus Professor of Medieval and
Arabic Philosophy, The Sorbonne, The University of Paris I

"compelling and thoughtful"

Carl Anderson opens the text of this compelling and thoughtful book with Jefferson's famous question about whether a nation can survive for long if it forgets that its freedoms and liberties are gifts derived from God.

In answering Jefferson's question he calls up George Washington's proposition that religious faith is not merely a private matter but is central to the country's inner workings and to what makes for a good society. And then he asks his readers the central question: *What should America be? Can its promise of liberty and justice for all be fulfilled?*

In providing answers, and woven into a rich narrative, is the inspiring story of the founding and work of the remarkable Knights of Columbus. Its founder, Father McGivney, answered Jefferson's question by insisting that Catholics had a duty to play their part and to use their gifs to enliven and animate civic society.

Through their extraordinary work, the Knights have remained true to these founding ideals, and use their skills and resources as gifts for the common good.

In returning to these old questions and challenges, Carl Anderson does so with new and fresh insights and contemporary answers. It's a book that should be read by anyone who wants to make a difference.

—David Alton,
Lord Alton of Liverpool, House of Lords

THESE LIBERTIES WE HOLD SACRED

CARL ANDERSON

SQUAREONE
PUBLISHERS

Cover Designer: Jeannie Rosado
In-House Editor: Joanne Abrams
Typesetter: Gary A. Rosenberg

Square One Publishers
115 Herricks Road
Garden City Park, NY 11040
(516) 535-2010 • (877) 900-BOOK
www.squareonepublishers.com

**Library of Congress Cataloging-in-Publication Data
is on file with the Library of Congress**

LCCN: 2020938680

ISBN: 978-0-7570-0504-6 (hb) / 978-0-7570-5504-1 (eb)

Printed in the United States of America

10   9   8   7   6   5   4   3   2   1

Contents

Acknowledgments

Since this is chiefly a book of speeches, I think it only right that I begin by thanking those whose dedication to the craft of public speaking has helped shaped my own. For four years I had the privilege of serving as a member of the White House staff of President Ronald Reagan. During that time, I got to know and admire colleagues such as Ben Elliott, Peggy Noonan, and Anthony Dolan—some of the best speechwriters of the modern American presidency. Ronald Reagan was truly the "Great Communicator" and he made it look easy. But the effortlessness he exhibited hid the hard work and personal sacrifice that was the daily price paid by those in the White House speechwriters office. Three decades later, I still found myself while working late into the night asking, "How would Ben or Peggy or Tony say this?" I have benefited immensely from the standard they set.

I left the White House staff in 1987 to serve in the newly created position of Vice President for Public Policy of the Knights of Columbus and to establish an office for the Order in Washington, D.C. Opening the Washington Office for Public Policy of the Knights of Columbus afforded me the opportunity to work closely for more than a decade with the senior executives of the Order, including my predecessor as Supreme Knight, the late Virgil C. Dechant, and others such as Charles Reisbeck and Robert Lane. One could not hope to have more dedicated Catholic fraternalists than these as colleagues. I owe them a great debt of gratitude.

This time in Washington was also a period of friendship and support by my brother Knights in the District of Columbia whose dedication and service has been a continuous inspiration to me. They are the best sign of Father Michael McGivney's genius of empowering men to respond to so many of the social evils of our day. In particular, I am grateful for the cooperation of friends such as James Tolliver, George Hanna, and Anthony Colbert, as together we worked our way "up the chairs."

Also, in 1987, I began to serve in another newly created position, Vice President of the Pontifical John Paul II Institute for Studies on Marriage and Family as I put in place the Washington campus for this graduate school of theology. This initiative was the result of my discussions with Pope John Paul II and the president of the Institute at that time, Monsignor Carlo Caffarra. The Institute had been established in Rome six years earlier by the pope, and I had been teaching there as a visiting professor since 1983. My association with the Institute—and, through it, with Pope John Paul II himself—opened up a unique window into his pontificate, theology, and understanding of the workings of the Vatican. This would lead to more than a three-decade relationship with the faculties in both Rome and Washington and theologians such as Cardinals Angelo Scola, Marc Ouellett, P.S.S., and Joseph Ratzinger. I will always be grateful to my faculty colleagues in Washington, David L. Schindler, Father Antonio Lopez, F.S.C.B., David Crawford, Joseph Atkinson, Michael Hanby, Nicholas Healy, Margaret Harper McCarthy, D.C. Schindler, and John Haas. And I am deeply thankful to those professors at the Dominican House of Studies who were instrumental in the early years of the Institute in Washington, Father Romanus Cessario, O.P., Father Gabriel O'Donnell, O.P., Father John Farren, O.P., and Archbishop Joseph Augustine Di Noia, O.P.

I am grateful to colleagues with whom I collaborated on earlier books: Father Jose Granados, dcjm, and Monsignor Livio Melina. Stanislaw Grygiel—who, with Jaroslaw Kupczak, O.P., was instrumental in establishing the Knights of Columbus in Poland—remains a dear friend whose counsel has been invaluable. Bishop Jean Laffitte remains a friend and colleague not only at the Institute but through our collaboration on the Pontifical Council for the Family and the Pontifical Academy for Life. I am deeply grateful for his guidance in bringing the Knights of Columbus to France.

My journey with this extraordinary academic community eventually led to the decision to establish the St. John Paul II National Shrine in Washington, D.C.

As Supreme Knight, it has been my privilege to be joined by a new generation of fraternal leaders whose counsel, expertise, and determination have been nothing less than stellar: Jean Migneault, Charles Foos, Deacon Kenneth Ryan, Pat Cipollone, Edward Mullen, Donald Kehoe, Paul Devin, John O'Reilly, Dennis Savoie, John Marrella, Charles Maurer, Logan Ludwig, Dennis Stoddard, John Kennedy, Anthony Minopoli, Ronald Schwarz, Michael O'Connor, and Patrick Kelly.

At the beginning of 2001, I traveled to the Basilica of Our Lady of Guadalupe in Mexico City with the Knights of Columbus Board of Directors to be installed as Supreme Knight. Many years after his first visit to the Basilica, Pope John Paul II would write, "To some degree, this pilgrimage inspired and shaped all the succeeding years of my pontificate."[1] I would say the same of my tenure as Supreme Knight; not the least of which is my collaboration and friendship with the postulator of the cause of Saint Juan Diego, Monsignor Eduardo Chavez, whose dedication led to our co-authoring *Our Lady of Guadalupe: Mother of the Civilization of Love* in 2009.

I am deeply grateful to Stephen Feiler—no one could ask for a more dedicated and talented assistant than he has been to me; he has been a tremendous help in ways too numerous to mention. Special thanks are due to my executive assistant for two decades, Kathleen Kowalczyk, for her patience and diligence. I have been helped immensely by the professionalism of my current assistant, Mary-Ann Luczak, as well as that of Julie White. A special thanks to Greg Mueller and Stephen Ford for their advice and suggestions, which have been invaluable. It has been a pleasure to work with Rudy Shur and Joanne Abrams at Square One Publishers. I am greatly obliged to them for their support and counsel, and for making this book so much better.

A great debt of gratitude is owed to my friend and colleague of many years William Gribbin, who for me remains the gold standard of dedicated public service in our nation's Capital. In a city defined by hubris and towering egos, Bill has always put principle above personality and effectiveness over the limelight. His friendship has been one of life's great gifts. So much of what is good in these pages is a result of his wise counsel.

For fifteen years, Andrew Walther had been one of my close associates on a number of the projects discussed in this book, and with his wife, Maureen, he has been invaluable in preparing these speeches for publication. His untimely death just weeks before the completion of this project was a great personal loss to me. He will be missed by so many.

Blessed Michael McGivney is widely recognized for his humility and confidence in entrusting the leadership of the Knights of Columbus to the laity. I have been blessed during most of my tenure as Supreme Knight by the dedication of a true spiritual son of our founder as our Supreme Chaplain—and for me that has made all the difference. Archbishop William Lori of Baltimore is a friend of nearly four decades whose companionship and steady compass I am grateful for beyond my ability to express.

Several years ago, during a visit to Vienna, my wife, Dorian, and I visited Antonio Canova's extraordinary tomb for Maria Christina of Austria, on which is inscribed the Latin phrase "Vxori Optimae." No two words could better describe what Dorian has been to me as we approach five decades of marriage. She has read every word of my speeches before delivery, and many were never publicly spoken because of her sound advice. Her contribution to this project has been paramount and is emblematic of a life of generosity to me and our family. This book is dedicated to her with gratitude for being the "best wife" and, through her, to our five children and eleven grandchildren, who each in their unique way has brought joy into our lives.

Introduction

"Can the liberties of a nation be thought secure when we
have removed their only firm basis, a conviction in the minds
of the people that these liberties are the gifts of God?"
—THOMAS JEFFERSON, NOTES ON
THE STATE OF VIRGINIA, QUERY XVIII, 1781

What should America be? Can its promise of liberty and justice for all be fulfilled?

These questions—over the past year—seem to be tearing our country apart. Is there a greatness or promise in our constitution that should be embraced, or has the American experiment failed to such an extent that it needs to be radically re-constituted?

This book, through a series of essays and speeches on the subject of the confluence of faith and public life, speaks to that question. In doing so, the arguments it makes have in mind those made by Reverend Dr. Martin Luther King, Jr., and generations of Knights of Columbus since the nineteenth century. Namely, that we should demand the fulfillment of the promises made in the Declaration of Independence and Constitution, and that doing so from a religious basis is not only appropriate, but wholly consistent with the original vision of America's founding.

It makes its case also mindful of a twentieth century that saw many nations "re-constituted" by revolutionary movements that often made situations far worse than they had been. Even where things were quite difficult to begin with, things seldom improved

1

after revolutionary change. One need only think of Northern Iraq in 2014, Cambodia in the 1970s, Eastern Europe and China in the 1940s, Germany in the 1930s, or Italy and Russia earlier in the century to understand that the fall of one order, no matter how problematic, could easily usher in years or decades of something far worse.

This is not to say the United States is perfect. Nor is it to say that the promises made in the U.S. Constitution have always been promises kept. However, having avoided the worst of the twentieth century's violent totalitarianism, and having made important advances in the protection of human rights, the United States still has much to offer anyone who lives in this great land, as well as much to offer those living in other countries. One could easily argue—as Dr. King did in his "I Have a Dream" speech—that "the magnificent words of the Constitution and the Declaration of Independence" are "a promissory note to which every American was to fall heir." And as he declared further: "we refuse to believe that the bank of justice is bankrupt. We refuse to believe that there are insufficient funds in the great vaults of opportunity of this nation."

Years earlier, in his "Letter from a Birmingham Jail," King also appealed to the founding documents of this country, writing:

> One day the South will know that when these disinherited children of God sat down at lunch counters, they were in reality standing up for what is best in the American dream and for the most sacred values in our Judaeo Christian heritage, thereby bringing our nation back to those great wells of democracy which were dug deep by the founding fathers in their formulation of the Constitution and the Declaration of Independence.

That Dr. King's efforts had a positive effect on racial justice in this country is undeniable. But how he advocated was important. He demanded the rights promised in the Constitution, and did so from a platform that was overtly religious.

Interestingly, King's approach of demanding that the equal rights America promised be applied regardless of race was closely mirrored by the Knights of Columbus' demand for the application of equal rights regardless of religion—work explicitly advanced by the Knights decades earlier.

As was stated at a Massachusetts' Knights of Columbus banquet in 1895: "We believe that the better Catholics we are, the better citizens we are also. Inspired by this spirit, we are tolerant of the opinions of others, and demand like toleration from others."

Father William Slocum, a priest who was a contemporary of Knights' founder Father Michael McGivney's in Connecticut, eulogized McGivney at a pilgrimage to his tomb in 1900 and exhorted the Knights: "As a Christian body, American citizens and lovers of justice, may you [Knights of Columbus] feel it your duty to say: 'Thus far and no farther shalt thou go.' You have a right to say, we want nothing but our rights and, before heaven, we will be satisfied with nothing less."

Again, and tellingly, from the earliest years, the effort had both a strong civic and a strong religious component. Like King's work, the Knights' work met with substantial success in bringing Catholics into mainstream American society, and securing their rights irrespective of their faith.

Although anti-Catholic bigotry still raises its head from time to time—especially directed at Catholic beliefs that run counter to a "politically correct" secular world view—few today realize just how despised a minority Catholics were in America in the nineteenth and early twentieth centuries. Targeted, and even at times killed by the Ku Klux Klan and other "nativist" mobs, Catholics—whether American-born or hailing from Ireland, Italy, or elsewhere—were often made to feel extremely unwelcome in the United States.

Coming of age during the Know Nothing and Klan-dominated moments in American history, the Knights had its work cut out for it, but having experienced the lack of freedom in places like British-ruled Ireland, the early Knights—mostly Irish-Americans—equated their commitment to patriotism with a desire to promote the Constitution's guarantee of religious freedom. In 1890, the Knights of Columbus and its founder were praised for inspiring appreciation and action. Eulogizing the Knights' founder, a young man whose family had personally benefitted from the priest's charity noted that "unrivaled civil liberty on the one side and unrivaled religious liberty on the other demand of us cultivation and exercise of the most ardent patriotism." Patriotism for the Knights from the earliest days was a response to promised rights, rights worth claiming and defending.

Both King and the Knights of Columbus brought to bear a uniquely Christian perspective on their work to advance equality in the United States. By this, their appeal was doubly resonant within the American context.

As America's founders had noted, religious belief was integral to the smooth functioning of the United States. Madison perhaps offered the best summary of this in 1798 when he wrote:

> We have no Government armed with Power capable of contending with human Passions unbridled by morality and Religion. Avarice, Ambition, Revenge or Galantry, would break the strongest Cords of our Constitution as a Whale goes through a Net. Our Constitution was made only for a moral and religious People. It is wholly inadequate to the government of any other.

The idea was not simply that the government was prohibited from imposing a particular denominational creed, but also that the government was only functional in a situation where it governed those who had religious and moral commitments.

President George Washington similarly held up religion and morality as essential to the country's functional inner workings, and expressed as much two years before Madison when bidding farewell to the nation as president. He said:

Of all the dispositions and habits, which lead to political prosperity, Religion and Morality are indispensable supports. In vain would that man claim the tribute of Patriotism, who should labor to subvert these great pillars of human happiness, these firmest props of the duties of Men and Citizens. [...] Where is the security for property, for reputation, for life, if the sense of religious obligation desert the oaths, which are the instruments of investigation in Courts of Justice? And let us with caution indulge the supposition, that morality can be maintained without religion. [...] reason and experience both forbid us to expect, that national morality can prevail in exclusion of religious principle.

Such thinking should not be taken as instrumentalizing religion, but as respecting its foundational force and influence in the life and future of the young nation.

Far from threatening to wall off faith from the public policy of the country—as is envisioned by some progressive secularists today—the country's founders saw faith as actually critical to, rather than undermining, America's civic enterprise. It should come as no surprise that the work for racial equality undertaken by Reverend King, and the work for religious equality undertaken by the Knights of Columbus were both based on Christian ideas, as was the abolitionist movement, which predated both.

Regarding what the interplay of faith and civic life looks like on the personal level, two of the questions that Knights' founder Father McGivney and the men who helped him launch the Knights of Columbus sought to answer were these—*Can a person be a good Catholic and a good citizen? And, if so, what does that look like?*

For nearly a century and a half, the Knights of Columbus has answered the first question affirmatively, and the second question by example. The Knights became the first large-scale Catholic organization of laymen in America to explicitly take on the importance of faith and citizenship. In so doing, it also became the first

Catholic organization through which laymen helped give the Catholic Church and Catholic Faith a major voice on key civic issues of the day. As such, the Knights had a real effect in a number of areas including:

- Helping put an end to prejudiced, anti-Catholic publications.

- Standing up to the Klan's bigoted efforts, including their attempts to outlaw Catholic education.

- Shaping opinion about global persecution of Christians.

- Introducing American servicemen to the good work of Catholics through free hospitality centers in the United States and Europe during World War I.

Building on the organization's history as a thought-leader in the area of civil and religious rights, as well as its charitable leadership, the addresses and writings in this book were designed to bring that wisdom and perspective beyond the Knights of Columbus, to diverse audiences. Some of what is contained here are addresses that helped shape American public policy, others pieces spoke directly to groups of individuals at more private events—such as the address to a Maronite (Eastern Catholic) convention—which nevertheless held a message deeply relevant to a much broader audience today.

Each speech or essay in this book had a path for change in mind, rather than simply being a record related to particular moments in time. Therefore, I invite you to view this book as representing a belief in the promises made by our country's founding documents and a demand that those promises be kept. Embracing and demanding the fulfillment of these promises informed by Christian principles has led—and can continue to lead—to respect for human dignity and authentic equality for all Americans. It is an idea and process that I believe most Americans can embrace to heal our country and its politics.

This book addresses areas that were not simply of great concern for American Catholics, but areas of great concern for the entire nation because of their great consequences—areas where lives have been taken, people have been jailed, voices have been silenced, and families have been pitted against each other with lasting consequences for this and the next generation.

Section 1 ("Domestic Religious Freedom, Conscience, and Secularism") begins with the fundamental freedom—religious freedom—which is increasingly squeezed out of the public square in our country. It presents the long-standing understanding and expectation that religion would serve a foundational role in our country. Further, it explores the impact that Catholics and others can have through faithful citizenship, and presents what the "Next Great Awakening" should look like if Americans are to develop faithful citizenship to overcome the challenges of today.

Section 2 ("International Religious Freedom") looks at a specific situation in which the United States' commitment to religious liberty as a universal human right (not simply one for Americans) has had a chance to protect that right for others: i.e., in the Middle East, where restrictions on religious freedom have progressed unchecked, creating one of the most deadly religious freedom situations of our generation, killing thousands, and making religious pluralism an endangered reality that may not survive there. The Knights of Columbus was and continues to be a key advocate and charitable support for religious minorities—including Christians, but for other persecuted religious minorities there as well. Our work and ideas literally shaped U.S. and international policy on the issue, and some of the addresses represent those efforts. However, the continuation of Christian citizenship in those lands depends on more than aid or public awareness, and some of the items here speak to the cultural, spiritual, and personal prerequisites needed, both in persecuted communities and in ally/advocate communities.

Section 3 ("Respect for Life") addresses a right that remains unfulfilled in the case of nearly one million people a year. This right to life is one of those "unalienable rights" which are "endowed by the Creator." Science has made clear that each unborn child is a unique human life. As with the other civil rights movements mentioned above, hard work is being done, often led by people of faith, to extend the equal protection of the laws and the promise of the Constitution and Declaration of Independence to these defenseless individuals who have yet to benefit from it.

Little wonder the U.S. Conference of Catholic Bishops has labeled this issue the "preeminent priority" of our time—an assessment with which Pope Francis strongly agreed in a meeting with American bishops in 2020.The issue of abortion and related issues are put in context of its foundational disregard for the humanity of the unborn child, as well as the growing technological advances that flirt with changing what a human is. The section ends with a discussion of suffering—a factor that contributes to how the "throwaway culture" defends abortion as a necessity, along with euthanasia, the maltreatment of the elderly and people with disabilities, and even suicide.

Section 4 ("Transcending Partisanship") speaks to the violent protests, election rancor, political polarity, and impasses for the last decade. It lays out paths toward genuine civic involvement with an eye toward change, both drawing on Martin Luther King's Christian-based ethic of non-violence as well as outlining the contributions that Catholic voters can make as a voice of reconciliation, even beyond election season. Recognizing the deeper origins of such internal combat, the section concludes with a deep dive into the essential spiritual element—mercy—which is often lacking in our interactions with those we considered flawed, and deeply needed in response to our own flaws.

Finally, Section 5 ("Love in Society") addresses the need for love as both a foundation for our society, and an exploration of civic life's impact on the family—the place where love, as well as the virtues entailed by citizenship, are first learned. The ideologies of the last two centuries is explored with a specific eye towards how they targeted the family, a fundamental "organization" whose framework predates those ideologies and their states. The results of family breakdown on children, as well as a more specific analysis of the material and spiritual contributions of grandparents, draw out these themes in concrete terms.

If, as Madison observed, the laws of this land are insufficient for any but a moral and religious people, then the heart of our county's divisions are not fundamentally legal, but religious and moral. Thus, an understanding of rights that—to paraphrase President John F. Kennedy—come not from the generosity of the state but from the hand of God, would be a good starting point for unity and a universal application of rights to all God's children. In short, our country will function best not by completely replacing the system we have with something of unknown quality, but by embracing at every level a sense of morality and religion, both committed to rights and justice based on love of neighbor.

After calling into question whether liberties could survive if "in the minds of the people" they were seen as anything but gifts from God, Jefferson noted: "Indeed, I tremble for my country when I reflect that God is just, and that his justice cannot sleep forever."

The justice he feared was a justice meted out in the absence of a proper understanding of the role of God in providing a foundation for these rights. These men were prescient, for from the French Revolution, to the Russian Revolution, to the killing fields of Cambodia, to Nazi Germany, a complete rejection of God quickly led to human bloodletting on a massive scale. By embracing a balanced approach to church and state, the United States avoided such a catastrophic outcome.

But as Jefferson, Madison, and Washington observed, it is the morality and religious sense of the people that is the necessary bulwark against tyranny. Little wonder that morality—built on religious principles—has moved the country ahead from abolition, to Catholic civil rights, to the Civil Rights Movement led by Dr. Martin Luther King, Jr.

To the extent that we would have this country function at its best, and deliver on its promises of equal rights, regardless of race or creed, faith should be embraced, not avoided. In awakening to this reality, we would help America achieve its promise of liberty, and justice for all. This, only "we the people," and especially "we the people of faith," can accomplish.

SECTION 1

Domestic Religious Freedom, Conscience, and Secularism

Includes the following chapters:

1. America and Religious Freedom

2. The Importance of Christian Witness in America Today

3. The Next Great Awakening

In 1909, the great French Catholic writer Charles Peguy observed, "For the first time since Jesus, we have seen, under our very eyes . . . a new world arise . . . constituted, or at any rate assembled . . . after Jesus and without Jesus."[2]

Peguy was speaking about recent events in the Europe of his day—a Europe profoundly transformed by the Enlightenment, which would become deeply wounded by the atrocities of atheistic political ideologies from its Germanic north, Italian south, Soviet east, and Spanish-Communist west.

More than a century later, we must admit that the cultural trend of a new world after Jesus and without Jesus has become more pronounced in Europe, as well as throughout the Western

Hemisphere. Europe's continued embrace and even promotion of secularism as the new "baseline" of political life continue, including the promotion of its derivative ideologies (often rooted in the failed experiments of the Soviet bloc) to the developing world.

The United States has in many ways been a late-comer to embracing radically secular or even atheistic political ideologies. The American "Enlightenment," which gave birth to the country in the eighteenth century, and the arising political philosophies, which continued to shape it at key moments in the nineteenth and twentieth centuries, strongly embraced the idea that rights protected by the state came from God.

Disagreeing so fundamentally on the place of God, the results of these two disparate Enlightenments existed in tension with one another. In the political realm in particular, in our lifetimes, we have seen religious hostility come to a tipping point, when hostility toward religious involvement in political life began gaining a vocal constituency among politicians—a trend that has grown, rather than reversed. This tension pulls at the social realms as well, and reaches into the worlds of family life, business, education, and healthcare as norm-changing mandates and ideals are put forward. Any citizen—and certainly anyone working for a cause with political implications—experiences the tensions in a personal way.

My experience was initially from the inside, rather than from the civilian sector. Prior to committing to the Knights of Columbus full time—a transition that occurred in the 1980s—I had worked in the world of men and women who call themselves "public servants." I considered my time spent on the Civil Rights Commission and on the staff of President Ronald Reagan a strong foundation for serving an international organization that had a strong record of faith and advocacy for freedoms of religious, racial, and civil nature—and a record (akin to John Kennedy's and Ronald Reagan's) of standing up for the rights of those persecuted for their faith by Communist regimes.

What I did not know at the time was that my experience in

public life was not the exception to the position of supreme knight, but historically had been the rule. From the beginning, the Knights of Columbus paired a strong ethic of non-partisanship with a robust dedication to civic responsibility. An early parade of Knights sported badges showing their political affiliations, driving home both the members' commitment to civic engagement and the diversity of political parties through which their engagement occurred. The Knights of Columbus has understood that the obligations of citizenship include civic and political improvement. With harmonious ease, the lives of the earliest supreme knights and early leaders wove together service to the Order and service through civic leadership. This included John Phelan—who served as Connecticut's secretary of state and as the Order's second supreme knight, simultaneously! His successor, James Hayes, was a rising star in the Massachusetts statehouse who served simultaneously as a Democratic senator there and as the Order's third supreme knight; his later successor Luke Hart served as an alderman and delegate for the Republican Party, while Francis Matthews went on from being supreme knight to hold the positions of Secretary of the Navy and Ambassador to Ireland for President Harry Truman.[3]

The Knights of Columbus not only was built by and attracted Catholic civic-minded men, but had as a purpose, in the words of one of the original incorporators, "to unify American Catholic citizens of every national and racial origin"[4] who, among other things, had a particular interest in defending the religious freedom of Catholics. Part of this effort was making the case for defending a place for Catholics in public life through the examples of its own members as model citizens.

Eulogizing Father McGivney in 1890, Edward Downes—brother of Alfred Downes, for whom Father McGivney had become guardian after the death of their father—noted the fact:

> Comfort and help are not the only fruits of our organization, its province is more far reaching. . . . The very name of our

order, bespeaking the wisdom of our founder, necessarily *inspires our members with renewed patriotism and makes us better citizens.* The name stands as a beacon light reminding us of the duties we owe our country, and *reminding us that unrivaled civil liberty on the one side and unrivaled religious liberty on the other demand of us cultivation and exercise of the most ardent patriotism.* [Emphasis added]

Despite being born on the east coast of the United States, the Knights of Columbus managed to overcome the predominantly Anglo narratives of American history. The Irish immigrant heritage of many of its founding members certainly brought a personal awareness of the tragedy of living as a Catholic amidst persecution under English Protestant rule. The Knights' appreciation for religious liberty furthered its international perspective by its almost immediate expansion to the west coast (with Hispanic missionary history), its early Canadian expansion (with both French-Catholic and English-Protestant heritage), and its early expansion to Cuba and the Philippines (which were eyed by the United States at times with an overtly anti-Catholic/pro-Protestant oriented colonization). The diversity of experiences drove home that the importance of religious freedom was not an American issue, but an issue of basic human rights, which ought to be protected in each homeland.

In particular, I think the Order's foray into Mexico made a significant impact. Our establishment in Mexico in 1905 further strengthened our racial and ethnic solidarity, which had already included African Americans and Native Americans. As Mexico became ground zero for the persecution of Catholics in the 1920s, our solidarity with them and with our brother Knights was important and helped bring international attention to the issue of the persecution and laid a foundation for a century of international work defending the rights of Catholics—and others—to practice their faith without fear of persecution.

As the Knights of Columbus has expanded during my tenure to new countries, the importance of civil responsibility, including in the face of the fragility of religious liberty and the responsibility to stand up for those persecuted for their faith, has been a common denominator.

Interestingly, each new country where the Order has established in the twenty-first century had an experience of a dominant culture harboring suspicion of Catholics or even actively undermining fidelity to Catholic teaching. Fulfilling an invitation by Pope John Paul II himself for the Order to establish in Poland, the Knights there, like other Polish Catholics, still bear the emotional and spiritual scars of decades of the hostile coexistence of Communist oppression and deep Catholic spirituality. Ukraine bears both old wounds and new from Soviet-era Communist oppression and its more current conflicts, and these experiences are shared in many ways in Lithuania as well. The bravery of Korean Catholics during the Sinyu Persecution and the persecutions that followed continues to animate the faith of the Church in that country, at a time when the reality of persecution looms across the border in North Korea. And in France, threats to the faith of Catholics come increasingly from virulent secularism and personal religious apathy that paint over the country's rich Catholic history with the visages of the anti-Catholic Enlightenment's grandchildren. This is without even mentioning the sporadic but undeniably persistent specter of real terrorism from secularist, anarchist, and jihadist sources. For example, the Observatory on Intolerance and Discrimination Against Christians in Europe, which documents such events, reported an average of more than 200 incidents in Europe each recent year[5]—the iceberg of hatred beneath more visible acts such as the brutal murder-by-stabbing of a Father Jacques Hamel at the altar and the attack at a Christmas market in Strasbourg. Such events show, perhaps not an exclusively anti-Catholic sentiment, but certainly an anti-Christian one. And the situation in France (400+ events since 2014), according to the

Observatory's executive director, makes it the "worst country in Europe" for Christians.[6]

In some ways, what is old is new again. The Knights of Columbus spoke out against the Secularism Law in France in 1905 and now are established there, showing in that country too what good citizens Catholics can be. Throughout World War II and during the Cold War, the Knights stood up for those persecuted by Nazi and Communist regimes in lands where we have taken root, like Poland, Ukraine, and Lithuania.

In the United States, the organization has again had to make the case that faithful Catholics—including Knights—have a role to play in this country and its public life—even as some in the Senate and elsewhere in government have publicly questioned that role.

What became obvious as my tenure progressed was that the need to protect the civil rights of Catholics—based on promises of religious freedom in the United States Constitution and Bill of Rights—remained important. In short, the understanding of Father McGivney and those first incorporators of the Knights of Columbus on this issue had continuing relevance nearly a century and a half later. Now as then, an organization is needed not simply to support men in their faith and help keep their families financially viable in times of tragedy, but also to unite Catholic men, regardless of race or political belief, with the understanding that love of God, love of neighbor, and love of country are all important and good, and that Catholics have as much right as any other person to live out faith, charity, and citizenship—as much as any other citizen, whether in the United States, in France, in Mexico, in South Korea, or in the Middle East.

1.

America and Religious Freedom

Dignitatis Humanae and the Rediscovery
of Religious Freedom Conference
John Paul II Institute for Studies on Marriage and Family
February 21, 2013, Washington, DC

A new way of looking at religious freedom, guaranteeing the free exercise of the faith for all, was central to the American founding. Despite this, that promise has been eroded by nineteenth- and twentieth-century philosophy, by certain domestic political trends, and even by some Catholics who have sought to reconcile secular values with religious ones in a way that privileges the former. Tracing the origins of America's religious freedom tradition as well as contemporary challenges to it, this speech made the case for Catholics—following well-formed consciences—to be a light to the world.

America's Religious Freedom Tradition

The importance of religious freedom and its underlying principles have shaped the United States and its citizens in profound ways. In 2012, speaking to the Bishops of the United States on their *ad limina* visit in 2012, Pope Benedict XVI raised with appreciation the place of religion in the country's chosen unifying identity:

> One of the most memorable aspects of my Pastoral Visit to the United States was the opportunity it afforded me to reflect on America's historical experience of religious freedom, and specifically the relationship between religion and culture. At the heart of every culture, whether perceived or not, is a consensus about the nature of reality and the moral good, and thus about the conditions for human flourishing. In America, that consensus, as enshrined in your nation's founding documents, was grounded in a worldview shaped not only by faith but a commitment to certain ethical principles deriving from nature and nature's God.[7]

I think all of us here would recognize in the pope's words the freedom we cherish so much in our country.

Unlike much of Europe, which has historically lurched between the extremes of theocracy and militant secularism, in the United States, we have experienced a form of American exceptionalism in regard to questions of religious liberty and especially in regard to the free exercise of religion.

Steven Waldman reminds us in his book *Founding Faith: How Our Founding Fathers Forged a Radical New Approach to Religious Liberty* that from the time of the Declaration of Independence to our Bill of Rights and shortly thereafter, a transformation took place in the United States in the way in which religion was treated.

Americans rejected the old European model of an established state religion in which religious minorities were only granted some level of *toleration* by government. They rejected the idea of merely tolerating religion.

Thomas Paine put the matter very clearly: "Toleration is not the *opposite* of intolerance but the *counterfeit* of it. Both are despotisms:

the one assumes to itself the right of withholding liberty of conscience, the other of granting it."[8]

James Madison and others would not accept the idea that Americans were to petition their government for permission to exercise their religion. Instead, he argued that the "free exercise of religion, according to the dictates of conscience" was a "natural and absolute right." This "shift[ed] the terms of debate from toleration to liberty," according to Waldman.[9]

In his famous "Memorial and Remonstrance," Madison wrote: "The Religion then of every man must be left to the conviction and conscience of every man; and it is the right of every man to exercise it as these may dictate. This right is in its nature an unalienable right."[10]

Madison's concern went beyond diversity or pluralism to something far more important:

> It is the duty of every man to render to the Creator such homage, and such only, as he believes to be acceptable to him. This duty is precedent, both in order of time and in degree of obligation, to the claims of Civil Society. Before any man can be considered as a member of Civil Society, he must be considered as a subject of the Governor of the Universe.[11]

We can, of course, debate the degree to which the Founders such as Madison were influenced by Christian or Enlightenment thinking and to what extent the English common law tradition, influenced by a fundamentally Christian understanding of natural law, was reflected in the mindset of the Founders. But it is clear that if Madison's statement above is reflective of the view of most, if not all, of the Founders, then their view of religious liberty arose not from an indifference to either truth or the Creator. Instead, it seems quite clear that their defense of individual conscience rested precisely upon the recognition of the demands that the truth sets upon each person's conscience because of his relationship to his Creator. Nor can one see this view as simply the consensus about a state-sanctioned civil right. To the contrary, the proposition was clearly one of an inalienable natural right rooted in the very core of the human person.

In his historic 1963 letter from a Birmingham jail, Reverend Martin Luther King, Jr. said that he and his followers "were in reality standing up for what is best in the American dream and for the most sacred values in our Judeo-Christian heritage, thereby bringing our nation back to those great wells of democracy, which were dug deep by the founding fathers in their formulation of the Constitution and the Declaration of Independence."[12]

Perhaps we need to remember also that King's letter relied upon the Catholic natural law tradition in his appeal to American public opinion, citing Saint Augustine that "an unjust law is no law at all."

And he asked, "How does one determine when a law is just or unjust? A just law is a man-made code that squares with the moral law or the law of God. An unjust law is a code that is out of harmony with the moral law." He answered, against citing another Catholic: "To put it in the terms of Saint Thomas Aquinas, an unjust law is a human law that is not rooted in eternal and natural law."

There you have the ancient teaching of the Catholic Church, summed up by a Baptist preacher under arrest for living by it. But to whom was King appealing with this argument from natural law? And why did he think that resting his case on the natural law thinking of Saint Thomas Aquinas would resonate within the American cultural and political environment of his day?

Every legal system rests upon a certain vision of the human person. As it was observed in *The Federalist Papers No. 51*, "What is government itself, but the greatest of all reflections on human nature?"[13] Obviously, our laws affecting religious liberty are no exception.

The *"Masters of Suspicion"*

To continue with the observation of Pope Benedict to the American bishops on their *ad limina* visit, he also said this:

> Today that consensus has eroded significantly in the face of powerful new cultural currents which are not only directly opposed to core moral teachings of the Judeo-Christian tradition, but increasingly hostile to Christianity as such.[14]

Sadly, most of us would recognize our country—or its current direction—in that statement as well.

I think that Paul Ricoeur's idea of the "Masters of Suspicion" is an essential, interpretive key to understanding the current controversy in the United States as well as the historical antecedents in Europe.[15] Ricoeur described Marx, Nietzsche, and Freud as the "Masters of Suspicion" because each in his own way cast Christianity under suspicion as a "system" that fundamentally distorts our perception of the human person, restrains our exercise of authentic freedom, and which, therefore, makes impossible the pursuit of true happiness.

Whether society considers Christianity to be the opium of the people, a slave religion, or an infantile delusion (as each of these men did respectively), such a society is hardly likely to give such a religion, its institutions, or its followers a privileged place. Neither is it apt to consider the free exercise of this religion to be a good thing.

The position of the "Masters of Suspicion" has been ascendant in Europe for much of the twentieth century and now is gaining ground in the United States. Many in government seem to be of the opinion that government's reflection of human nature should be of the person devoid of his very soul—and of the religious ideals that nourish that soul.

Seeing this trend, Pope Benedict said to the American bishops last year:

When a culture attempts to suppress the dimension of ultimate mystery, and to close the doors to transcendent truth, it inevitably becomes impoverished and falls prey, as the late Pope John Paul II so clearly saw, to reductionist and totalitarian readings of the human person and the nature of society.

He added:

The seriousness of these threats needs to be clearly appreciated at every level of ecclesial life. Of particular concern are certain attempts being made to limit that most cherished of American freedoms, the freedom of religion. Many of you have pointed out that concerted efforts have been made to deny the right of conscientious objection on the part of Catholic individuals and institutions with regard to cooperation in intrinsically evil practices. Others have spoken to me of a worrying tendency to reduce religious freedom to mere freedom of worship without guarantees of respect for freedom of conscience.[16]

Professor Stephen Carter of Yale Law School has warned that the "potential transformation of the Establishment clause from a guardian of religious liberty into a guarantor of public secularism raises prospects at once dismal and dreadful."[17]

One of the examples that Professor Carter cites is the litigation from a number of years ago that challenged the tax-exempt status of the Catholic Church because of its pro-life advocacy. Carter speculated that such a precedent could lead to similar challenges to churches on the basis of advocacy of civil rights or other politically sensitive issues. But then he suggested that:

Maybe there are not any principles involved. Maybe it is just another effort to ensure that intermediate institutions, such as the religions, do not get in the way of the government's will. Perhaps, in short, it is a way of ensuring that only one vision of the meaning of reality—that of the powerful group of individuals called the state—is allowed a political role.

Then he observes this: "Back in Tocqueville's day, this was called tyranny. Nowadays, all too often, but quite mistakenly, it is called the separation of church and state."[18]

Saint Thomas More: Model for Conscientious Citizenship

Carter argues that a central role of religion in American democracy is "the role of external moral critic and alternative source of values and meaning," especially when these conflict with those of the state.[19] He then concludes with this observation:

> In a state that does little regulating—the state, for example, that the Founders envisioned when they wrote the First Amendment—this tension will but rarely be apparent. As the apparatus of government grows, and its control over the lives of citizens increases, the situations in which meanings are imposed become of necessity far more numerous, and conflicts between the visions imposed by the state and the visions imposed by the religions become more frequent. A pervasive, totalitarian state will of course find these conflicts threatening, which is why religious liberty is among the first freedoms to go when statist dictators take firm hold. A state that loves liberty and cherishes its diversity, however, should revel in these conflicts, welcoming them as a sign of political and spiritual health.[20]

Indeed, a political and legal culture that works to drive our Catholic institutions from carrying out their charitable work focuses our attention on the life of Saint Thomas More. He is an appropriate guide, for he used all his brilliance as a lawyer to avoid conflict with King Henry VIII. Yet, finally, when direct conflict could no longer be avoided, he laid down both his family's security and his very life.

Clarence Miller, the editor of the *Yale Edition of the Collected Works of Thomas More*, recalls the various reasons that have been given for More's martyrdom:

> The integrity of the self as witnessed by an oath, the irreducible freedom of individual conscience in the face of an authoritarian state, [and] papal supremacy as a sign of the supra-national unity of Western Christendom. . . . All of these are true as far as they go. But in the last analysis, More did not die for any principle, or idea, or tradition, or even doctrine, but for a person, for Christ.[21]

In 1929, G.K. Chesterton wrote that "Thomas More is more important at this moment than at any moment since his death, even perhaps the great moment of his dying; but, he is not quite so important as he will be in about a hundred years' time."[22]

In the life of More we see the truth recognized in *Gaudium et Spes*: that "in the depths of his conscience, man detects a law which he does not impose on himself, but which holds him to obedience."[23] This is the natural law that resonates in man's conscience. But in the matter of Christian witness, we can say something further: in the depths of his heart, a Christian detects a love which he does not impose on himself, but which holds him to obedience.

More was a layman; and last year when speaking to the American bishops, Pope Benedict was very clear that the struggle for religious freedom must be joined by the laity as well as the clergy. He said:

> Here once more we see the need for an engaged, articulate and well-formed Catholic laity endowed with a strong critical sense vis-à-vis the dominant culture and with the

courage to counter a reductive secularism which would delegitimize the Church's participation in public debate about the issues which are determining the future of American society. The preparation of committed lay leaders and the presentation of a convincing articulation of the Christian vision of man and society remain a primary task of the Church in your country; [and] as essential components of the new evangelization.[24]

The loyalty and action of the laity is especially important today because we find ourselves in a virtual legal "Wonderland" where the government seems willing to give institutions rights of conscience that it denies to individuals. But how long may we expect the First Amendment to protect institutions when its protections are denied to individual Americans? What we have seen during the year-long controversy over the so-called HHS Mandate and what we now see in its present iteration is precisely an exercise of that despotism of toleration about which Thomas Paine warned us.

The relationship between conscience and truth in contemporary culture was addressed by Cardinal Joseph Ratzinger in a 1991 lecture sponsored by the National Catholic Bioethics Center and the Knights of Columbus.[25] He first observed that the conscience of post-modern man considers itself entirely *subjective* while, at the same time, being *infallible* in its judgments. This subjective conscience is also self-justifying, setting itself in opposition to any outside authority.

This type of conscience acts "not as a window through which one can see outward to that common truth," according to Ratzinger, but as a "protective shell, into which man can escape and there hide from reality."[26]

The post-modern conscience is thus vulnerable to prevailing societal opinions; it mirrors them and becomes ultimately enslaved by them. The notion of truth as a reference point is abandoned, and in its place, we find the concept of progress. Ironically, progress itself "is" the infallible truth. And with objective truth sufficiently out of the way, power becomes the only category that matters. The strong are then free to dominate the weak. This dynamic was later described by Pope John Paul II in more detail in his encyclical *Evangelium Vitae*.[27]

In *Evangelium Vitae*, Blessed John Paul calls for "a general mobilization of consciences and a united ethical effort to activate a great campaign in support of life."[28] This mobilization of consciences is at the center of the encyclical's vision of evangelization. It is also the foundation of John Paul II's approach to social justice and the law. *Evangelium Vitae* was not the first time the Holy Father proposed such a role for conscience in the transformation of society. In reviewing the reasons for the collapse of Marxism throughout Eastern Europe, *Centesimus Annus* asserted that "the fundamental error of socialism is anthropological in nature," since socialism rejected "the concept of the person as the autonomous subject of moral decision."[29] *Centesimus Annus* made clear that the encounter between Christianity and any political order must be focused within the conscience of each person. The encyclical asserts that the mission of the Church in confronting such a culture is "to increase the sensitivity of consciences."[30]

In his examination of the relationship between conscience and the Magisterium, Cardinal Ratzinger recalled the work of another great English witness to conscience—Cardinal John Henry Newman.[31]

Newman's conversion to Catholicism cost him dearly and came about as a need to obey the truth in his conscience. In a letter to the Duke of Norfolk, Newman wrote, "If I am obliged to bring religion into after-dinner toasts . . . I shall drink—to the Pope, if you please—still, to Conscience first, and to the Pope afterward."[32]

In explaining this statement, Ratzinger noted that Newman was not falling into modernity's trap of presupposing the opposition of conscience to authority. Rather, Newman had such high regard for truth that conscience, as the "presence of the voice of truth," takes priority over other claims. In this way, conscience is the "over-coming of mere subjectivity in the encounter of . . . man with the truth from God."[33] The natural law speaks to man in the innermost reaches of his heart. This original memory of the good and the true—what Ratzinger called the "inner ontological tendency"—has been implanted in each of us.[34]

It is for this reason, Ratzinger asserted, that Cardinal Newman was right; the toast to conscience must come before the toast to the pope, because "without conscience there would not be a papacy. All power that the papacy has is power of conscience."[35]

The task before us then is not only to re-capture a Catholic understanding of conscience, but to do so in the context of American culture. Conscience is not only a reference point for theological reflection; it is also a principle deeply imbedded in our political founding. In fact, the centrality of conscience was well-regarded by the framers of the U.S. Constitution. In 1802, President Thomas Jefferson called the Establishment and Free Exercise Clauses of the First Amendment the "expression of the supreme will of the nation [on] behalf of the rights of conscience."

Jefferson's view of the government's obligation to respect the rights of religious believers was articulated two years later in a letter he sent to the Ursuline Sisters of New Orleans. In 1804, the United States purchased the Louisiana Territory from France. The Ursuline Sisters—having recently experienced the anti-clerical excesses of the French Revolution—were fearful of how the predominantly Protestant and Anglo-Saxon nation would treat their school, orphanage, and hospital. The Ursuline superior in New Orleans wrote Jefferson to get his assurance that they would be allowed to continue their charitable work. In a handwritten letter, Jefferson responded that the "principles of the constitution and the government of the United States are a sure guarantee . . . that your institution will be permitted to govern itself according to its own voluntary rules, without interference from the civil authority." Jefferson closed the letter with these touching words: "Be assured . . . [of] all the protection which my office can give . . . I salute you, holy sisters, with friendship and respect. Thomas Jefferson."[36]

Secular versus Religious Consciences

Given today's political environment, it is hard to imagine the president writing a letter of this kind to a religious hospital, giving his assurance that they could govern themselves "without interference from the civil authority." In fact, as one contemporary observer has noted, "It is simply incomprehensible to many people in positions of power . . . that the same [Catholic] vision that inspires widely respected compassionate care would also compel closure or sale of a facility to avoid complicity in providing abortions."[37]

We have all heard quite a bit about the dictatorship of relativism. Perhaps it is time that we also discuss the despotism of tolerance.

In a previous era, Jacques Maritain observed that Christians had advanced toward a more just and humane society through what he termed the "evangelical inspiration" of the secular conscience.[38] Yet today, the effect of pervasive secularization has accomplished the reverse—the secularization of the Christian conscience. Or perhaps more precisely, secularism prevents the adequate formation of the Christian conscience. It prevents the formation of the type of conscience needed to evangelize society as Maritain envisioned.

We must ask ourselves: What does it mean to form a Catholic conscience disposed toward conforming one's life to the imitation of Christ? And we must also ask: Why are so many Catholics and Catholic institutions so unwilling to preserve a genuinely Catholic conscience in the face of countervailing pressure?

The task of conscience formation was historically accomplished through a combination of institutions such as the family, parishes, and Catholic schools and universities. And it has become obvious that in many ways these structures are no longer accomplishing this mission.

I would suggest that a turning point in the secularization of the

Catholic conscience occurred in the summer of 1964, when members of the Kennedy family and their political advisors invited a group of theologians to Hyannis Port to discuss a political stance that would justify the legalization of abortion.[39] That November, Senator Edward Kennedy would run for re-election in Massachusetts and Robert Kennedy would seek the Senate seat in New York.

One of the priests involved, then-Jesuit Father Albert Jonsen, has written a detailed account of the gathering.[40] According to Jonsen, the group included Father Robert Drinan, S.J., the Dean of the Boston College Law School; Father Charles Curran; and Jesuit theologians Father Josef Fuchs, S.J., Father Giles Milhaven, S.J., and Father Richard McCormick, S.J. Milhaven later recalled that the group worked for a day and a half at a nearby hotel. They arrived at a consensus that Catholic politicians "might tolerate legislation that would permit abortion . . . if political efforts to repress [it] . . . led to greater perils for social peace and order." In the end, according to Milhaven, the theologians "all concurred on certain basics . . . that a Catholic politician could in good conscience vote in favor of abortion."[41]

In *We Hold These Truths*, Father John Courtney Murray, S.J., had made a similar argument in regard to the legalization of contraception. Jonsen credits Murray's work with influencing the thinking of the so-called "Hyannis Port colloquium" on abortion. Murray wrote about the issue in the context of the Comstock law and the Connecticut statute that criminalized the use of contraceptives. He said this:

Perhaps the heyday of reformist confusion of law and morals was the notorious "Comstock Era," the 1870s. And doubtless the most famous relic of the era is the Connecticut birth-control statute. . . . (T)he Connecticut statute confuses the moral and legal, in that it transposes without further ado a private sin into a public crime. The criminal act here is the private use of contraceptives. . . . It is "indefensible as a piece of legal draughtmanship."[42]

Of course, what Murray failed to mention was that the federal Comstock Law included not only contraception, but also abortion.

He then concluded, "But what matters here is the mentality exhibited, and the menace in it. Protestant moral theory . . . seems never to have been able to grasp the distinction between private and public morality."[43]

Obviously, the analysis also rests in part upon one's understanding of intrinsic evil, moral absolutes, and the common good. The view on such matters by theologians such as Fuchs, McCormick, and Curran needs no review in this setting. But we might do well to reflect on the implications of that understanding for one's view of the exercise of conscience and religious liberty.

Thus, what we might well describe as the "deconstruction" of the Catholic political conscience nearly four decades ago had a very definite theological grounding.

The question today is whether it is possible to reconstruct a Catholic conscience among Catholics in general and among Catholic public officials in particular?

Some time ago, Michael Novak reminded us that one of the great achievements of Jacques Maritain was that his scholarship had "inspired" the Christian Democratic parties of Sturzo, de Gasperi, Schuman, and Adenauer.[44] Because of that evangelical inspiration, Maritain contended that "the secular conscience has understood the dignity of the human person and has understood that the person, while being part of the State, yet transcends the State because of the inviolable mystery of his spiritual freedom."[45] We would do well to consider whether a new generation of political leadership might draw a similar inspiration from the work of John Paul II and Benedict XVI. We should consider whether it is still possible to speak in such a way in our national discourse. And we should consider also whether we can expect anyone to do so if Catholics do not.

During Pope Benedict's visit to the United States, he noted that, unlike much of Europe, secularization in America has not yet spawned a wholesale disrespect for religion and its role in public life. The fact that the most modern society in the world is also one of the most religious societies confounds the proponents of "secularization theory"—the idea that as modernity advances, religion must necessarily retreat.

While in America, Pope Benedict XVI warned that we cannot rely on this traditional religiosity of Americans since America's unique brand of secularism tends to "reduce religious belief to a lowest common denominator."[46] Faith becomes a lukewarm acceptance that there are certain moral values which increasingly seem to have little relevance for everyday living.[47]

Speaking to university students in the mid-1960s, Father Joseph Ratzinger said this: "It has been asserted that our century is characterized by an entirely new phenomenon: the appearance of people incapable of relating to God." Then he continued:

> I believe the real temptation for someone who is a Christian . . . does not just consist in the theoretical question of whether God exists. . . . What really torments us today, what bothers us much more is the inefficacy of Christianity: After two thousand years of Christian history, we can see nothing that might be a new reality in the world. . . . What is all this array of dogma and worship and Church, if at the end of it all we are still thrown back onto our own poor resources? That in turn brings us back again, in the end, to the question about the gospel of the Lord: What did he actually proclaim and bring among men?[48]

In other words, Father Ratzinger's question brings us back to the issue presented by the "Masters of Suspicion": What is the "reality" that Christianity brings into the world? Do we experience something new and is there a visible difference in the way Christians live in contrast to the secular society that surrounds them? And part of that difference must be in the way Christians think about one's conscience.

Thomas Jefferson described religious liberty as "the most inalienable and sacred of all human rights."[49] It seems to me that no matter what we think of Jefferson's personal views of religion or lack thereof, we have no reason to doubt the sincerity of his commitment to religious liberty. Ronald Reagan once observed that, "We're all Jefferson's children."[50] An overstatement perhaps, but for better or worse there is truth in the observation. We are called to evangelize our culture and we must do so amidst the bright spots and shadows that the Founders have left us.

Nonetheless, there is occasion for hope that there is still in the legacy of the Founders a passion for liberty in the hearts of many Americans. In recent days, it has fallen upon Catholics in America to reawaken a sense of the importance of religious liberty and sanctity of conscience among our fellow citizens. We may all in some sense be Jefferson's children, but as Catholics, the more pressing question is whether we are that generation open to the message and inspiration of John Paul and Benedict. Are we capable of both preserving what is true in our own tradition as Americans and at the same time bearing witness to what is new that the Gospel brings among men? Before we may truly be "a light to the Gentiles," we must all do more to nurture that flame within ourselves.

2.

The Importance of Christian Witness in America Today

John Carroll Society
April 18, 2009, Washington, DC

The audience for this 2009 speech to the John Carroll Society—named for the patriot who was America's first bishop—included Chief Justice John Roberts. The speech lays out the case that Americans need to be vigilant in protecting their religious freedom rights, while also urging them to heed Pope Benedict's words to "be saints" and to proclaim the gospel by personifying it in a world often filled with confusion.

The Return of the Know-Nothings?

Since 1951, the John Carroll Society has been a vital part of Catholic life in our nation's capital—witnessing to the faith in a town that sometimes doesn't seem to understand Catholicism or religious witness very well.

You know, several weeks ago, I found myself facing a situation much like one faced by John Carroll.

Last month, many of us in Connecticut stood up to lawmakers in the "Constitution State" who were rushing to consider legislation to impose "lay trusteeism" on the Catholic Church.

This bill would have stripped bishops and pastors of their authority over many parish and diocesan decisions and put boards of "lay trustees" in charge.

This presented a problem Catholics in the United States hadn't had to deal with for about 150 years—when the Know Nothings passed a similar bill in New York.

But John Carroll knew about "trusteeism." In the words of Monsignor John Tracy Ellis: "For the quarter century of John Carroll's rule, and for years thereafter, this attempt . . . to usurp . . . the rights [of bishops] was, perhaps, the most harassing problem with which the bishops had to deal in the United States."[51]

Laws—like the Know Nothing bill in 1855 or the proposed Connecticut bill today—have a drastic effect on our religious liberty as people have to consider the state's reaction to the practice of their faith.

But non-Catholics and Catholics—bishops, priests and laymen—all stood up and stood together. After the outcry, the legislators tabled the bill.

This episode reminds us of another issue Bishop Carroll had to deal with regularly: explaining and defending one's faith in a nation that sometimes doesn't understand it. In defending the practice of faith in the public square, all of us have something in common with John Carroll.

Despite its founding by a variety of religious groups unwelcome in England, including the Quakers, the Catholics, and the Puritans, this land wasn't always—as we know—the land of First Amendment religious freedom.

John Carroll had to contend with people like John Jay, who was both the first Chief Justice of the United States and a famous anti-Catholic. Shortly before becoming chief justice, Jay argued vociferously for a law in New York that would have excluded Catholics from public office.[52]

Jay failed in that attempt, but in 1777, he was chief author of

New York's Constitution, which banned Catholic immigrants unless they renounced the pope.[53]

Confronted with such hostility, as patriot and priest, John Carroll was the public face of a distrusted religious minority, and he left us a shining example of living the faith *and* defending religious liberty.

Catholic Models for Cultural Engagement

Today, there are fewer *direct* assaults on religious liberty—although the Connecticut bill reflected an astonishing ignorance of the history of religious discrimination in America. But if direct attacks are infrequent, the subtle pressure to marginalize religious values and voices from the public square has increased.

Catholic Church history is interesting in this regard. Historically, Catholics have followed two cultural models. First is the Catholic nation-state, with its roots in the monarchies of Europe. We may call this model the "embrace": with Church and state intertwined. The second model is the ghetto: a minority of Catholics, surrounded by cultural hostility of varying degrees.

Emerging from years of immigration, the ghetto long characterized the American Catholic experience. It allowed Catholics to maintain their identity in spite of cultural challenges.

It gave Catholics—as a group—a strong sense of cultural identity and a shared public morality. For the individual Catholic, it provided common first principles and the opportunity to develop a well-formed conscience.

Yet this strong identity encountered strong opposition. As late as the 1920s, Al Smith was facing the wrath—and burning crosses—of a resurgent Ku Klux Klan simply because of his religion. Catholics responded by swelling the ranks of organizations such as the Knights of Columbus, dedicated to being both faithful Catholics and patriotic Americans.

The election of John F. Kennedy signaled the end of this ghetto experience. Yet today, Catholics—and religious people in general—face a new, troubling, and as yet unresolved challenge.

The French philosopher Jacques Maritain wrote that one of the great accomplishments of Christianity in modern society had been what he called the "evangelization of the secular conscience." But perhaps today the process has been reversed: with society's progressive de-Christianization do we not also see a de-Christianization of distinctly Catholic consciences?

How do we maintain our distinct religious identity in the midst of a secular culture doing its best to decrease the influence of faith?

In the 1980s, Joseph Cardinal Ratzinger surveyed this dilemma and concluded: "In the long run, neither embrace nor ghetto can solve for the Church the problem of the modern world."[54]

Whether we like it or not, all of us have to engage a world that isn't just outside anymore. It is inside our homes, on our television sets, on the Internet, everywhere we turn. There is no longer a religious ghetto into which we can retreat.

In this context we might recall the words of Cardinal Ratzinger in 1997. He said the Church must "fight against being subjectivized . . . [it] must try to continue to speak its message publicly." To do that, he said, we need "people who are inwardly seized by Christianity, who experience it as joy and hope, who have thus become lovers, and these," he said, "we call saints."[55]

In a speech in 2000, entitled *The New Evangelization: Building a Civilization of Love*, Cardinal Ratzinger said that "evangelizing is not merely a way of speaking but a form of living." And to make that form of living possible, he insisted that "we must also offer a community of life, a common space for the new style of life."

So, what is to be done? Three things.

First, our faith lives or dies in our parishes and places of worship.

So we must strengthen these as the primary place people can find spiritual nourishment and fraternal communion—where the experience of God is made truly alive and present. Then we must communicate that experience.

This is the cornerstone of Christian renewal—within both the Church itself and the larger society. Associations such as the John Carroll Society and the Knights of Columbus are thus very important. They offer this "common space for the new style of life." Our members are able then to breathe new energy into their parishes.

We must be preachers of the Word like Saint Francis of Assisi, who said, "Preach, and if necessary, use words."

Second, we must also be able to "use words."

During the past thirty years we have been blessed with two magnificent popes who have opened an extraordinary new discourse with contemporary culture. We must follow their lead and "use words" as they have, thus entering into the thinking and pastoral mission of these great popes.

A principal reason I wrote the book *A Civilization of Love* was to encourage people to take seriously these efforts of John Paul II and Benedict XVI.

Early in his pontificate, John Paul focused on the question of human dignity through the lens of human love, first during his addresses, which came to be known as the Theology of Body, and then in his apostolic exhortation on the family: *Familiaris consortio*. In this way, he developed a vision of the person based on the Christian understanding of human love.

As John Paul made clear repeatedly, the human person was created out of love, for love, and with a life unintelligible if cut off from love—only the vocation of love is adequate to do justice to the dignity of every person.

This is the reason it is possible to think about our civilization in terms of love. And as Pope Benedict has suggested, the building blocks of the civilization of love are the *theological* virtues of faith, hope, and charity.

To a cynic, such a society might be too idealistic to be taken seriously. But then what are we to say of our Lord's answer when asked to sum up the law and the prophets? His answer was simple and we all know it—love of God and love of neighbor. This presents the source and summit of the civilization of love. Indeed, if we are to take seriously this command of love of neighbor, what society is adequate other than a civilization of love?

This brings me to my third observation: our Christian witness cannot be separated from our charity. Many of us have long lived the faith in public at many levels. And though we do not usually think, for example, of Blessed Teresa of Calcutta as an "evangelist," her example reminds us all of our fundamental responsibility to bring Christ into our culture through personal and corporate witness.

Politics will continue to remain the "art of the possible,"[56] but what will be *possible* can be determined in large part by the values of our culture and our ability to transform them. We should remember that the early Christians transformed society by their rhetoric, apologetics, and their witness.

Pope John Paul II in his apostolic exhortation *Christifideles laici* reminded us that charity towards one's neighbor is a specific duty of the laity: the most immediate way Christians lift up the temporal order.[57]

And here is where Pope Benedict has made a profound contribution in his encyclicals *Deus caritas est* and *Spe salvi*. They offer a theological blueprint for building the civilization of love by focusing on the virtues of faith, hope, and charity—virtues fundamental not only to every Christian life, but to every humane society.

A democratic society such as ours—founded largely on Enlightenment principles of autonomy and equality—has difficulty at times understanding both an apostolic Church—a Church with a hierarchy of pope, bishops, and priests—and the public place of religion.

Yet in America we have a unique advantage. We have not, like so many countries—particularly in Europe—experienced the political embrace of Church and State. Such nations that did so have now more or less accomplished a total divorce in the name of pluralism, resulting in a radical secularism in many European countries.

We must be both a nation of citizens and a nation of believers. With Christianity in decline in Europe, what happens to Catholicism in America will affect the future of Catholicism around the world, and that future will depend upon the integrity of the Catholic conscience of Catholic laymen and laywomen.

One year ago this week, here in Washington, Pope Benedict signaled the need for a sound moral formation, calling upon us to embody an identity grounded in a uniquely faithful way of thinking.

At the White House, he praised American history, noting: "From the dawn of the Republic, America's quest for freedom has been guided by the conviction that the principles governing political and social life are intimately linked to a moral order based on the dominion of God the Creator."[58]

As people of faith, we must never relinquish this fundamental conviction of American democracy. And we should ask whether the easy distinctions some make between private and public morality in the marketplace or in the public square are consistent with this conviction.

In Washington, Pope Benedict asked us to resist the temptation to "subjectivize" or privatize the reality of Christianity. He said: "Only when [our] faith permeates every aspect of our lives do Christians become truly open to the transforming power of the Gospel." And unless we ourselves are open to this transforming power, how can we hope society will be?

National opinion surveys sponsored by the Knights of Columbus and conducted by The Marist Poll found that a year later, people still want to hear Pope Benedict's message. According to the poll, 63 percent of Americans and 71 percent of Catholics want to hear him discuss the need to serve the less fortunate. And 57 percent of Americans and 64 percent of Catholics want to hear him address the need for ethics in our social and business life.

Additionally, the pope's approval rating among Americans is nearly 3 to 1 in his favor. Approximately 60 percent are favorable, and only 20 percent are not. Among Catholics, his numbers are the envy of every politician—76 percent to 11 percent.

He has achieved this with little, and often hostile, news coverage. But people still seek the truth. And it falls to us to join him in the new evangelization, to accept the invitation of his episcopal motto, to be with him, "co-workers in the truth."

Pope Benedict's message—summarized by the theme of his American trip *Christ Our Hope*—resonates, because Americans see his preaching of the Gospel as consistent. This has opened up an opportunity for us to build new bridges among people of faith.

In reflecting on how to do this myself, I often think of these words of Benedict which in closing I share with you: "May the Holy Spirit make you creative in charity, persevering in your commitments, and brave in your initiatives, so that you will be able to offer your contribution to the building up of the 'civilization of love.'"[59]

May we all continue to do our part as "co-workers in the truth."

3.

The Next Great Awakening

SPEECH

National Catholic Prayer Breakfast
April 19, 2012, Washington, DC

This speech was delivered to Catholic political, business, and religious leaders from around the country at the height of the controversy over the Affordable Care Act's HHS Mandate, which sought to force Catholic employers—including the Little Sisters of the Poor—to provide coverage for contraception, sterilization, and abortion-inducing drugs. It sought to remind Americans of the great tradition of religious freedom in the United States, while also urging Catholics to follow the example of Saint Thomas More, who—while on death row in the Tower of London—prayed for his persecutors, that they, and he, would be together with God in heaven. Citing the effect of great religious awakenings in the past, the speech noted that in the face of hostility to religion in some quarters and even in corridors of power in Washington, America might well be on the cusp of a new "great awakening."

We come together at the National Catholic Prayer Breakfast to publicly offer thanks for the blessings of American liberty, a freedom which, in its extent and its endurance, is unique in human history.

We also come to publicly affirm our determination to preserve that liberty, for us and for our fellow citizens, and to ask the Lord's guidance in doing so.

There are times when we need that help more than others.

This is such a time.

I venture to say that, never in the lifetime of anyone present here, has the religious liberty of the American people been as threatened as it is today.

Of some things, we should not need to be reminded. There are some truths and some historical realities which should not need repeating.

But in today's society and in this year's official Washington context, we must repeat them.

We must remind our fellow Americans, and especially those who exercise power, that religious liberty—the freedom guaranteed by the First Amendment—has been essential to the founding, development, and improvement of the American Republic.

Before there was an American Revolution, there was what historians call the First Great Awakening, which swept through the colonies and transformed their outlook.

The Second Great Awakening led to the abolition of slavery, as well as the other great reform movements of the nineteenth century.

A third wave of religious energy led to reforms in education, labor, and women's rights.

Alexis de Tocqueville observed the profound connection between religion and liberty in our national life. "Religion does not give [Americans] their taste for freedom," he said. "It singularly facilitates their use of it."

We may ask: Is this historical connection between Christianity and liberty an accident of history or is it something fundamental?

Our Founders answered that question unequivocally. They declared we are "endowed" by our "Creator" with inalienable rights.

Washington's Farewell Address insisted that religion and morality are "indispensable supports of our political prosperity," warning that "reason and experience both forbid us to expect that national morality can be retained without religion."

Adams asserted that "Our Constitution was made only for a moral and religious people. It is," he said, "wholly inadequate to the government of any other."

Those views have echoed down through our history. Perhaps most notably in 1961, when President Kennedy, in his Inaugural Address, spoke of the rights for which our "forebears fought," namely "the belief that the rights of man come not from the generosity of the state, but from the hand of God."

According to a poll we conducted for the fiftieth anniversary of that speech, 85 percent of Americans still agree with Kennedy's statement.

No one here needs to be reminded that this belief was the driving force behind the life's work of the Reverend Martin Luther King, Jr.

In his historic letter from the Birmingham jail, Reverend King said that he and his followers "were in reality standing up for what is best in the American dream and for the most sacred values in our Judeo-Christian heritage, thereby bringing our nation back to those great wells of democracy, which," he said, "were dug deep by the founding fathers in their formulation of the Constitution and the Declaration of Independence."

But perhaps we do need to be reminded that King's letter relied upon our own Catholic natural law tradition.

He cited Saint Augustine that "an unjust law is no law at all."

And he asked, "How does one determine when a law is just or unjust? A just law is a man-made code that squares with the moral law or the law of God. An unjust law is a code that is out of harmony with the moral law."

He then went on to say, "To put it in the terms of Saint Thomas Aquinas, an unjust law is a human law that is not rooted in eternal and natural law."

There you have the ancient teaching of the Catholic Church, summed up by a Baptist preacher under arrest for living by it.

When you visit the new memorial to Dr. King on our national mall, read carefully the fourteen quotations inscribed there.

You will not find a single reference to God.

Not one.

Imagine how those in authority must have searched to come up with fourteen quotes of Dr. King without one mention of the Almighty.

There is no more shocking symbol of the ongoing campaign to drive religion out of our public life.

King's statue looks across the Tidal Basin to the Jefferson Memorial dedicated to the president who is now championed by secularists for inventing a "wall of separation" between Church and State.

Ironically, while the King Memorial was scrubbed of any reference to our Creator, in Mr. Jefferson's memorial, the walls tell us that "The God who gave us life, gave us liberty."

And they ask us, "Can the liberties of a nation be secure when we have removed a conviction that these liberties are the gift of God?"

A great deal hinges on how we answer that question.

On the occasion of receiving the Nobel Prize for Literature, Alexander Solzhenitsyn spoke of the ideological manipulation of history that occurred in Russia under Soviet Communism.

It was, he said, "a closing, a locking up, of the national heart, [and an] amputation of the national memory."

He warned that when this happens, a nation "has no memory of its own self. It is deprived of its spiritual unity. And even though compatriots apparently speak the same language, they suddenly cease to understand one another."

Solzhenitsyn devoted his life to prevent the militant atheists in his country from destroying the soul of the Russian people by rewriting their history.

How would Solzhenitsyn have viewed the controversy surrounding the King Memorial?

Would he have seen it as preserving the spiritual unity of

America or as one more symptom of a trend to separate Americans from their religious heritage?

In 1954, the Knights of Columbus was instrumental in having Congress place the words "under God" in our Pledge of Allegiance.

Those words were placed in our pledge in part to mark a stark contrast between the ultimate source of our rights and the pretensions of the atheist totalitarian dictatorships of the twentieth century.

These pretensions were well summarized by Benito Mussolini in 1919 when he said: "Everything within the state, nothing outside the state, everything for the state."

Yet today we find a new hostility to the role of religious institutions in American life at a time when government is expanding its reach in extraordinary ways.

And it is not only because of the Obama Administration's HHS contraception mandate. It may have gotten the most attention, but it wasn't the first.

Arguing before the U.S. Supreme Court in *Hosanna-Tabor v. EEOC* last year, the Administration sought unprecedented limits on the autonomy of churches and religious institutions.

The Administration argued that if any "ministerial exception" in employment exists it should be strictly "limited to those employees who perform *exclusively* religious functions."

That caused Chief Justice John Roberts to ask during oral argument whether even the pope could meet the Administration's definition of a religious minister.

The Supreme Court *unanimously* disagreed with the Administration saying, "We are unsure whether any such employees exist," because even the highest-ranking churchmen have "a mix of duties."

Similarly, the HHS mandate allows only the narrowest exemption for religious institutions.

The exemption exists only for institutions that, among other things, hire and serve only members of their own faith.

As Cardinal Daniel DiNardo put it: "Jesus himself, or the Good Samaritan . . . would not qualify as 'religious enough' for the exemption, since they insisted on helping people who did not share their view of God."

Christians are called to reach beyond their own denominations in teaching "all nations," considering everyone their "neighbor," and doing "good to those who hate" them.

So in a country where three quarters of the population professes to be Christian, the Administration insists upon a religious exemption that Christ himself cannot meet.

In the *Hosanna-Tabor* case, the Administration sought to impose a new definition of ministry so narrow that ministers didn't fit it.

In its HHS mandate, the Administration insisted on an exemption so narrow that organizations can qualify only by violating the teaching of their church.

Consider if the Administration's view in the *Hosanna-Tabor* case had prevailed.

Churches and religious institutions would have found themselves at the mercy of what the Supreme Court unanimously characterized as "government interference with an internal church decision that affects the faith and mission of the church itself."

Precisely the same can be said of the HHS mandate.

A government willing to affect the faith and mission of the church is a government willing to change the *identity* of the church.

And what can we expect in the future?

The National Right to Life Committee makes a compelling case that the Obama Administration's "accommodation" for the HHS mandate—if accepted—paves the way for mandated coverage of "abortion on demand."

But if the HHS mandate and the *Hosanna-Tabor* case have been among the most egregious assaults on religious liberty, they are not the only ones.

Last year, the Department of Health and Human Services denied renewed funding of the Catholic Church's work with victims of human trafficking.

The Conference of Catholic Bishops had successfully administered the program for five years, but after the ACLU filed suit demanding that the program refer women for abortions and contraception, HHS restructured the program.

As a result, highly qualified providers such as the Catholic Church are now barred from the program because they cannot, in good conscience, provide what HHS calls the "full range" of reproductive services—namely abortion and contraception.

Once again, the Administration's logic is consistent: faith-based groups may apply only if their "faith and mission" are acceptable to the government.

Earlier, the Obama Administration applied a similar standard to *individual* rights of conscience when it "rescinded most of a federal regulation that protected workers who refuse to perform services they find morally objectionable."[60]

Health-care workers now face the choice of holding onto either their religious beliefs or their jobs.

In other words, if the health-care institution provides services contrary to Catholic moral teaching, Catholic doctors and nurses need not apply.

And so, we see a new government intolerance of religion.

Perhaps this is why Cardinal Francis George has referred to the Obama Administration as "the most secularist administration we have ever had in this country."

During his visit to Washington, Pope Benedict XVI reminded us that: "Christians are easily tempted to conform themselves to the spirit of this age." The spirit of our age is profoundly secular. And secularism accepts religion—if it accepts it at all—only on its own terms.

Under this view, religion is subordinated to the political interests of the secular state. And it is precisely this subordination of religion to the state that the First Amendment seeks to prevent.

Let us be clear: we value religious liberty not only because it protects our personal autonomy. We also value religious liberty because of the *good* that religion brings into the life of the individual believer and into the life of our nation.

Before he was elected pope, Cardinal Josef Ratzinger wrote that "neither embrace nor ghetto" can solve for the Church the problem of secular society.[61] Instead, Cardinal Ratzinger counseled that we must constructively engage secularism.

The question for us is, "How do we as Catholics go about doing this in the United States today?"

Last year, the Secretary of Health and Human Services told a NARAL luncheon, "We are in a war." I sincerely hope we can put away such partisan rhetoric. We do not need a government that sees itself at "war" with its own citizens. We should counsel a different approach.

Awaiting execution in the Tower of London, Saint Thomas More wrote a prayer, which we have included in our Knights of Columbus prayer book. During this national prayer breakfast we can make that prayer our own.

> Almighty God, have mercy . . . on all that bear me evil will,
> And would me harm,
> And their faults and mine together . . . vouchsafe to amend
> and redress,
> Make us saved souls in heaven together,
> Where we may ever live and love together with Thee and Thy
> blessed saints. . . ." Amen.

As Christians we are called to be witnesses. But to be true witnesses we must preserve our Catholic identity—and like Saint Thomas More—preserve it, especially from the heavy hand of government.

We are also called to sustain our witness through prayer. How appropriate then that our bishops have called upon us to take up a great fortnight of prayer for religious freedom from the vigil of the Feasts of Saint John Fisher and Saint Thomas More to July 4th.

During the current HHS controversy, some have asked, "What kind of Christians would impose such a government mandate on our religious institutions?"

In December, 1941, with Britain in mortal peril and America reeling after Pearl Harbor, Winston Churchill addressed the United States Congress. In that worst of times, he scorned the enemies of freedom and defiantly asked, "What kind of people do they think we are!"

Today, with the same defiance, we can declare, "What kind of Catholics do they think we are!"

Do they really expect us to go gently into that dark night they are preparing for religious liberty in America?

Do they not know that people who believe in "one holy, Catholic, and apostolic church" can never agree to compromise our Church by entangling it in intrinsically evil acts?

Do they not see that faithful Catholics will never accept cynical political strategies of "divide and conquer" to separate us from our bishops?

You and I have reason for hope.

We have been successful in the past.

Consider, for example, the national campaign in the 1920s by the Ku Klux Klan to close our Catholic schools. They succeeded in the State of Oregon until the Knights of Columbus and others succeeded in having the law declared unconstitutional by the U.S. Supreme Court. In its landmark decision in *Pierce v. Society of Sisters*, the Court protected the rights of parents—of all denominations—to guide the education and moral upbringing of their children.

When we seek by such means to preserve our own identity as Catholics, we are not a divisive force in society. To the contrary, actions that respect our religious diversity benefit all Americans.

Earlier this month we observed the anniversary of the death of Blessed John Paul II. On that occasion many of us again recalled his words at the beginning of his great pontificate: "Do not be afraid. Open wide the doors for Christ." We live in a time when, from the standpoint of religious liberty, it seems that there are more doors closing, than doors that are opening.

John Paul II often spoke of "a new springtime" of the Gospel. If he had been an American, he might have spoken of a new Great Awakening in America—one in which Catholics could play a greater role than ever before.

Every great religious renewal in America has led to an advance in civil rights—from the Declaration of Independence and the Bill of Rights to the end of slavery and the pursuit of racial equality. But all of this has been achieved in the face of established power structures strongly and often violently opposed to these rights.

So this is a time for choosing—choosing whether as Catholics we will stand together to keep open the doors of religious liberty.

If we do so, then we will make possible the next great awakening in America that will bring us closer to building that culture of life and that civilization of love about which John Paul II so often spoke.

May we, like Blessed John Paul II, be not afraid in our choosing.

SECTION 2

International Religious Freedom

From its earliest days, the Knights of Columbus has advocated for Catholic civil rights around the world as well as for the religious freedom of other believers being persecuted for their faith. The Knights spoke out for Catholics being targeted by U.S. government policy in the Philippines and Cuba after the Spanish-American War. It spoke out against the French Secularism Law of 1905. Following World War I, the Knights helped provide concrete support to the Armenian and other Christian communities targeted by the Ottoman Turks. Then, in the 1920s, as persecution of the Catholic Church in Mexico reached a fever pitch, the Knights became the principal advocates for Catholics there. The efforts were noticed by the American president and secretary of state–both of whom met with Supreme Knight James Flaherty. Pope Pius XI lauded the Knights' efforts on behalf of the persecuted in the papal encyclical *Iniquis Afflictisque*, and slowly, the persecution abated.

In the 1930s, the Knights continued to speak out against the persecution of Catholics, by Nazis and Communists, but also, even before World War II began, on behalf of Jews in Germany. Throughout the Cold War, the Knights' work continued, as it provided moral, temporal, and strategic support to those behind the Iron Curtain. Two notable examples—among many—show the depth of the Knights' work in this area. The first was our work on behalf of Cardinal Joseph Mindszenty in Hungary. During his show trial and imprisonment by the Communist Government in Hungary, the Knights were outspoken in his defense in writing and speeches and through participation in public rallies on his behalf. In 1956, he was liberated from prison during the Hungarian Revolution, but when the Soviets crushed that uprising, he had to flee to the United States Embassy in Budapest. There he remained for fifteen years, with his room and board funded each month by the Knights of Columbus.

For centuries, a religion that had been the core of many "confessional states," the Catholic Church only recently laid out its case for religious freedom. As Christian states gave way to pluralistic ones, and following the atrocities of the Holocaust, and in the midst of the persecution of believers during the Cold War, Catholic teaching on religious freedom took the important step of addressing the modern world with the Second Vatican Council's document *Dignitatis Humanae*, which laid out the Catholic position on religious freedom, and was influenced in large part by future cardinal, pope, and saint Karol Wojtyła.

When Cardinal Wojtyła of Krakow became Pope John Paul II, the Knights were again ready to help defend the rights of persecuted believers. During 1979, the Knights funded the filming of Pope John Paul II's visit to Mexico City. The films were then smuggled into Poland to provide the faithful there with a model of how they might react in receiving the Polish Pope. As history has recorded, the pope's reception by the Polish people was unprecedented, and in that trip, the seeds were planted for the collapse of the country's Communist regime a decade later.

Having been involved in both domestic and international religious freedom work during my time in public service, this issue had long been a priority for me, and when I became supreme knight, the issue remained a priority. While persecution had been ticking up globally, when the extent of the ISIS campaign of genocide began to become known in 2014, the world finally took notice. Taking a leadership role in helping people understand what was happening was the Knights of Columbus. Our work in educating the public—and the American government—about what was happening to Christians resulted in a declaration of genocide by Secretary of State John Kerry in 2014, and helped shape unanimous declarations by the House of Representatives and the Senate. Further advocacy resulted in the Iraq and Syria Genocide Relief and Accountability Act—which also passed both Houses of Congress unanimously—and explicitly directed that funding could be provided to religious minority communities and entities in the region.

From 2014 on, this issue became a subject of many of my speeches, as well as my congressional testimony, columns, op-eds, etc. Some of the speeches laid out the Catholic position, others spoke to the facts on the ground, still others explored the history of Christianity in the Middle East, and all advocated that the faith of our brothers and sisters in Christ be respected, along with their right to practice their faith free from coercion.

4.

The Global Crisis of Religious Freedom and *Dignitatis Humanae*

SPEECH

Given at "Under Caesar's Sword: An International Conference on Christian Response to Persecution" December 12, 2015, Pontifical Urban University, Rome

In late 2015, a conference was held at the Pontifical Urban University, co-sponsored by the Center for Civil and Human Rights at the University of Notre Dame; the Religious Freedom Project at the Berkley Center for Religion, Peace, and World Affairs at Georgetown University; and the Community of Sant'Egidio.

That ISIS had committed genocide against Christians and others was now very clear, and this speech sought to lay out both the Catholic foundation for the importance of religious freedom and the need for a coherent response from the West to the growing threats that Christians face.

As we come to the end of this conference, I would like to suggest that *Dignitatis Humanae*, the Second Vatican Council's Declaration on Religious Freedom, can address the global crisis of religious freedom in two significant ways.

First, a greater understanding of *Dignitatis Humanae* can re-energize an appreciation for religious freedom in Western societies in a way that will better enable them to respond to the global crisis of religiously motivated violence and coercion. Second, *Dignitatis Humanae* provides universal principles applicable to non-Western societies in a way that will better enable Muslims and others to confront violent extremism among their co-religionists.

The facts about international religious persecution are, in a word, grim. Over three quarters of the world's people live in countries where religious freedom is virtually non-existent. Millions of human beings are vulnerable to violent persecution—unjust imprisonment, forced conversion, forced exile, torture, rape, and murder—because of their religious beliefs and practices.

There are many victims of violent religious persecution around the world from a wide variety of religious and ethnic groups. But the data from studies by the Pew Research Center and others show clearly that those suffering the greatest persecution are Christians.

Violence by radical Islamists against Christians is placing at risk the very presence of Christianity in Iraq and Syria. It is putting enormous pressure on Christian and other minorities across the Middle East. And it poses an increasing danger to Muslims and to Islam itself. Violent Islamist extremism is not the only threat to Christians as events in India during the past several decades make clear. But it is certainly the most widespread and the most virulent.

Indeed, we are witnessing the genocide of Christian communities in Iraq and Syria that threaten the disappearance of Christianity in those countries. But there is also increasing violence and coercion against Christian minorities elsewhere in the Middle East, North Africa, and South Asia. From Sudan to Pakistan to India, hundreds of thousands of Christians are at risk of violent death.

The global crisis of religious freedom constitutes a global humanitarian crisis of immense proportions.

But this crisis goes beyond the humanitarian. It extends to

questions of international stability and peace. The absence of religious freedom and the presence of violent religious persecution fuels deep fissures in societies, de-stabilizing both nations and entire regions.

Much religious persecution occurs by the acts of governments. But increasingly, violent persecution stems from the actions of non-governmental movements—often encouraged or tolerated by governments.

Notwithstanding, the official foreign policies of the United States, Canada, and the European Union—policies that are rhetorically committed to advancing international religious freedom—have had too little impact on the global decline of religious freedom or the increase in religious persecution, including violent religious extremism.

At the root of this failure is another significant problem. Religious freedom itself is in decline throughout the West. This decline is encouraged by a toxic combination of increased government hostility toward religion, particularly Christianity, and militant secularism—a combination that in many Western countries was unthinkable as recently as thirty years ago.

Western governments that diminish religious freedom at home have understandably proven to be unwilling or unable to convince non-Western societies to respect religious freedom—even when the violations of religious freedom in those societies reach the level of deadly persecution.

It is difficult to sell a product in which one no longer believes.

Of course, Western governments still *claim* to believe in religious freedom.

But today many officials of the United States government no longer profess an expansive notion of religious freedom or speak about it as did those who drafted America's Bill of Rights, that is, as the "first" freedom of democracy—a freedom absolutely necessary for every human being and for every free society. America's founders sought to protect an expansive notion of the "free exercise" of religion. Today, many in government more often speak of a narrowly defined freedom of worship (rather than a robust free exercise of religion).

And many Europeans take an even more restrictive view of religious freedom.

Increasing numbers of Westerners see religious freedom as a mere claim of privilege by religious people or more often by religious institutions. And they see this claim as one that should be limited by more important rights.

People stop protecting what they no longer value.

Often a limited view of religious freedom is accompanied by an expansive view of government's right to determine what is permissible for religious communities to believe or practice.

More troubling still is the perception—often advanced by militant secularists—that religion itself is not an expression of human flourishing, but, to the contrary, is an impediment to freedom and wellbeing.

For too many in the West, religion—particularly Christianity—is no longer seen as a solution to society's problems, but as the problem itself.

Some in the West would have us proceed as though the only way to remove the threat of religious violence is to remove the influence of religion from society.

The approach creates a two-fold problem.

First, the secular proposal of a "godless" society without the influence of faith communities is a non-starter with all the world's great religions. At the same time, the proposal of a "godless" society appears to validate the claim of religious extremists around the world who maintain Western values to be fundamentally hostile to religion.

The unintended consequence of this view has dramatically weakened the West's effectiveness in winning hearts and minds in the confrontation with violent religious extremism.

The theological wellsprings of the very idea of religious freedom lie in the sacred texts of Judaism and Christianity. Distilled through those texts, religious freedom came to political fruition in the same Western nations where it is now in decline and whose governments no longer appreciate its benefits.

The first book of the Jewish and Christian scriptures makes it clear that *every human being* is created in the image and likeness of God. This is at the foundation of our understanding of the dignity and equality of every person. And it is the starting point for the Second Vatican Council's Declaration on Religious Freedom, *Dignitatis Humanae.*

Taken together with the teaching of Jesus that each person must render unto Caesar what is Caesar's, but never to Caesar what is God's, these principles form the basis for the Catholic claim to *libertas ecclesiae* ("freedom of the church"), religious freedom that must not be interfered with by secular authority of the state. For the greater part of two millennia this principle has stood as a barrier protecting both individuals and institutions from the claims of the absolutist state.

But I would emphasize that these principles of human dignity, equality, and the rights of conscience, while developed in the West, did not originate in the West. They were not in the first instance Western—they were incorporated from a Middle Eastern Judeo-Christian outlook into Greek and Roman societies that had very different traditions.

At a time of increasing globalization, those of us in the West would do well to reflect upon this historical fact—especially at a time when those Western nations formed by the two-thousand-year history of Christianity are no longer willing or capable of persuading non-Western nations of the intrinsic value of religious freedom.

Nor are these societies willing to specifically defend Christians *as such.* The United States, for instance, is willing to call what is happening to the Yazidis genocide, but not what is happening to the Christians—despite the fact that it is qualitatively the same.

This is the clear implication of the virtually total failure of the West to make reasonable accommodation for the immigration of Eastern Christian refugees from Syria and Iraq.

Up until now [late 2015], Pope Francis has been alone among world leaders in using the term "genocide" to describe what is happening today to Christians in Iraq and Syria. At the U.N. in September, he called for international action.[62] And in a recent homily, he said: "Perhaps more than in the early days [Christians] are persecuted, killed, driven out, despoiled, only because they are Christians."[63]

He added: "Today too, this happens before the whole world, with the complicit silence of many powerful leaders who could stop it."[64]

Except for the pope, the leaders in the West fear to call what is happening to the Christians in the Middle East genocide. But if it is not genocide, what is?

The United Nations Convention on the Prevention and Punishment of the Crime of Genocide defines it as follows:

"genocide means any of the following acts committed with intent to destroy, in whole or in part, a national, ethnical, racial, or religious group, as such:

(a) Killing members of the group;

(b) Causing serious bodily or mental harm to members of the group;

(c) Deliberately inflicting on the group conditions of life calculated to bring about its physical destruction in whole or in part;

(d) Imposing measures intended to prevent births within the group;

(e) Forcibly transferring children of the group to another group."[65]

The concept of genocide, after all, was first conceived of by the Jewish lawyer from Poland, Raphael Lemkin, because of the terrible events that befell *Christians* during and after World War I. Most in the West have forgotten, if they knew at all, that 100 years ago, Christians in Iraq and Syria endured the "Sayfo" (year of the sword) and perished in the same wave of Ottoman persecution that saw the genocidal slaughter of Armenian Christians.

Historian Philip Jenkins has written: "If the word genocide has any meaning whatever, it certainly applies to these events," that took the lives of as many as "1.5 million Christians."[66]

What, then, is to be done?

First, we need to be realistic about the ideological dispositions of many Western governments that render them incapable of adequately responding to the global crisis of religious freedom, so we must work to make *Dignitatis Humanae* understood in the West.

Second, we need to be realistic about both the necessity of military action in some cases and the limits of such action in others. Confronted with mass murder, the international community must resoundingly demonstrate that violence will be contained, halted, and punished. If the World Court can try deposed rulers accused of genocide, it can put on trial those who are guilty of religious massacres. That cannot be done by issuing subpoenas. Pope Paul VI famously said, "If you want peace, work for justice."[67] Well, justice for persecuted Christians will not be had until the leaders of free nations are as courageous as the men and women of their armed forces.

We all know that, while military force can defeat terrorists militarily and drive them away from their "caliphate," it is not sufficient. The cause of the crisis is not military. Nor is it economic. The cause is a religious sensibility that insists upon violence.

Military action cannot impose a solution because a solution cannot simply be imposed. Judaism, Islam, and Christianity have all shown that they cannot be forced to change their beliefs, tenets, and traditions from the outside. Change of this magnitude can only come from within the faith community.

Even today, Muslim thinkers in the Middle East who seek to address this question by integrating non-violence into popular interpretations of the Koran and the Hadith are often blocked by the absence of religious freedom. Anti-blasphemy, anti-apostasy, and anti-defamation laws ensure that their views cannot be heard in a sustained way.

These laws not only harm Christian and other minorities. They ensure that often Muslim reformers have no voice as well. They help make change impossible.

These laws often enjoy broad support in Muslim-majority societies by ordinary citizens who believe that those who offend Islam must be punished, either by state action or, if necessary, private violence. The Christian activist Shahbaz Bhatti was murdered in Pakistan primarily because he opposed the anti-blasphemy laws; the same was true of his Muslim Pakistani counterpart Salman Taseer.[68] But even when Muslim citizens condemn such violence, these laws ensure that violent ideologies survive and flourish.

Muslims who live in countries that respect religious freedom bear a heavy burden. They are challenged to be more—rather than less—active. Following the Paris attacks, we saw many Muslims condemn terrorism and assert that Islam is a religion of peace. This is both brave and helpful. And perhaps *Dignitatis Humanae* provides a roadmap for those Muslims with the necessary learning and credibility needed to offer interpretations of the Koran and the Hadith that counter those espoused by the extremists. Furthering such interpretations could demonstrate *in a way persuasive to all Muslims* that Islam can and should build societies grounded in the respect for the dignity of all people.

The flourishing of the Middle East and Islamic civilization especially pronounced during the periods of cultural interchange and relative harmony between Muslims and Christians provides a starting point that highlights that far from something to fear, religious freedom provides a fertile cultural environment.

The advancement of religious freedom by Muslims would not

only hearten many non-Muslims in the West, but more importantly, it would have a credibility in Muslim countries that is only possible when made by Muslims themselves.

It would be foolish to underestimate the obstacles to this course. However, one practical reality is emerging that could open opportunities for Muslim reformers and Western policy-makers to support them: the greatest victims of Islamist violence are Muslims themselves and the nations of the Middle East.

It is when Muslims themselves reject religious violence in the name of their religion that nations in the region will be able to avoid the blights that come with intolerance: an unsustainable cost in human lives, intellectual atrophy, economic stagnation, and political failure.

Today, conflicts between radical Islam and non-Muslims are for the most part centered on an encounter with the West. But historically, Islam has also had violent encounters with both China and India. It is not beyond the realm of possibility that the spread of religious violence in the name of Islam may one day foster a future alignment of nations beyond that occurring among France, Russia, and the United States.

Islam is not without resources in developing doctrines of non-violence and religious freedom. Daniel Philpott has written of the "seeds of freedom" in Islam, which include the Koranic verse, "there is no compulsion in religion."[69] There are also important seeds in some of the historical experiments of cultural interchange between Christians and Muslims, and there is the success of Muslim-majority countries like Senegal in moving toward religious freedom.

And we tend to forget that in this cultural interchange, Christianity has proven able to work together with—and even influence—Islam in a way that achieved greatness. Philip Jenkins notes:

> It was Christians . . . who preserved and translated the cultural inheritance of the ancient world—the science, philosophy, and medicine—and who transmitted it to centers like Baghdad and Damascus. Much of what we call Arab

scholarship was in reality Syriac, Persian, and Coptic . . . Syriac-speaking Christian scholars brought the works of Aristotle to the Muslim world. . . . Syriac Christians even make the first reference to the efficient Indian numbering system that we know today as 'Arabic.'. . . Such were the Christian roots of the Arabic golden age.

Two unanswered questions are whether Western nations have the will to encourage this dynamic, and whether Western nations can provide an atmosphere in which Muslim leaders can undertake the discussion necessary to bring about a process of reform.

Here is where *Dignitatis Humanae* can play a decisive role.

As the Second Vatican Council acknowledged, the Catholic Church was late in developing its doctrine of religious freedom. Its experience in doing so, however, should provide a reason for hope for Muslims working to develop an Islamic doctrine of religious freedom.

I would suggest six principles established in the Declaration that could assist both Western policy makers and reform-minded Muslims.

First, religious freedom has staying power because it is gift of God, not of the state. The right of religious freedom, said the Council Fathers, "is known through the revealed word of God and by reason itself."[70] It is an inalienable right. Retrieving this fundamental idea—the very engine of Western democracy—will be critical to retrieving the commitment of the West to religious freedom.

Second, to protect religious freedom is to protect its free exercise in *public* matters as well as private. The Declaration teaches that "Injury . . . is done to the human person and to the very order established by God for human life, if the free exercise of religion is denied in society, provided just public order is observed."[71] All the great religions of the world are premised upon an insight that their faith community is called not only to a specific way of praying, but to a specific way of living. A notion of religious freedom that excludes the "free exercise of religion" and substitutes instead the narrow concept of freedom to worship is universally inadequate.

Third, religious freedom extends to religious communities and faith-based civil-society organizations as well as individuals. The Declaration observes, "the social nature of man . . . requires that he should . . . participate with others in matters religious; that he should profess his religion in community."[72]

Fourth, religious freedom does not mean an indifferentism that assumes all religions are the same, or equally true. It is difficult to overemphasize this principle in the context of the current crisis. By linking religious freedom with each person's responsibility to seek the truth, the Declaration grounds religious freedom at the very heart of human dignity and not simply as the consequence of a philosophical skepticism.

Fifth, all religious and faith-based communities have an equal right to make their respective claims in society. Notwithstanding their reaffirmation of the Catholic Church's centrality in the lives of men, the Declaration does not reassert a claim for a *privileged* position in the civil order. Instead, it affirmed the right of all religious communities, lay and religious, Christian and non-Christian, to equality in the civil order.

The Declaration proposes for all faith-based communities a broad spectrum of civic rights, including the right to select, train, and place clergy; communicate with "religious authorities and communities abroad," raise funds, own property, erect buildings, and "establish educational, cultural, charitable, and social organizations, under the impulse of their own religious sense."[73]

Sixth, the religious freedom asserted by the Declaration has important limits. It is not a license for violence or any other act contrary to the moral law. This qualification is vital for Muslim-majority states that will have to balance the desire to give Islam a significant public role with the responsibility to guarantee religious freedom for all religious minorities.

The right to the exercise of religious freedom, according to the

Declaration, is "subject to certain regulatory norms [including] respect both for the rights of others and . . . for the common welfare of all." It also states that "[S]ociety has the right to defend itself against possible abuses committed on the pretext of freedom of religion. It is the special duty of government to provide this protection."[74]

Let me close by noting that when *Dignitatis Humanae* was promulgated at the Second Vatican Council in 1965, most Catholic-majority nations, such as Spain, Chile, and the Philippines, had authoritarian governments that were widely believed to be incapable of protecting the rights of non-Catholic citizens and religious groups.

But during the ensuing decades, the world witnessed what Samuel Huntington called "the third wave of democratization," in which many of these Catholic nations began the transition from authoritarianism to free and stable societies.[75] Huntington (citing George Weigel) and others have flagged *Dignitatis Humanae* as one of the necessary catalysts to this transition.[76] Stimulated by the apostle of religious freedom—Saint John Paul II, who had significantly influenced the drafting of *Dignitatis Humanae* during the Council—Catholic-majority nations the world over began to embrace its principles.

A document like *Dignitatis Humanae* could not have been written just 100 years before. Yet the Catholic Church saw its views of religious freedom advance substantially in just over a century.

In his book *Principles of Catholic Theology*, Josef Ratzinger spoke of three of the Second Vatican Council's texts—*Gaudium et Spes*, *Dignitatis Humanae* and *Nostra Aetate*—as "a kind of counter-syllabus" to the nineteenth century Syllabus of Errors.[77]

If Catholic thought in this area can so develop, it is not unreasonable to hope and suggest that other religions could see similar developments of thought as well. If it is true for Christianity in Ratzinger's words that "neither embrace nor ghetto can solve for Christians the problem of the modern world," the same can be said for Islam or any other populous religion, which must navigate in our pluralistic and often secular world.[78]

How religion can engage in constructive engagement is something Christianity has pioneered, and can help others do as well.

In this way, *Dignitatis Humanae* can be a document of hope, not only for its theological contributions and policy implications, but for its historical importance as a document that charted a course few might have considered just a century before.

If today, Catholicism can eschew and condemn the concept of violence in the name of religion, there is no reason that other religions cannot do the same as well.

Islam, it is true, has no pope or magisterium that can take the lead in moving toward religious freedom. What Muslims do have is two competing visions of Islam: a religion of peace, and a religion of violent jihad. One of those visions is eventually likely to triumph over the other, but it is an open question as to which.

Addressing this dichotomy is one of the great issues of our day—both for the Muslim-majority world and the Christian-formed West. If we do not work together, the results will be catastrophic for us all.

Today, we benefit from the remarkable leadership of Pope Francis who has spoken out about the genocide of Christians, has condemned violence and killing in the name of religion, and has spoken strongly about the need to enhance religious freedom. He has spoken this message in the West—in Europe and the United States, and just last month, he became the first pope in history to visit an active conflict zone when he visited Africa, where he urged an end to violence. We might all ask ourselves whether we have done enough to add our voices to his.

As we celebrate its fiftieth anniversary, *Dignitatis Humanae* provides us with a unique platform from which we can address both the East and the West. We might consider that it creates an intellectual space in which all persons of good will can meet, find a common ground, and affirm a common dignity.

Perhaps working together, Christians and Muslims can create together a second Arabic golden age—as they did centuries ago.

5.

Atrocities
in Iraq and Syria
Relief for Survivors
and Accountability
for Perpetrators

Presented at a hearing before the Helsinki Commission
September 22, 2016, Washington, DC

Following Secretary of State John Kerry's 2016 declaration that ISIS was committing genocide against Christians and other religious minorities, there was substantial debate over what the U.S. Government's humanitarian response should be. One response was a visit to Iraq three months later by Congressman Chris Smith—who co-chaired the Helsinki Commission—along with members of the Knights of Columbus to see the situation, confronting displaced Christians first hand. This trip and this congressional testimony became part of the basis for another act, H.R. 390, the Iraq and Syria Genocide Relief and Accountability Act of 2018. That act would pass both the House and Senate unanimously and would authorize the government explicitly to assist communities, including Christians, targeted for genocide by ISIS.

Thank you, Mr. Chairman, and members of the Commission, for this opportunity to testify. Congress and the Administration have our appreciation for their declarations of genocide that speak on behalf of victims, who often feel that the world has forgotten them.

Mr. Chairman, you, Ms. Eshoo, Mr. Fortenberry, and Mr. Franks are to be commended for your leadership in introducing H.R. 5961 [of 2016], *the Iraq and Syria Genocide Relief and Accountability Act.* In testimony in May, I outlined six principles for averting the extinction of Christians and other minorities in the Middle East.

I am grateful that H.R. 5961 makes progress in all six of these areas. Thank you, and be assured of the full support of the Knights of Columbus in your work to bring this bill to the President's desk with all deliberate speed.

I would like to speak to you today about three matters.

First, our government's humanitarian aid bureaucracy is often not making aid available to communities that need it most.

Section 5 of the bill directs the Secretary of State in consultation with Administration officials to prioritize relief particularly for those groups and individuals targeted for genocide, to identify their vulnerabilities, and to work with humanitarian and faith-based organizations to address these needs. It seems that it is more of a mindset than anything else that has resulted in the need for this section.

Our representatives have met with U.S. and U.N. officials in Iraq and in Washington to ask them all the same question: "Why aren't the communities that were victims of this genocide receiving public aid?"

The main answer has been that the current policy prioritizes individual needs but does not consider the needs of vulnerable communities—even when they have been targeted for genocide and risk disappearing altogether.

But regardless of the reason, the outcome is the same. Such a policy increases the likelihood that the complete eradication of these groups from the region—which was the intent of the genocide—will succeed.

We know that many Christian and Yazidi victims of genocide do not receive public aid.

And here we have a fundamental inconsistency in the U.S. stance toward the genocide.

On the one hand, we have the unanimous policy of the elected branches of the United States government stating that a genocide is occurring. On the other hand, we have an aid bureaucracy that is allowing the intended consequence of the genocide to continue, even though it is in our power to stop it.

Responding to a genocide requires a different approach. Fortunately, the bureaucratic roadblocks are mainly cultural, not statutory.

What the bureaucracy needs is an immediate change of mindset. Legislation—or the threat of legislation—may be helpful in hastening this, but even now, it does not have to be this way.

As this bill proceeds to a vote, our legislative and executive representatives need to deliver to our diplomatic and aid entities a clear and simple message:

In the midst of this genocide, saving Christians—and other communities that face extinction—in Iraq and Syria is part of your mission. There is nothing unconstitutional, illegal, unethical or unprofessional about prioritizing their right to survival *as communities.* They are innocent victims of a genocide. If these victim communities are not receiving aid, you are not fulfilling your mission. And helping them is inconsistent with the best of American and U.S. State Department tradition.

In fact, exactly a century ago, during and following World War I, the United States government helped assist Christians in the region with direct aid as they suffered what Pope Francis has called the first genocide of the twentieth century.[79]

Chartered by an act of Congress, and recipient of more than $25 million in direct U.S. government "supplies, services, and cash," the

Near East Relief organization constituted a collaboration of the State Department and American religious entities on the ground in the Middle East. It is widely credited with having been key in saving religious pluralism in the region during and following World War I. And I am proud to say that the Knights of Columbus was among the groups that supported this humanitarian effort in the 1920s.[80]

The organization sought to save the Christian populations of Iran, Iraq, Syria, and Armenia from "immediate and total destruction."[81]

There is no reason that such a prioritization and partnership—assisted by direct government funding—could not exist today to save Yazidis, Christians, and other small vulnerable indigenous groups.

To be clear, we have had the assistance of many people who are working within this system and are trying to help, and many officials are advocating within their entities for a change in the status quo. But they are often limited by a bureaucracy that is resistant to initiative and resists change.

What is lacking may be legislation, but it is also leadership. With this bill, Congress is providing leadership—and it is time for the aid community to respond. If they do not, the officials from the State Department, USAID, and their private partners that have not prioritized aid to Christians and Yazidi communities need to continue to hear directly from Congress and from the President and from the American people that public aid needs to flow to these communities now.

Second, on the subject of aid I would like to reiterate that, in addition to the funds provided in this bill, Congress should explore a stand-alone emergency appropriations bill to respond to this genocide in an even more direct and comprehensive manner.

It seems that few situations could be as worthy of such a measure as the genocide Congress has declared unanimously to be ongoing.

My third point is that the aid we provide must be an investment in a more peaceful future in the region. This cannot happen unless the system of religious apartheid there ends. Christians and other religious minorities are entitled to equal rights and the equal protection of the laws as enumerated in the Universal Declaration of Human Rights.[82]

Our tax dollars to governments in the region must not be used to rebuild a discriminatory system that imposes second-class citizenship upon religious minorities. U.S. aid for reconstruction, military, and other purposes should be contingent on the application of full and equal rights of citizenship to every citizen of Iraq and other countries in the region, as defined by the Universal Declaration.

This agenda demands from us a new approach to issues of human rights in the region.

When we speak of human rights, we are referencing those rights enumerated in the Universal Declaration of Human Rights. When governments in Muslim-majority countries speak of human rights, they may be thinking of those rights as defined—or as confined—by *Sharia*. The interests of the region, and our own interests demand that we not mislead ourselves or allow others to mislead us in this regard.

Our own laws, including the International Religious Freedom Act of 1998,[83] recognize these realities, and require our government to act. Christians in the Middle East region have a natural and universal right to practice their faith freely and openly. They must receive protection from civil authorities when they do so. They and other minorities must have religious freedom. Without it, pluralism will certainly die, and with it all hope for stability in the region. If civil authorities in the region cannot supply this protection, they are not suitable partners for our aid.

Only with such policies will we be able to break the cycle of persecution culminating in genocide, which has afflicted these communities for far too long, and which threatens international peace and security.

Mr. Chairman, thank you very much for your leadership and that of the members of this Commission.

6.

Christians of the Middle East Are a Precious Patrimony of Humanity

SPEECH

Upon receiving the Lifetime Achievement
Award from In Defense of Christians
September 8, 2016, Washington, DC

The Knights had worked closely with In Defense of Christians (IDC) on the genocide report and campaign to get the U.S. government to recognize that ISIS's actions were genocide. After the genocide designation by Congress and Secretary John Kerry, but before the government had prioritized attention to religious communities targeted by ISIS, this speech focused on the need to ensure that government aid not exclude these communities (including via Congressional legislation, which successfully came to fruition with H.R. 390, the Iraq and Syria Genocide Relief and Accountability Act). The speech—given at IDC's dinner in 2016—also challenged both presidential candidates (Hillary Clinton and Donald Trump) to prioritize this issue as well. At the same time, it urged that dialogue on human rights be based on the Universal Declaration of Human Rights, because the meaning of human rights language coming from different political and/or religious perspectives might not always have the meaning assumed by those in the West.

It is an honor to receive this award this evening. I accept it on behalf of those Christians in the Middle East, who have lost everything—except their faith. They are the ones who deserve an award for providing for the rest of us a witness of authentic Christianity.

Today we celebrate and honor their triumph of faith, hope, and love over trials so terrible most of us cannot imagine them. These Christians persevere through an everyday heroism; and despite the tragic costs of that heroism, they continue to hope.

And their hope includes a faith in us—that our own efforts when joined with those of others will be sufficient to allow their witness to continue.

In the past year, much has happened. Our government has declared with one voice that Christians, Yazidis, and other religious minority groups face genocide. Both sides of the aisle are to be commended for the unanimity of this message from Congress, our State Department, and the U.S. Commission on International Religious Freedom.

The Knights of Columbus was pleased to assist in this determination through our public awareness efforts and the report we produced at the request of the State Department on the situation confronting Christians in the region.

But there is still much for us to do.

At the Knights of Columbus' international convention last month, Patriarch Ignatius Youssef III Younan of the Syriac Catholic Church noted: "The very existence of Eastern Churches, those churches that come from the apostles' time, is at stake." He also said Christians there are an "endangered species."[84]

And he noted an important difference between this genocide and the genocide committed against both his people and the Armenian people in the early twentieth century. Then, that savagery was little known and seemed far away. Today's campaign of murder is happening, as he said, "before the eyes of the whole world, and the global indifference is stunning!"[85]

We also must face this reality: even in those areas where genocide by the sword may have ended, the lingering effect on the genocide survivors continues. We might say that many survivors now face a new genocide by attrition. Many of those who have lost everything now live as refugees who cannot find employment or housing or adequate medical care or clothing, or education for their children. They will inevitably lose hope. Under such conditions these Christian communities will gradually but surely fade into oblivion.

But a genocide that some began by the sword cannot be allowed to succeed through indifference.

A legal genocide designation is simply a diagnosis. By itself it is not a cure.

However, the United States can provide that cure if we have the political will to do so.

First, fragile indigenous religious communities must be preserved. And that requires money. The Knights of Columbus and other religious organizations have filled the void to the extent possible. But we are told that up until now, in many places, including in Erbil, Christians have received no financial support from our government or from the United Nations. Currently, individual needs are prioritized. But the fate of minority religious communities that could entirely disappear receives no consideration. This has been confirmed to us directly by U.S. and U.N. officials on the ground in Iraq.

This must end now.

Congress should immediately authorize emergency appropriations that will actually reach these endangered communities. The current aid channels have failed. We can no longer rely exclusively or even primarily upon government delivery systems in the region. Steps must be taken to ensure that financial aid is delivered directly to these threatened indigenous communities. This will require opening new delivery channels and new partnerships with religious organizations.

The idea that we should help everyone is noble. But the idea that we should help only individuals and ignore communities facing extinction is not. Victims and survivors of genocide should be prioritized.

Second, the system of religious apartheid in the region must end. Christians and other religious minorities are entitled to equal rights and the equal protection of the laws as enumerated in the Universal Declaration of Human Rights.

Our tax dollars to the region must not be used to rebuild a discriminatory system that continues to impose second-class citizenship upon religious minorities. U.S. aid for reconstruction, military, and other purposes should be contingent on the application of full rights of citizenship to every citizen of Iraq and other countries in the region.

Tonight, I call upon leaders of both political parties, as well as candidates for president, Hillary Clinton and Donald Trump, to commit themselves to this simple agenda: to promote the international affirmation of their human rights in keeping with the Universal Declaration of Human Rights, both as individuals and as distinct societies within their national framework, and to end the second-class citizenship of religious minorities in the Middle East; and, to help preserve their ancient communities, which should be considered part of the cultural heritage of all humanity, including by direct government funding for those communities who were targeted for genocide.

This agenda demands from us a new realism in our approach to issues of human rights in the region.

Dialog is, of course, necessary if we are to make any progress in this regard. But dialog is possible only when all the participants agree upon the meaning of the words they use.

When we here speak of human rights, we are referencing those rights enumerated in the Universal Declaration of Human Rights. When Islamic governments speak of human rights, they may be thinking of those rights as defined—or as confined—in the *Sharia*-based Cairo Declaration. Realism demands that we not mislead ourselves or allow others to mislead us in this regard.

Third, we need a clear-eyed view of the history of Islamic cultures and their failure or rejection of secularization. The following observation by Professor John Owen of the University of Virginia deserves serious consideration. He writes:

> We must grapple with the following unsettling fact: secularism has been tried in the Middle East, and in many places it has not worked. Islamism is in fact a reaction to secularism, imposed many decades ago by Europeans and Muslim secularists. Those who say that the Middle East must go through what the early modern West went through must recognize that that has already happened. What is more, far from killing off traditional Islam, secularization transformed it into a potent, variegated modern ideology. All over the Muslim world, Islamist groups and parties—some extreme, some moderate, all determined to weaken secular government—draw support. Nowhere is the irony more striking than in lands where secularism was tried with the most determination.[86]

We must understand how this recent history conditions our efforts for equal rights for Christians and other minorities in the Middle East. It makes our task even more formidable. This is not the place to address the central, and the most challenging, question facing us: To what extent can governments recognize and truly respect human rights if they are also committed to an Islam that totally organizes life on both the political and social levels of their countries. This discussion must soon be undertaken in this country and throughout the non-Islamic world.

Today, the Christians of the Middle East are a brilliant example to the world—and especially to Christians. They forgive their tormentors and practice their faith in spite of what, for many of us, are truly unimaginable costs.

These Christians, many of whom speak the language of Jesus, exemplify a Christianity that is not dying, but instead reflects the face of The One Who Lives. They love one another, they lay down their lives for one another, and they return good for evil.

The United Nations has designated many sites throughout the world as World Heritage Sites because of their importance as a patrimony of humanity. To my mind these Christians in the Middle East are a precious patrimony of humanity.

Their witness to their beliefs should inspire people of all faiths— or of none. In a world crippled by relativism and uncertainty, our brothers and sisters in the Middle East offer the example of complete, selfless commitment.

They inspire us to renew our Christian identity, reaffirm our Christian solidarity, and proclaim to the world that we are one with them. If their witness leads us to do that, then they will have given us, from the riches of their poverty, the greatest gift. That will be the renewal of our Christian faith, here in our own country and throughout the world.

7.

The U.S. Government's Genocide Recovery and Persecution Response Initiative in Iraq

SPEECH

Given at the U.S. Department of State
Ministerial on Religious Freedom
July 17, 2019, Washington, DC

Having advocated for years for an aid policy that did not leave out those targeted for genocide, I was honored to speak at the U.S. State Department's Ministerial on Religious Freedom in the summer of 2019. While the American government had placed greater focus on religious minorities targeted by ISIS, new threats had emerged, in particular, Iranian-backed militias, which saw in Christian towns places to occupy and expand their influence. The Ministerial was an important indication of the American government's commitment to international religious freedom. It brought together high-level government "ministers" from countries around the world as well as bipartisan representatives from within the American political scene. The event made clear that, even in a time of extreme partisanship, some core principles, including international religious freedom, were a unifying force.

Good morning. It is an honor to address you today on the issue of genocide recovery and persecution response in Iraq.

Last year, Vice President Pence announced the Genocide Recovery and Persecution Response Initiative. This is an important step forward for the United States, and we are grateful for his leadership and that of the White House, the State Department, and USAID on this issue. We are also pleased that our organization has been able to provide important input to this and the previous administration on the response to religious persecution, and has worked successfully for unanimous passage by both houses of Congress on not one, but two bills addressing this genocide and its aftermath.[87]

Beginning in the nineteenth century, the Knights of Columbus began its advocacy on behalf of religious freedom—here at home and around the world. We were born against the backdrop—and in some ways as a response to—the rampant anti-Catholicism of nineteenth-century New England, and our members in the United States, including candidates for president like Alfred E. Smith and John F. Kennedy, found themselves suspect in some quarters because of their faith.

Our organization took religious freedom seriously around the world, speaking out on behalf of persecuted Armenian Christians a century ago and working in support of President Wilson's response. We supported Mexican Catholics persecuted by their government in the 1920s and 1930s and urged action by Presidents Coolidge and Roosevelt. Also in the 1930s, we urged President Roosevelt to take action on behalf of Jews in Germany, and went on to work in support of those whose religious freedom was suppressed behind the Iron Curtain during the Cold War.

More recently, we have turned our attention to religious communities targeted for genocide—particularly in the Middle East—becoming involved in assisting and advocating for those targeted by ISIS in 2014. To date, we have committed about $25 million to support persecuted communities in Iraq, Syria, and the surrounding region.

In 2016, we led the effort to have ISIS's crimes declared genocide by Congress and by then-Secretary Kerry, providing the state department with a nearly 300-page report detailing the evidence and legal analysis supporting that determination.

We have built on that work with this administration—and with Congress. We have urged more efficient means of assisting those communities targeted for extermination by ISIS—especially since many of these minority communities had been overlooked in terms of US government and UN humanitarian aid and reconstruction.

This administration's work to rectify such oversights and to provide assistance to those communities who faced genocide is an important step forward for how the United States can and should respond to such situations.

While the now-common individual-needs approach has noble goals, in this case, it clearly overlooked shattered communities in danger of extinction. The administration's willingness to rethink strict adherence to this model based on the reality of the aftermath of ISIS's genocide is commendable. The fact that infrastructure and other projects have focused on targeted communities will be key to their survival. It is also consistent with U.S. government practice historically. After World War I and World War II, those religious minorities that faced genocide received a level of priority from the United States government. It is good that the United States is doing so again in this instance.

For the government and targeted communities, the Knights of Columbus has been able to serve as a mediating institution, to use a term popular some decades ago. We have provided points of contact and connectivity between the American government, other actors, and the religious minority communities targeted by ISIS. We have helped to bridge gaps, clarify solutions, and bring key stakeholders together from government, UN, NGOs, and victimized communities to find strategies that work in light of the reality of the situation.

While we have not taken government money in our more than 135-year history, we have worked closely with the U.S. government on post-ISIS relief and reconstruction efforts, signing an MOU with USAID to help better coordinate responses to persecution and genocide, including better information sharing.

This public/private partnership in the humanitarian arena has allowed government funding to address big-ticket infrastructure items, while allowing us the flexibility to quickly do projects that regulations make difficult for the government. For instance, we have focused on rebuilding homes in the town of Karamles, one of the few success stories for returns to the portion of the Nineveh region controlled by Baghdad.

Let me also say this. Regulatory reform is badly needed. USAID was founded by Knight of Columbus and U.S. President John F. Kennedy in 1961. The regulatory constraints on USAID have only grown since. While many of the regulations probably make sense in isolation, the vast maze of regulations can mean that comprehensive solutions are elusive. Only certain problems can be solved in this context, and they may not always be the most important ones. MOUs with private organizations can help, but so would legislation, giving more flexibility in humanitarian crisis situations, particularly situations of genocide.

One final note. During a visit to Iraq earlier this year, I was told repeatedly that security is the primary concern of those trying to return home after ISIS. The Knights of Columbus along with other organizations, and the United States and other countries, including Hungary, have spent millions of dollars to assist returns by targeted communities to Nineveh—the place that has been their home for millennia.

But this is being threatened by the unaccountable PMF [Iranian-backed militias known as Popular Mobilization Forces] forces, which the government of Iraq in Baghdad seems unwilling or unable to control. Reports of abuse by PMF forces is common. As a result, minority communities fear to return, and every day more slip away from Iraq.

If the destruction of these communities by ISIS is completed by the PMF, Baghdad will bear responsibility for the loss of its minorities.

Before I visited Iraq in March, I met with Pope Francis who told me that the Middle East without Christians is not the Middle East. The Iraqi ambassador to the United States often says something similar: Iraq without its minorities is not Iraq.

Keeping the authentic identity of Iraq, and of the Middle East more generally, is a priority for all of us, but it is the particular responsibility of the national governments there. They owe it to their people to protect *all* of their people, regardless of the faith they profess. We stand at a critical juncture, and we urge Baghdad and the other governments of the Middle East to take the protection and preservation of their minority communities seriously.

As this ministerial makes clear, the world is watching.

8.

To Build a Civilization of Love in the Middle East
"Beloved, rejoice in so far as you share in the sufferings of Christ"

SPEECH

Given at the 54th National Apostolate
of Maronites Convention
July 1, 2017, Greenville, South Carolina

Delivered to the annual convention of the Maronites in the United States, this speech focused on the power and unique witness in the Middle East of Christian forgiveness. Given the unique infrastructure of the Maronite Church and the relative stability (until recently) of its Lebanese homeland, the speech also laid out a particular path by which Maronites could put their specific advantages to work on behalf of all the Christians in the region.

Christianity in Non-Western Contexts

I would like to begin my remarks today by reflecting not on the situation in the Middle East but on the history of seventeenth-century Japan.

Perhaps some of you have seen Martin Scorsese's recent film *Silence,* based on the book by the same title by the Japanese Catholic author Shusaku Endo. As we know, Saint Francis Xavier brought Christianity to Japan in 1549, and even though many Christians were persecuted in the years that followed, in less than a century, there were approximately 300,000 Japanese Christians. Thereafter, an even greater persecution of Christians occurred in which thousands of Japanese Christians were killed—on one occasion as many as 30,000.[88]

The martyrdom by burning of fifty-five Japanese Christians including little children was recounted by an English visitor to Japan in the early 1600s. It provides a telling example of the suffering and witness of these Christians. As their execution drew near, the martyrs sang the *Magnificat* and *Laudate Dominum omnes gentes*, and at their death, the many thousands of Christians present for the executions sang the *Te Deum*.

In 1632, the leader of the Jesuit Mission to Japan, Father Christovao Ferreira, renounced the Christian faith and began cooperating with the Japanese authorities in the suppression of Christians.

Silence recounts the story of two young Jesuit missionaries who travel to Japan to ascertain whether the rumors about Father Ferreira's apostasy are true. The film is an extraordinary portrayal of the persecution of them and the Japanese Christians they meet.

There are many aspects of the book and the film that we could consider, but for me the dramatic high point is the confrontation between Father Ferreira and the young Jesuit who has come to find him, Father Rodrigues.

Father Ferreira describes himself as "an old missionary defeated by missionary work" and says, "The one thing I know is that our religion does not take root in this country." But the young Jesuit replies, "It is not that it does not take root. . . . It's that the roots are torn up."[89] He cites as proof the many thousands of Japanese Christians who have accepted death rather than renounce their faith.

Father Ferreira responds that it is not really Christianity that has taken root in Japan. "The Japanese did not believe in the Christian

God but in their own distortion. . . . In the minds of the Japanese," he says, "the Christian God was completely changed."[90]

Earlier, Father Rodrigues confronted the Shogun's inquisitor who also had told him that a foreign religion like Christianity would not be accepted in Japan. Father Rodrigues replies that if Christianity is not true everywhere, it is true nowhere.

This brings me to the point that I wish to make here. It seems to me that part of the importance of the film and its popularity in some quarters is precisely the impression that it creates of a Christianity that is too conditioned by Western culture and its intellectual tradition to take root in other parts of the world.[91]

And further, in an era of increasing sensitivity to diversity and globalization, whether this depiction of a Westernized self-limited Christianity—a stereotype to be sure—is gradually taking hold in too many parts of the West, even among some Christians.

If this is so, then we should ask ourselves today: what is the role of the Christian witness and suffering that has been the hallmark of the Maronite Christians in the Middle East? And especially, what are the lessons that Christians in the United States can learn from their experience and testimony?

The Unique Potential of Maronite Witness

I think we must explore the meaning for us of today's martyrs of the Middle East. Especially, what do they teach us about the call of Christian discipleship for Catholics living in the United States today?

Surely these men and women stand as beacons of light for their fellow Christians in the Middle East. But it seems to me that they offer all of us a beautiful example of what it means to be a universal Church that must today become a true global church.

It seems to me further, that while Maronite Christians—and all of us—have a responsibility and a mission to help preserve Christianity in the Middle East, Maronite Christians today have a special mission to their fellow Christians in the West, and especially in the

United States, to deepen their own understanding of the path of Christian discipleship and witness.

And because of your unique history and experience, I think that in many ways you have a unique contribution to make to the Christian community in the United States.

For nearly five decades, popes going back to Paul VI have called on us to build a civilization of love. The need is certainly enormous around the world, and especially in the Middle East. The rise of ISIS has brought a brutality and hatred of our faith on a scale unique in recent memory. But even when the terror group and its allies are defeated militarily, there is only one thing strong enough to counter its ideology—that is the witness of Christian love and forgiveness.

In the words of Lebanese Statesman Charles Malik—"You may win every battle, but if you lose the war of ideas, you will have lost the war. You may lose every battle, but if you win the war of ideas, you will have won the war."

Building a Culture of Love and Forgiveness

Love and forgiveness are central to our faith, and always have been. We believe in a God who is love, whose son died for us out of love, and who forgave his killers. We believe that as his disciples we should imitate him.

Christians have practiced this from the beginning.

In some ways, the blueprint for building a civilization of love is simple. It is the great commandment: love God completely, and our neighbors as ourselves (Matthew 22:37–39).

Lived authentically, Christians have witnessed to this from the beginning and in so doing, converted not just the Middle East to Christianity, but also substantial populations of the Roman Empire and eventually of Europe, America, and much of Africa and Asia, as well.

Those in this room certainly know what a Christian bishop from Syria pointed out to me: Saint Paul did not convert the citizens of that country. Rather, the Syrian Christians baptized Saint Paul!

And I would add this. They had to forgive him before they baptized him. When asked to visit Paul, Syrian Christian Ananias' first reaction was to remind the Lord that Paul had persecuted Christians. Ananias had to forgive, then embrace his former persecutor.

As Saint Augustine would write several hundred years later, hating an evil person resulted in two people (the hater and the hated) being evil.

Of course, the Maronite Church has its roots in Syria, even if its home now is predominately in Lebanon. And we know from *The Acts of the Apostles* that Saint Paul was cared for by the Christians in Lebanon during his travels (*Acts 11:19*).

Saint Maron, for whom your Church is named, certainly was a pioneer in building a civilization of love. He was famous not only for his acts of self-denial as a man who lived alone, exposed to the elements to be closer to God, but also for healing the physical and spiritual infirmities of the many who sought him out.

Although Saint Maron lived apart from the world, he ministered to it with a Christian love and charity that focused on the needs of those who sought him out.

His disciples did the same. They continued his work of healing, while also gathering together a group of blind beggars and caring for them. In other words, from its very beginning, charity was foundational to the Maronite Church.

That loving charitable impulse—an impulse that can change the world through love—continues in the Maronite Church today. Recently, I read Patriarch Rai's new encyclical. It was impressive in a number of ways, but perhaps most impressive were the charitable endeavors of the Maronite Church it listed just in Lebanon:

- 275 schools serving 192,000 students and tuition subsidies of $31 million.

- 5 universities serving 22,000 students with financial aid totaling nearly $14 million.

- 12 hospitals, serving nearly 300,000 patients.

- 25 medical clinics.

- 9 childcare centers.

- 5 centers for people with special needs.

- 10 nursing homes.

- And another 9 charitable organizations.[92]

In short, the charity and service that show our faith in action in a transformative way are already an essential component of the Maronite Church. Little wonder that your infrastructure has helped provide a safe haven in Lebanon for many of your fellow Christians from Iraq and Syria. The Knights of Columbus has supported efforts on behalf of persecuted Christians, through which we have donated more than $12 million to Christian refugees in Lebanon, and also in Iraq, Syria, Jordan, and Egypt. And we will continue this year to do more.

The charitable infrastructure that the Maronite Church has established is today a providential resource for peace in the region. Because of what you have accomplished, you are stewards of hope and you have a vital role in building a new future in the Middle East. Your charity during a very uncharitable time wonderfully reflects what Pope Benedict XVI wrote in *Deus Caritas Est*: What is required among Christians today is "a heart [that] sees where love is needed and acts accordingly."[93]

The Maronite Church is also a remarkable symbol of unity. It is unique among the Eastern churches in having always been loyal to the pope, even when that meant suffering persecution from other Christians. That unity matters not only theologically, but also because it shows that our Catholic faith is able to transcend regional, linguistic, and cultural differences.

Forgiveness: A Uniquely Christian Witness

Pope Francis recently spoke words that I think will resonate with every Maronite and every Christian in—or from—the Middle East. He said this: "Here is the secret to this mission: the presence among us of the Risen Lord, who with the gift of the Holy Spirit, continues to open our minds and our hearts, to proclaim his love and his mercy even in the most resistant areas of our cities."[94]

This is the history of Christians indigenous to the Middle East. There are few areas more resistant to God's love and mercy than terrorist or extremist controlled regions of the Middle East. And yet, Christians stay whenever possible. Why?

From many conversations with those from the region over the past few years, one reason is this: Christians stay because they understand that without them, the future of the entire region would suffer. When they live out their faith authentically, Christians bring a unique sense of forgiveness and love. They are a bright light pointing the way to a civilization of love.

For an authentic witness of our Christian faith—based on love— stands in stark contrast to hatred, murder, slavery, and pillaging. And while revenge creates a cycle of violence that is often hard to break, forgiveness ends the cycle of violence and shows the path to building a civilization of love and a society of peace.

Today, many Christians in the Middle East have given up everything but their faith, for their faith. But even having lost so much, these heroic men and women have given a great gift to their fellow citizens and to the world. The gift they have given is the example of faith embodied in acts of forgiveness and mercy—the fundamental building blocks of peace, and an important component of building a civilization of love.

Consider the following examples of the witness of Christian faith that directly counter ISIS's ideology of hate.

A young girl burned to death by ISIS in Mosul told her mother to "forgive them" before she died of her injuries in a hospital.[95]

Twelve-year-old Myriam surprised the world when, speaking of ISIS, she told ABC's *20/20* "Yes I forgive them." Then she added this: "Jesus said 'forgive each other, love each other the way I love you,' that is what we need to learn. Forgiveness."[96]

In Egypt too, we have seen such forgiveness. The widow of Naseem Faheem, a guard at St. Mark's Cathedral who was killed in the bombing there said: "I'm not angry at the one who did this. . . . I'm telling him, 'May God forgive you, and we also forgive you. Believe me, we forgive you.'"[97]

Egypt was collectively shocked at her words, for the importance of this Christian witness of forgiveness is not lost on those of other faiths. For example, Iraqi Muslim religious leader Ali Al-Yacoubi has noted: "Our Christian brothers must be thanked for they are an element of peace and coexistence for Iraq, because 'despite having suffered a lot,' they have never responded to attacks with violence, but have continued to promote unity in a country that 'has to be of and for everyone.'"[98]

Writing in *The City of God*, Saint Augustine observed: "Let this city bear in mind, that among her enemies lie hidden those who are destined to be fellow citizens, that she may not think it a fruitless labor to bear what they inflict as enemies until they become confessors of the truth."[99]

When we hear of the quiet conversions or of apologies from former persecutors, we have some idea of the power this witness is having.

The truth is that we stand at a crossroads for the future of Christianity—and pluralism—in the Middle East. Either Christianity will survive, continuing to offer a witness of forgiveness, charity, and mercy, or it will disappear, impoverishing the region religiously, ethnically, and culturally.

The Christian witness has been profound—not only in terms of forgiveness, but also in terms of charity to others in need as well.

This continues day in and day out, in acts great and small.

On a Knights of Columbus trip to Iraq last year, a member of our team was told by a Yazidi family that with the exception of one kilo of lamb delivered in 2014, *all* of the assistance they have received was from Christians. Though they have next to nothing themselves, we hear reports over and over again of Christians reaching out to care for those with even less.

We see the same charitable witness in Lebanon, where many Iraqi and Syrian Christians have fled to Lebanon seeking safety.

The efforts of the Maronite community there on behalf of these Christian refugees have been impressive and important.

So has the fearlessness of Lebanese Christians in the face of attacks from ISIS on some of their towns.

Despite years of occupation, war, and abuse, Lebanon is the only country in the region where a sizeable percentage of the population is Christian, and yours is the only Church in the region with such a strong and wide-ranging Church-based charitable infrastructure.

Despite the many problems Lebanon has faced for the past four decades, the Maronite Church has continued to focus on helping its brothers and sisters in need and building for the future with such institutions.

Such infrastructure not only means that Maronites can help other Christians that flee to Lebanon, but it also means that Maronites have something unique to offer in terms of helping these communities to rebuild when the time comes.

Necessary Responses from Church and State

If Christianity is to survive in the Middle East, all of us—whether we are Maronites in Lebanon or Roman Catholics in North Carolina—all of us have certain responsibilities. If we want a civilization of love to spring up where hatred and genocide ruled before, all of us must take action based on our faith.

First, we must live out that faith authentically. Like Saint Maron, our own comfort should be less important to us than our relationship with God and the needs of our neighbors.

Second, we must love our neighbor as ourselves especially in their time of greatest need. This means we must support Christians in countries like Iraq or Syria or Egypt or Libya—and, at times, Lebanon—who face persecution and death for their faith. That support must have financial, spiritual, and advocacy components. We must do another thing as well: we must forgive those who wrong us.

Third, the unity we have with our Church must extend to one another too. We must foster a sense of brotherhood among Christians—those who worship and believe just as we do and those who differ in some way from us as well. Too often as Christians, a lack of unity places us in a vulnerable position. Christ's prayer that we may be one should start with each one of us. We should lead the way with our example in terms of our actions in public life.

Those three steps are the key to the building a real civilization of love.

Within the Knights of Columbus, we speak of these three components as our principles of Charity, Unity and Fraternity—all guided by our faith.

- **Charity** puts our love of God into action by helping those most in need, following Christ's mandate that having loved God completely, we also turn our attention to loving our neighbor as ourselves.

- **Unity** keeps us connected to our Church and to each other, and aligns all we do to our faith.

- **Fraternity** joins us to each other in the common cause of doing good for our neighbor—to live as brothers seeking to care for each other.

Soon after our founding, we added a fourth principle: patriotism, love of country.

And whether we hold an American passport or a Lebanese one, we—and our countries—have something important to offer in this case.

America is widely understood to be a pluralistic society and a democracy. Those in the Middle East know that the same is true of Lebanon. It is a pluralistic society and a democracy in a region where both are rare.

This is an important example, because historically, when Christians and Muslims are able to work together in a common cause, when pluralism is given a chance in the Middle East and Christians are allowed to contribute, the results can be incredible for the entire world.

Consider the words of Professor Philip Jenkins, who writes:

It was Christians . . . who preserved and translated the cultural inheritance of the ancient world—the science, philosophy, and medicine—and who transmitted it to centers like Baghdad and Damascus. Much of what we call Arab scholarship was in reality Syriac, Persian, and Coptic. Syriac-speaking Christian scholars brought the works of Aristotle to the Muslim world . . . Syriac Christians even make the first reference to the efficient Indian numbering system that we know today as 'Arabic,' and long before this technique gained currency among Muslim thinkers. Such were the Christian roots of the Arabic golden age.

Imagine if the Christian witness would plant the roots of a new Golden Age—a civilization of love taking root where Christianity itself first took root—in the Middle East.

Perhaps it is simply a fantastic idealism—totally removed from the ways of the world. But as Christians, we are called to be in the world, not of it. And if we think of the history of Ireland and the waves of conversion that have been experienced in Europe or Spain and the conversion of Latin America, perhaps it is not so fantastic.

But this can only happen if we act on our faith in our personal lives and if we act on our faith in our public lives as well, including in what we urge our elected leaders to do.

There is no reason why we should accept a government in the U.S. that ignores the plight of Christians in the Middle East.

In the United States, we must urge our government to ensure that U.S. foreign assistance actually reaches those from the communities targeted for genocide by ISIS. We must also insist that the American government condition our military and government-to-government foreign assistance on the principle of equal citizenship, regardless of faith. As a regional example, our government might well cite Lebanon.

And Maronites too have an enormous responsibility, for no civilization of love or interfaith cooperation can take root in the region without Lebanon.

Living in the only Middle Eastern country with a substantial percentage of the population that is still Christian, Maronites have a particular opportunity to shape a future for democratic pluralism and a particular responsibility to do so in a sustainable way that becomes an undeniable regional model.

In addition, Maronites have something unique to offer on the topic of Christian unity and should further strengthen the unity of Christians in Lebanon, and of Lebanese Christians with those of the neighboring countries.

Maronites who have the benefit of a Church-sponsored charitable infrastructure should use that experience to help other Churches in the Middle East to build such infrastructure themselves and should put that infrastructure at their service when possible.

Finally, as participants in a functioning, pluralistic democracy that is quite unique within the Middle East context, Maronites are well positioned to help those from other countries in the region to consider government options that unify rather than divide citizens.

I would add that Roman Catholics in the West share many of these responsibilities, even if they are in some ways culturally limited as outsiders of the region.

In the months and years ahead, if we would see a civilization of love in our lifetime or in our children's, each of us must act to ensure that the Christian community that baptized Saint Paul, the Christian community of Syria, survives, and that the voices of forgiveness and pluralism in the region are not silenced.

Only an authentic witness to love is strong enough to overcome the hatred and genocide of ISIS.

And we can do another thing too. We can learn from—and deepen—our own faith on the basis of the example of Christian forgiveness and Christian witness that these persecuted Christians have shown to their neighbors, and to the world.

This does not mean that we are to instrumentalize Christianity, that is, to use our Christian faith as a way of empowerment—in order to be more successful in the ways of the world—or perhaps better to achieve success in these matters as the world measures success.

No, as Christians we are called to a moral, personal, and spiritual mission that is to be measured by a calculus that is not of this world.

As Maronites, your roots are in Syria, your homeland is in Lebanon. Your allegiance is to the pope, and you pray in the language of Jesus. Your history has been at times painful and your ancestors themselves have had to flee at times, but that experience—together with your strong faith authentically lived—may well be the key under a Divine Providence that unlocks a better future in the Middle East and around the world.

9.

The Christian Witness of Mercy and Forgiveness Is the True Path to Peace in the Middle East

SPEECH

Upon receiving the Path to Peace Award
from the Path to Peace Foundation
October 12, 2016, New York, New York

The Path to Peace Foundation was founded almost three decades ago to support the work of the Vatican's Permanent Observer Mission of the Holy See to the United Nations. In 2016, the Knights of Columbus and I received the Path to Peace Award for the Order's work on behalf of persecuted Christians in the Middle East and for the Knights' "humanitarian work throughout the world." The speech focused not just on what the Christians of the Middle East have suffered and not just on what steps governments had taken and should take to help them, but it also highlighted that the witness to forgiveness by Christians in that region was itself "a path to peace."

Calling Genocide by Its Rightful Name

The Knights of Columbus and I are honored to receive the Path to Peace Award tonight. But I must say that the ones most deserving of an award, and of all the support we can give them, are the Christians in the Middle East, especially in Iraq and Syria.

The Knights of Columbus came to work on behalf of these Christians first through charity and humanitarian assistance in 2014. As ISIS began its campaign of destruction, we began a campaign of assistance. With the generous support of our members and the public, the Knights of Columbus was able to direct millions of dollars to those who had been forced to endure or flee this persecution.

As Christians, we understood that our brothers and sisters in Christ who were being killed for their faith by ISIS were martyrs. As citizens, we understood the importance of providing the proper legal definition for this slaughter, and the only adequate legal term was genocide.

It was the word that had been used by Pope Francis to describe the situation last year.[100] It was the word that had been used by the Iraqi and Kurdistan Regional governments, and by the European Parliament.[101] And it was the word that justice, and legal precision, demanded should be used by the United States.

Advocating as we were for the use of this term and with solid contacts in the region from our humanitarian work, the State Department came to us and asked us to provide evidence of the genocide facing Christians. We did so, sending one of our team to Iraq to interview witnesses and creating a nearly 300-page report produced with the help of the group In Defense of Christians.

The effort and surrounding public awareness campaign were effective, and Congress—unanimously—and the State Department, have declared the persecution of Christians, Yazidis, and other religious communities in the region, to be genocide.

For the Knights of Columbus, taking action that included humanitarian advocacy and public awareness came naturally.

We had done the same for Mexican Catholics persecuted by the government of Plutarco Calles ninety years ago, raising the issue publicly, advocating on behalf of the persecuted, and assisting the refugees. A century ago, we assisted efforts on behalf of the victims of what Pope Francis has called the twentieth century's first genocide—the Christians of Armenia and the Middle East during and following the First World War. The efforts of the American government, in concert with those of American church groups and religious organizations, helped to save religious pluralism in the region at that time. Before World War II, we advocated on behalf of the Jews in Germany. And during the Cold War, we supported religious freedom for those behind the Iron Curtain. We did the same at home, standing up to the Ku Klux Klan to defend Catholic education in the 1920s.

And in our efforts at home and abroad, we continue this work today.

We do this because we understand that true peace is possible only when the fundamental rights and dignity of every person are respected. We continue to believe that fundamental human rights must include the freedom of conscience, the free exercise of religion, and equality under the law.

The work of bringing the United States government to recognize the genocide of Christians opened a unique path to peace. In one of the most partisan years anyone can remember, our government spoke in a unanimous and bi-partisan way in support of those being persecuted for their faith in the Middle East.

The recognition that some issues, such as fundamental human rights, transcend politics, may be the first step on a path to political peace in our country.

Forgiveness: A Path to Peace

An even greater path to peace is opened by preserving Christianity—and religious pluralism—in the Middle East.

Christianity there has a long history of not only living the faith but also of forgiving and even embracing persecutors. As Archbishop Jeanbart of Aleppo is fond of pointing out, Saint Paul did not convert the Syrian Christians, they baptized Saint Paul.

And I would add this. They had to forgive him before they baptized him. When asked to visit Paul, Syrian Christian Ananias' first reaction was to remind the Lord that Paul had persecuted Christians. Ananias had to forgive, then embrace his former persecutor.

For two thousand years these Christians have lived heroically. Pope Francis recently said: "Here lies the secret of [the Christian's] mission . . . to proclaim [God's] love and mercy even in the most resistant areas."

This is the history of Christians indigenous to the Middle East. They forgive, and by doing so they open the path to peace.

Today, they have given up everything but their faith, for their faith. But even having lost so much, they have given a great gift to their fellow citizens and to the world. The gift they have given is the example of forgiveness and mercy—the fundamental building blocks of peace.

Consider the following examples.

A young girl burned to death by ISIS in Mosul told her mother to "forgive them" before she died of her injuries in a hospital.[102]

Twelve-year-old Myriam surprised the world when, speaking of ISIS, she told ABC's *20/20* "Yes I forgive them." Then she added this: "Jesus said 'forgive each other, love each other the way I love you,' that is what we need to learn. Forgiveness."[103]

Father Douglas Bazi, whom I am honored to have worked with, was held for nine days by terrorists and tortured. They knocked his teeth out and broke his back with a hammer. During this ordeal, he prayed the rosary on the ten links of the chain that hung down from his shackled hands. And in between the torture sessions, he ministered to those torturing him. When one of the torturers asked what Father Bazi would do if they crossed paths on the street at some point in the future, Father Bazi said, "I will buy you a cup of tea."

Such witness of mercy and forgiveness stands in stark contrast to the blood feuds and stories of revenge that are far too common in the region.

And the importance of the Christian witness of forgiveness has not been lost on their fellow countrymen.

Muslim religious leader Ali Al-Yacoubi has noted: "'Our Christian brothers must be thanked for they are an element of peace and coexistence for Iraq, because 'despite having suffered a lot,' they have never responded to attacks with violence, but have continued to promote unity in a country that 'has to be of and for everyone.'"[104]

With these words in mind, I believe we stand at a crossroads for the future of Christianity—and pluralism—in the Middle East.

Either Christianity will survive and offer a witness of forgiveness, charity, and mercy, or it will disappear, impoverishing the region religiously, ethnically, and culturally.

The Christian witness has been profound. And it continues day in and day out in acts great and small. On a trip to Iraq in May, a member of our team was told by a Yazidi family that with the exception of one kilo of lamb delivered in 2014, *all* of the assistance they have received was from Christians. Though they have next to nothing themselves, we hear reports over and over again of Christians reaching out to care for those with even less.

The Christian witness of mercy and forgiveness is the true path to peace in the Middle East.

It is important that governments around the world—including our own—have recognized that what is happening to Christians is genocide. Tonight, we call upon the U.N. to do so as well. It is important to have diagnosed the problem. But it is important that the United States and the international community now provide the cure.

Needed Actions

A true path to peace in the region requires the presence of Christians within a pluralistic society in which they are full and equal citizens. This means they must survive, and they must be treated equally.

First, there must be direct funding made available for those communities who are victims of genocide. Both U.S. and U.N. officials in Iraq have confirmed to us directly that they prioritize aid to individuals in the most need, but do nothing for groups—even if the groups have been targeted for genocide and now are in danger of extinction.

The idea that we should help everyone is noble. But the idea that we should help only individuals and ignore communities facing extinction is not. Victims and survivors of genocide should be prioritized.

The current aid channels have failed. We can no longer rely exclusively or even primarily upon government delivery systems in the region. Steps must be taken to ensure that financial aid is delivered directly to these threatened indigenous communities. This will require opening new delivery channels and new partnerships with religious organizations.

This was done during and following the First World War, in a public private partnership between the United States government and individuals and religious groups. It could be done again. If it is not done, the genocide begun by ISIS will likely succeed by our own inaction.

Second, with enormous amounts of government and military assistance flowing into the region from the United States and others, we have the leverage to insist that real equality—based on the Universal Declaration of Human Rights—be implemented for religious and ethical minorities.

The regime of second-class citizenship faced by Christians in much of the region before the advent of ISIS, has been seen as the breeding ground for the genocide. We must insist that Christians and other non-majority communities are no longer marginalized.

Dialog is, of course, necessary if we are to make any progress in this regard. But dialog is possible only when all the participants agree upon the meaning of the words they use.

When we here speak of human rights, we are referencing those rights enumerated in the Universal Declaration of Human Rights. When governments of Muslim-majority countries speak of human rights, they may be thinking of those rights defined—or as confined—in the Sharia-based Cairo Declaration. Realism demands that we not mislead ourselves or allow others to mislead us in this regard.

The first step on the path to peace in this region has been taken: Christians have forgiven their persecutors. The second step must be a level of government funding directed to those communities that have faced genocide, so that they, and their witness, can survive. The third step must be the creation of real equality regardless of religious belief.

If we take these steps, we will not only have saved the faith of a people, we will have ensured that their witness of mercy and reconciliation—which is the only authentic path to peace—continues to be a leaven in this region.

Allow me to add one final thought. Earlier this evening, we heard Bishop Habash chant the words of the Our Father in Aramaic—the language Jesus and His apostles spoke. Let us commit ourselves to ensuring that this prayer continues to be said in this language, in the lands Jesus and His apostles walked, until He comes again.

Published Articles and Editorials

The multifaceted demands of the persecution crisis in the Middle East necessitated a variety of responses from advocates such as the Knights of Columbus. Direct contact with those in the Middle East—refugees, relief workers, and especially those entities like the Chaldean Catholic Archdiocese of Erbil, which coordinated much of the response—was, of course, essential in identifying and meeting needs in a volatile landscape that could quickly change. Political contact with stake-holding nations and government entities likewise helped to shift policy and quicken foot dragging. But reaching the public—which has an increasingly powerful voice both in terms of the potential for direct giving and widespread media impact—was crucial. It amplified the voice of the victims and helped maintain needed attention.

In light of this last need, the following opinion pieces and editorials (a selection of the several that were published online and in print) aimed to keep both civilians and civil servants apprised of the continued needs and political realities—both those abroad and the corresponding consequences of domestic policies.

10.

The Next Big Threat to Iraq's Christians

Iran-backed militias are keeping minority groups from returning home post-ISIS

OP-ED

Wall Street Journal, April 12, 2019

Before visiting Iraq last month, I met with Pope Francis. He told me that "a Middle East without Christians is not the Middle East." Baghdad's ambassador in Washington often says that "Iraq is not Iraq without its minorities." Consider these sentiments as Christian towns in Iraq increasingly look neither Christian nor Iraqi—but Iranian.

The public identifies the threat against Christians in Iraq and Syria as emanating from Islamic State. After a hard-fought war, ISIS is no longer a territorial power. But the religious minorities persecuted under the caliphate remain in peril, thanks to the Iraqi government's tolerance of Iranian influence.

Five years ago, ISIS swept through Northern Iraq, killing and displacing hundreds of thousands of Christians, Yazidis, and other religious minorities. The Obama and Trump administrations each declared ISIS's actions "genocide." The proof lay not only in the dead, but in the collapse of communities that had survived for millennia. There were as many as 1.5 million Iraqi Christians before 2003. Today some 200,000 remain.

The explosion of ISIS across Iraq was intense but burned out quickly. The group swiftly took control of the ancient Christian homeland of Nineveh in 2014 but was forced out within three years. With their towns liberated, displaced Christians hoped to return, rebuild, and work for a better future. The Knights of Columbus, the Catholic service organization that I lead, has committed $25 million to help with rebuilding and returning to the area.

The Trump administration also promised to prioritize the needs of these minorities after previous aid programs had overlooked them. Water and power facilities, schools, hospitals, and other public works have been refurbished and rebuilt, courtesy of the U.S. government. Groups like the Knights of Columbus have rebuilt homes and other structures as well. But during my visit, I learned of new threats that could undermine these projects and keep Christians from returning home.

As ISIS fell, a different menace took its place. Iranian-backed militias known as the *Hashd al-Shaabi*, or Popular Mobilization Forces, quickly took root in the devastated, previously Christian towns. Baghdad claims power over the Nineveh region, but in reality, the militias control much of it. They have made life nearly unbearable for Christians attempting to return to towns like Batnaya, where the Popular Mobilization Forces have stripped Christian family homes of plumbing, wiring, and other metal.

Locals, church leaders, and American and Kurdish government officials warn that the Iranian-backed groups have extorted Christian families and seized their property. Credible reports of violent crimes have emerged. Iranian proxies now are conducting a program of colonization in the Iraqi sector—building homes and centers for the use of Iraq's Shiite majority in historically Christian towns.

Iran has two goals. First, it wants to build a "land bridge" to Syria through Iraq. Second, it aims to alter fundamentally the demography of Nineveh in favor of Tehran. The Christians are at best collateral damage. Fearing for their lives, without even a semblance of the rule of law in their hometowns, many are fleeing the country rather than face the militias.

The genocide ISIS conducted is now being facilitated and even actively continued by Iran's proxies with the tacit support of the Iraqi government. The situation is beyond demoralizing for anyone who has stood by Iraq's minorities and prayed for their triumph after years of adversity.

Plenty of aid has been directed to the Nineveh region. But it will be undermined unless the country's overall security situation improves. This is one reason that it is important that these fragile communities are supported throughout the country: in Nineveh, but also in Kurdistan and in Southern Iraq.

American officials, including Vice President Mike Pence, have urged Iraq to remove these irregular militias and take control of the region. Prime Minister Adil Abdul-Mahdi has proved unwilling to comply so far. The U.S. government is not amused by Iraq's dalliance with Iranian proxies. Neither are those who have advocated for and supported displaced communities.

Washington's designation of Iran's Islamic Revolutionary Guard Corps as a foreign terrorist organization should encourage Baghdad to rethink its embrace of Iran-backed militias. If Iraq wants Iraq to remain Iraq, it should get serious about protecting minorities before it is too late.

11.

ISIS Crimes Against Christians Amount to Genocide

Canada should lead on the question of genocide by ISIS, rather than following a U.N. commission's misguided exclusion of Christians from such a designation

OP-ED

Co-authored with Archbishop Bashar Warda
(Chaldean Catholic Archbishop of Erbil, Iraq)
Vancouver Sun Times, August 5, 2015

Canada should be commended for its leadership in recommending that the United Nations Security Council investigate ISIS's crimes.

Having shown such leadership, Canada should also lead on the question of genocide by ISIS, rather than following a U.N. commission's misguided exclusion of Christians from such a designation.

The idea that some religious groups have been targeted for genocide by ISIS—but Christians have not—is both false and dangerous.

This is all the more obvious since the recent murder of a priest by ISIS in France.

Based on the overwhelming evidence, Christians have been included in genocide designations by the European Parliament, the U.S. State Department, the U.S. Congress, parliaments and officials of a number of European governments, as well as the Iraqi cabinet and the Kurdish Regional Government.

The evidence offered to exclude Christians relies on an ISIS propaganda narrative that Christians are given the choice of paying "jizya"—a "tax" historically offered in exchange for protection by a Muslim ruler—rather than facing the "convert or die" ultimatum confronting non-Christian groups like Yazidis.

It's just not true.

ISIS's former leader Abu Omar Al-Baghdadi publicly revoked any special treatment of Christians years ago (he was killed in a joint U.S.-Iraqi forces mission in 2010).

ISIS has applied the term "jizya" even to include kidnapping, rape, and confiscation. It has used the handful of Christians left in its domains as human shields.

Scholar Alberto Fernandez, former U.S. State Department coordinator for strategic counterterrorism communications, has stated "jizya" is a "Salafi Caliphate publicity stunt," not a classical application of the concept.

Reverend Emanuel Adelkello (a priest with the Syriac Catholic Church) negotiated with ISIS as they invaded Nineveh. When interviewed for the nearly 300-page report on genocide the Knights of Columbus prepared for the U.S. State Department, he said: "[Jizya] was only put forward initially as a ploy from which ISIS could keep the Christians there to further take advantage of them and abuse them. There was specific concern that the intention was to keep women there so that they could be taken freely by the ISIS fighters. The ISIS fighters [said] that, according to the Koran, it was their right to take the Christian women as they pleased."

Rape and kidnapping, of course, are hallmarks of genocide.

Iraq's Christian population has plummeted by nearly 90 percent, Syria's by almost 70 percent. In the land where it first took root, Christianity could be stamped out entirely—within our lifetime.

Unlike ISIS's "jizya" propaganda, its official magazine *Dabiq* promises to "conquer your Rome, break your crosses, and enslave your women." Its videos encourage viewers to "terrorize the Jews and burn the slaves of the Cross."

Such threats and actions aren't special, preferential treatment. They are genocide.

It is time for both Canada and the U.N. to join the international consensus, supported by a majority of the Canadian people at a rate of two to one in our recent K of C-Leger poll.

When twenty-one Coptic Christians were beheaded in orange jump suits, it showed, in a single photo, ISIS's genocidal intent against Christians.

Reflecting on this, Coptic Orthodox Bishop Anba Angaelos warned that "if Christians are excluded from the classification of genocide, my concern, my fear, my expectation is that we will be responsible for a greater and more ruthless campaign of persecution against them. . . . People will see that the international community has supported one group against another and they will see that other as fair game."

12.

A Year Ago We Declared ISIS Genocidal. Why Are Its Victims Still Waiting for Aid?

Time is running out to preserve these historic communities.

OP-ED

Washington Post, March 21, 2017

On March 17, 2016, then-Secretary of State John F. Kerry announced to the world that the Islamic State was committing genocide against Christians and other religious minorities in the Middle East. It was an important statement, because it was only the second time our government had declared genocide in an ongoing situation—the first was Darfur, where some estimate that more than 300,000 people have been killed to date.

Congress, too, spoke, with the House passing a resolution March 14 that the Islamic State was committing genocide against religious and ethnic minorities, including Christians and Yazidis, by a vote of 393 to 0. The Senate unanimously followed suit later last year.

The Reverend Douglas Bazi, then stationed in Irbil in Kurdistan, ran a refugee center there for Christians displaced from the

Nineveh Plain. He knew well the kidnapping, torture, and confiscation they had endured because he himself had been captured and tortured in Baghdad in 2009 by a different group of extremists. Sitting with me in the gallery of Congress as the bipartisan genocide resolution passed, he said using the right vocabulary was the "first right step." But, he added, it needed to be followed up with the right action.

One year after our country used the right word, he and the other Iraqi Christians are still waiting for the next step: meaningful action.

Despite the genocide designation, our government spent the rest of 2016 operating on a business-as-usual basis. The largest displaced Christian community in Iraq—in Irbil—received no U.S. government or U.N. aid before the genocide designation. And they have received none since.

On a visit to Iraq last spring, one of our executives spoke to Yazidis who said they had been similarly overlooked.

Both the U.N. and the senior U.S. government officials there told our representative that this was the case because they prioritized *individual* needs, not group needs. When pressed, they admitted that they did not take into account the needs of communities—even if they had suffered genocide. This means that, when being considered for aid or resettlement, those who are the targets of genocide do not have their status as communities marked for extermination taken into account.

Unfortunately, ignoring the identity of these targeted groups plays into the hands of genocidal regimes. Such an attitude could well be a death sentence for these minority communities. What the Islamic State couldn't accomplish, misguided aid policies just might: eliminating entire ethnic and religious minority groups from their historic homes.

The region's Christians seem to be reaching a tipping point. Estimates vary, but the Christian population of Iraq has fallen from more than 1 million to less than 250,000 in recent years due in large part to the onslaught of the Islamic State. Syria's Christian population has fallen precipitously as well. For these historic religious communities, extinction is a real possibility.

Dating back to World War I, the United States has rightly extended a helping hand to threatened groups. Armenian and other Middle Eastern Christians targeted by the Ottoman Empire received tens of millions of dollars in humanitarian aid from the U.S. government and the American people, and Jewish survivors of the Holocaust received priority in resettlement. More recently, America has helped survivors of the Darfur genocide in the aftermath of their ordeal. The U.S. government has put more than $7 billion into Sudan since 2003, and USAID alone has provided more than $2.7 billion in humanitarian assistance for Darfur in that time frame, according to the organization Genocide Watch.

But in Iraq, many genocide survivors are still waiting for help. The tens of thousands of displaced Christians in Irbil, and Yazidis that Christians are caring for there, have received no U.S. government assistance—despite being direct targets of the Islamic State's genocide.

Allowing these current genocide survivors to suffer for the past two years has been a gross injustice and a blight on America's foreign policy record. Overlooking these people after a declaration of genocide is unconscionable, and in fact, it is de facto discrimination against the Islamic State's most vulnerable victims.

Since the 2016 election, Iraqi Christian leaders have reported that they perceive a new openness to helping them among American officials. This is commendable. Now openness should become concrete action.

Just less than a year ago, then-presidential candidate Donald Trump said: "We left Christians subject to intense persecution and even genocide." He added: "We have done nothing to help the Christians in the Middle East. Nothing. And we should always be ashamed for that lack of action." He was right that our country should be ashamed of how little it has done. And while his administration inherited this problem, now it is in a position to fix it. The

Trump administration should right the wrongs these shattered communities have endured through our country's inaction by immediately taking three helpful steps.

First, ensure that no community that suffered genocide is overlooked by—or excluded from—U.S. government aid programs. At a minimum, we should do here what we did for Darfur through USAID. Second, the United States must demand that the United Nations also assist all communities that suffer genocide by including them in humanitarian and reconstruction aid. And finally, we should continue to work with the international community to defeat the Islamic State and bring the perpetrators of this genocide to justice.

Congress should also act by swiftly passing H.R. 390—the Iraq and Syria Genocide Emergency Relief and Accountability Act—co-sponsored by Representatives Christopher H. Smith (R-N.J.) and Anna G. Eshoo (D-Calif.). This bill would help ensure that much-needed aid reaches these decimated communities. Under this legislation, the U.S. government would be required to direct some aid to entities specifically assisting displaced people from communities of religious and ethnic minorities targeted for genocide.

The new administration should begin to right this wrong and chart a different course. It can quickly end this de facto discrimination, and in so doing, help save ancient ethnic and religious communities that otherwise could cease to exist.

13.

A Mass Christian Exodus from the Middle East Would Be a Catastrophe

OP-ED

New York Post, November 15, 2019

What happens in the next few weeks in Iraq, Syria, and Lebanon is crucial for Mideast Christians—and the stability and pluralism of these countries and the wider region.

Christianity was born in the Middle East, yet Jesus Christ's followers there face a perilous moment. The Christian share of the population has shrunk to about 5 percent (if that), down from more than 20 percent at the turn of the last century. The decline attests to a century of their ruthless persecution—bookended by the genocide committed by Turkey a century ago and the recent one attempted by ISIS.

In Iraq, protesters are demanding an end to sectarian government and equal citizenship for all regardless of ethnicity or religion. Recent years have seen ordinary Iraqis get squeezed between the Sunni totalitarians of ISIS and Shiite Iran's imperial hegemony. They are fed up with both.

Which is why protesters are calling for the abolition of Iraq's dependence on Islamic law in favor of an overtly civil state. The message has drawn Christian support, including from the Chaldean Catholic patriarch and other bishops and priests, who have marched alongside Muslim citizens. The protests have remained peaceful despite hundreds killed, primarily by Iranian-backed militias.

The future of the Iraqi state hangs in the balance. Either it will become more sectarian under the influence of its more powerful neighbor—or it will become the pluralistic country sought by thousands marching in the streets, including Christians.

Meanwhile, Turkey launched an incursion into northeast Syria, home to many Christian communities, with Turkey's militia allies in Syria including Islamist terrorists, according to Christian leaders and credible regional observers.

Ankara has protested the recent bipartisan congressional resolution to recognize the Turkish genocide against Armenians and other Christians, and it has done little to alleviate concerns that its actions in the region will restage elements of those dark days when it comes to Christians and other regional minorities.

Most Christians in northeastern Syria are either the descendants of people who fled from the Turks during and after World War I, or they are people who fled there in the past few years from ISIS. When Turkey attacks a Christian neighborhood in Qamlishi (as it did at the start of its operation), or when its proxies attack a Christian church (as they did in October), or when newly resurgent Islamist terrorists kill Armenian Catholic priests—Mideast Christians and their allies are reminded of the worst of the last century's barbarous acts.

Then there is Lebanon, where recent protests have targeted both widespread corruption and the Shiite terrorist organization Hezbollah, which serves as Iran's proxy in that country.

So far, the Lebanese state's response has been largely nonviolent. But there is a real fear among the Christians that if the Lebanese economy collapses, the largely Christian-controlled Lebanese army may fall. The ensuing economic chaos in Lebanon may plunge the country into crisis and the mass exodus of the last statistically substantial group of Christians in any country in the Middle East.

Many Christians persecuted elsewhere in the region have fled to Lebanon. If Lebanon were to lose its gift for pluralism, that could spell the end of the concept in the rest of the region.

The governments of Turkey, Iraq, Lebanon and Iran bear much responsibility for what happens from here. So does the United States, historically the principal outside power in the region. To its credit, the Trump administration has worked to ensure that religious minorities, which have faced persecution in much of the Middle East, aren't overlooked.

The United States must play a decisive role in these issues through diplomacy. It must continue to press the countries of the region to end corruption, to put the needs of their people first and, in short, do the right thing. Governments in the region still listen closely to Washington, and we must continue to press for the protection of persecuted religious minorities. The well-being and physical security of indigenous Christian communities must be treated as a permanent agenda item in all U.S. aid and military assistance discussions with regional governments.

Because if the Christians go, so will any hope of a stable Middle East.

SECTION 3

Respect for Life

Each age has its great debate, its great struggle on behalf of the key rights of society's most forgotten or helpless individuals. An important measure of decency and goodness of any society is its respect for the life and dignity of the people within it.

Historically, as today, the marginalized have seen their lives valued less than the lives of others. Societies that practiced slavery or human sacrifice certainly provide public and jarring examples of such abuses of the right to life and dignity of other people, but in our own society, too, very real abuses exist. Today, such abuses generally happen in the shadows. The elderly and sick are offered assisted suicide; the unborn are seen as disposable, and a million each year are thus never born. The rights of other groups, including the poor, immigrants, minorities, and people of faith, are at times abused as well—whether by governments or individuals.

In the late twentieth century, and into the twenty-first, no issue has been more important in the United States than abortion. The reasons for this are twofold. First, abortion is the leading cause of death in the United States, leaving heart disease a distant second. Second, abortion is the issue of the day in which an entire class of people have been denied their humanity—completely. The very personhood of the unborn is denied, and the consequence in the United States alone has been 50 million deaths.

America is a country that has shown great persistence, openness, and eventual ability to struggle for the oppressed and marginalized. For example, so strong was the conviction towards justice that the country fought a civil war in no small part to free black men and women enslaved and considered by some to be less than human. A century later, the country underwent a further purification through the rightly-celebrated civil rights movement that made great strides in overcoming legal segregation and rampant racism.

In the past decades, it has been heartening to be part of America's continued passion for justice today in the fight against abortion—a fight which, like the fight against slavery in years past, occurs on a battlefield in which bad law provides aircover to the side of injustice. It has been heartening, too, to be a part of the growing majority who see the issue for what it is. Indeed, though some pundits and politicians want to tell us that the issue is "settled law," the hundreds of thousands who annually march for life prove otherwise. What the Supreme Court imposed cannot be settled law because a law that denies life and human dignity is simply not a sustainable law. Considering the magnitude of the lives lost in this dehumanizing of the unborn, it remains one of the most politically charged topics in our country's political debates today. In fact, the most searched term alongside both "Hillary Clinton" and "Donald Trump" in the days leading up to the 2016 election was "abortion."

For the Knights of Columbus, commitment to those on the margins runs deep—from the widows and orphans of Irish immigrants in nineteenth-century New England to those persecuted for their faith in Mexico, the Middle East, and by Nazi and Communist regimes. With such a record, it is not surprising that the Knights of Columbus was early in its vocal defense of the rights of the unborn. As abortion began to gain legal recognition in the country, the organization's members and leaders directed passionate rhetoric and substantial financial resources to defend the unborn from falling victim to legalized abortion, which was considered a serious backsliding in terms of their human rights. Not only my predecessor (Virgil Dechant) but my predecessor's predecessor (John McDevitt) were outspoken champions of life from the early 1970s onward. And that commitment to the life and dignity of every person, born and unborn, by the Knights of Columbus has continued unabated.

Today, the Knights of Columbus continues its work on behalf of the unborn and their families. In addition to providing practical support for pregnant women and families, the Knights has shaped hearts and the debate on abortion in impactful ways. Most notably, thousands of pregnant women have been given the chance to see for themselves the life within them, through the more than 1,300 ultrasound machines donated by the Knights to pregnancy resource centers around the country. Our surveys, in partnership with The Marist Poll, have helped redefine the debate over abortion by exposing and highlighting the vast consensus that exists in favor of substantial restrictions on abortion—a fact too often neglected before our polling effort highlighted it.

Despite the consensus, during the past decade, the Obama Administration and various state governments have sought to coerce religious organizations into cooperating with this evil. Not surprisingly, we and other Catholic and non-Catholic faith-based organizations resisted these attempts. Courts would ultimately vindicate the rights of people of faith, but the legal and legislative battles themselves showed that what starts with denying the rights of one group (the unborn) swiftly spreads to denying the rights of other groups (like those who believe the unborn have rights).

At the end of the day, abortion in the United States today is *the* defining issue in terms of how we deal with the most vulnerable. With abortion persistently promulgated as a right, a freedom, and a "fix" for ending the life of one in favor of the ease of life of another, the abortion issue has defined and in many cases become the common battleground for other issues, including conscience and the dignity of even those who suffer—issues that might be challenged and defined in other areas, but that are, in the United States, deeply conditioned either explicitly by abortion or implicitly by trends making abortion a legal reality—if by no means, a universally accepted one. Abortion's toll—both in terms of lost lives and lost values—makes it not enough to say we are for the threatened, the marginalized, or the "little guy," if that definition excludes the most threatened, the most marginalized, and the smallest of all.

Thomas Jefferson famously said that "eternal vigilance is the price of liberty." If we would protect the unalienable rights to "life" and "liberty" on which this nation was founded, we would do well to continue to be vigilant in our defense of the rights of the unborn, and of those who—whatever the price—refuse to be coerced into overlooking their plight.

14.

An Unparalleled Cause

SPEECH

Upon receiving the Great Defender of Life
Award from the Human Life Foundation
October 27, 2016, New York, New York

The magnitude and the seriousness of abortion made the fight to end it a life-long cause for both my wife, Dorian, and me. Fortunately, my years both in Washington and at the Knights of Columbus afforded many opportunities to try, in practical ways, to make a difference. The following speech was given on the occasion of receiving the "Great Defender of Life Award" from the Human Life Foundation. From the earliest years, many great partners have been found. One of the earliest was James McFadden, who founded the Human Life Foundation and its journal, which were instrumental in giving a reasoned voice on matters related to defending the life of every person, and making such ideas and news available. Shown not only in his foundation's work but also in seeing and pursuing the need for building a multi-faith coalition on life, Jim's personal qualities—strategic vision, tactical know-how, steely political realism, humility, uncompromising intellectual rigor, indomitable commitment to the cause of life—were not only a force to be reckoned with, but an inspiring model for anyone who believes that every human person, including the silent, forcibly patient unborn children, deserve the chance to live. It was in that spirit that I offered the following remarks.

The Greatest Poverty

We are often told that poverty and inequality—as well as the threat to peace presented by these disruptions—are some of the most important to address.

According to one of the world's foremost experts on poverty of all time, there is no greater poverty than that experienced in America. In her speech to Harvard's graduates in 1982, Mother Teresa explained that the poorest of the poor weren't in the slums of India. Calling abortion "one of the greatest poverties," the humble saint added: "A nation, people, family that allows that, that accepts that, they are the poorest of the poor."

Mother Teresa saw that the inequality of rights assigned to the unborn resulted in great poverty. She also regularly warned that this was likewise a threat to peace.

In 1994, at the National Prayer Breakfast, attended by congressional leaders of both parties and by President and Mrs. Clinton, Mother Teresa made a direct plea to the American people, saying: "I feel that the greatest destroyer of peace today is abortion, because it is a war against the child, a direct killing of the innocent child, murder by the mother herself. And if we accept that a mother can kill even her own child, how can we tell other people not to kill one another?"

The saint continued: "Any country that accepts abortion is not teaching its people to love, but to use any violence to get what they want."

How much of the violence we see today, and how much of the coarsening of our culture is the result of a legal system and way of thinking that says some lives don't matter—that some human beings have no rights at all.

We confront this greatest of poverties because our country has legally embraced what theologians might call "a structural sin," namely a legal system that denies the humanity of the unborn, and allows their innocent lives to be destroyed.

There are many threats to life in this country. All are to be resisted, but none comes close qualitatively or quantitatively to the devastation of abortion—the legal regime that has resulted in the intentional deaths of 50 million innocent human beings.

The American Consensus on Abortion

The Court's decision in *Roe v. Wade* didn't end the debate and it didn't settle the law. Instead, it left a country deeply uncomfortable with the decision and it galvanized a movement in favor of the civil rights of those who could not speak for themselves.

That decision did something else, too. It undermined the credibility of our Supreme Court in the way that *Dredd Scott, Plessy v. Ferguson,* and *Buck v. Bell* had done before it. Two of those cases denied human rights to African Americans. The third denied rights to those with intellectual disabilities, allowing their forced sterilization and opining that "three generations of imbeciles [was] enough." In each of these cases, as in *Roe,* the Court usurped for itself the role that the Declaration of Independence leaves to God—that all are created equal, and endowed by our Creator with certain unalienable rights—including life, liberty, and the pursuit of happiness. And it usurped that role with disastrous consequences.

If you doubt this, you have only to turn to the early volumes of *The Human Life Review* to see numerous legal scholars conclude not only that *Roe v. Wade* is bad constitutional law, but that it makes very little pretense of being constitutional law at all.

Roe and its companion case of *Doe v. Bolton* opened the door to virtually unrestricted abortion. And since that time the smallest and most common-sense restrictions have been blocked by pro-abortion politicians or by federal courts.

But that hasn't changed the fact that Americans remained unconvinced.

Forty-three years after *Roe,* our polling with Marist has found that a strong majority of Americans say abortion is morally wrong.

They do so by twenty points. And eight in ten would restrict abortion to—at most—the first three months of pregnancy, and a majority would limit it to the rarest of cases, to cases of rape, incest, or to save the life of the mother, or would not allow it all.

We may see these positions as imperfect given our strong belief in the value and dignity of every human life, but it is undeniable that if our politicians had the courage to act on this American consensus, we could eliminate almost all abortions in the United States.

Beyond the Cuomo Standard

Instead of embracing this consensus, we see too many politicians, including some who are Catholic, embracing ever more radical— and unpopular—positions.

Some pro-abortion candidates now want to repeal the Hyde Amendment even though almost two-thirds of Americans disagree.

Others use as a fig leaf their own "personal" opposition to abortion, but won't allow what they say is a religious belief to influence their public policy.

Let us be clear. The unique life of the unborn child isn't a matter of faith, it is a matter of science as the world-famous geneticist Jerome Lejeune made clear in testimony before Congress and in the pages of *The Human Life Review* more than four decades ago. The intentional killing of an innocent human being is wrong *not* simply as a matter of religious belief. It is always wrong because intentionally killing the innocent is always a grave injustice.

When the late Governor of New York, Mario Cuomo, pioneered this "personally opposed" argument in 1984, he claimed that he couldn't impose what he considered a minority view on the majority of Americans. It was a poor argument then.

It is an even poorer argument today, when eight in ten Americans support substantial limits on abortion. The position these politicians say they support in conscience could be acted on with overwhelming majority support, but instead they impose a political orthodoxy that is the minority view, violating their own conscience and the will of the majority.

The entire personally opposed argument also throws away the principled position of John F. Kennedy before the Houston Ministerial Association in 1960. There, Senator Kennedy had said that a conscientious public official should resign his office if he concluded that enforcing a law would violate his conscience.

It seems this principled position has gone by the wayside. Today, all that seems necessary—and politically expedient—is to "sincerely" register in a public forum one's personal opposition to a morally offensive law, and then one is morally free to defend and even promote the law one has concluded privately is gravely immoral. It is, of course, the very opposite of sound moral reasoning. It reflects the kind of counterfeit morality that one suspects Nelson Mandela and Martin Luther King spent much of their lives struggling against.

This doctrine has for decades proved politically useful, but may in the future be less tenable. Most Americans today agree that abortion is morally wrong. And huge majorities want restrictions on abortion. But still, these "personally opposed" politicians insist on violating both their own conscience and those of the majority of Americans.

I have not endorsed any candidate in any of this year's elections. But I have argued that we should not vote for any candidate who supports abortion and opposes abortion restrictions.

When confronting the greatest poverty in the world, the number-one cause of death in our country, the greatest destroyer of peace, the cornerstone of violence, and the denial of human rights to an entire class of people, and which has resulted in death on such a massive scale, I do not see how it is even remotely possible to build a culture of life and a just society by electing people who defend such a regime.

The reason is twofold.

First is the simple math that tells us that no other issue takes as many lives—all of them innocent—as abortion. Heart disease comes in a distant second.[105]

Second, compromising on this issue for the sake of other issues has not moved pro-abortion politicians in the direction of life. To the contrary, it has moved them further away—as the recent campaign to overturn the Hyde Amendment demonstrates. Those Catholics and other people of faith who think they have more influence as "insiders" with pro-abortion politicians have failed to deliver.

If Catholics were to stand together with other people who support life to make abortion the preeminent human rights issue of our time and to treat it as a truly non-negotiable priority, imagine how different our country would be.

In 1976, this almost happened. We could have had pro-life Democrat Sargent Shriver, who ran against Jimmy Carter in the primary, as president. If Shriver had won the primary and beaten Gerald Ford, it seems very unlikely that four years later, Ronald Reagan could have put together a coalition of blue-collar Catholics and values voters to defeat a pro-life Catholic President Shriver as he did defeat President Carter in 1980.

If this had happened, we might have had two parties committed to restricting abortion. We might have been able to have an ongoing debate over the rest of the important issues in Catholic social teaching. We might have been able to have a rational discussion of how to best tackle issues like immigration, the environment, poverty, the economy, and foreign policy.

I believe we can create such a moment again. If we stand together and say no politician, of any political party will get my vote unless he or she commits to policies that legally restrict abortion.

Quite simply, if enough of us did that, both parties would have to listen. And that would be real change.

The Eloquence of Practical Response

But this isn't just an election year. For Catholics, it is also the Year of Mercy. And for all of us who value the life of each person—including the life of every unborn child—we think of abortion not just as a political issue, but as a personal one.

Mother Teresa told us we should fight abortion with adoption, and everyone who would reduce abortion should commit to helping women in crisis pregnancies and by supporting adoption. In my book *A Civilization of Love: What Every Catholic Can Do to Transform the World*, I mentioned that years ago, Dorian and I brought into our home a young unmarried pregnant girl who lived with us throughout her pregnancy, and who we helped place her child with a loving Catholic couple through a private adoption. What I did not mention in the book was that the individual who assisted in that private adoption by finding the adopting couple was Jim McFadden.

We can be proud that for decades the pro-life movement has assisted women in choosing life by—among other things—making sure they have access to a full range of prenatal health-care options including the chance to see the child in their womb via ultrasound. In this regard, I am tremendously proud of the Knights of Columbus initiative of placing the most technically advanced ultrasound machines in crisis pregnancy centers.

Since this program began in 2009; we have placed 720 machines with a value of more than $35 million.[106] Of course, we do not know the exact number of lives that these machines have saved. But if each machine is decisive in convincing just one mother each week to keep her baby, these machines will save more than 37,000 lives each year. And they will keep doing this year in and year out.

Emotionally and spiritually, we must also accompany women. Whether they are pregnant, have had their child, or have had an abortion, we need to continue our support of ministries like Project Rachel. We have a responsibility to accompany women who face these challenges in ways that encourage them to see that the choice for life is at the same time a choice for their own fulfillment.

There is so much for us to do to bring about a culture of life in our politics, our economics and how we respect the inherent dignity of each human being. There must be a comprehensive, holistic approach that looks forward to the day in which each person is truly welcomed and accepted.

In beginning these remarks, I mentioned that my wife, Dorian, and I have been working continuously in the pro-life cause since we were in college together. Since that time, I have had the opportunity to be involved in numerous pro-life initiatives including the Helms Amendment, the Hyde Amendment, the Human Life Bill, the Mexico City Policy, various Human Life Amendments to the Constitution, litigation such as *Harris v. McRae,* the Bork and Scalia nominations to the Supreme Court, and initiatives such as our own ultrasound machine program. In all these efforts, the person whose advice I have relied upon the most has been Dorian. And there have been several times in the past decades where I have asked her whether we have done our part and whether it is time to move on to other matters. Her answer has always been: "There is so much still to do, we can still make a contribution, we must stay the course." So tonight, I would like to give my own, personal Great Defender of Life Award to my wife, Dorian.

Earlier, I mentioned the influence of a former governor of New York. In closing, I would like to quote another governor of New York—Teddy Roosevelt—whose words have always provided guidance for me and which I think are particularly appropriate for those of us committed to the cause of life. He said: "In any moment of decision, the best thing you can do is the right thing. . . .The worst thing you can do is nothing."[107] He also said: "Do what you can, with what you have, where you are."[108]

Let us continue together in what Ronald Reagan once described as "the long march for life" confident that we are in the right and that in America, despite all obstacles, right will ultimately prevail.

15.

Compassion and Post-Abortion Response

SPEECH

Given at the Project Rachel 25th Anniversary Dinner
September 18, 2009, Milwaukee, Wisconsin

One of the most telling developments of the case against abortion is that, over the years, strides in science, medical technology, and psychology have continued to affirm the prolife cause. By shining a brighter light on the humanity of the unborn child, such advancements have continued to reveal the unborn child's unique and permanent place in the lives connected to it. Science continues to reveal the unique ways a developing unborn child strives for life, as well as the permanent connectedness of an unborn child and its mother; medical technology continues to improve the threshold of viability earlier and earlier, as well as to give more detailed first pictures and 3D imaging of the unborn child, literally revealing the face of a person to be loved. And in psychology, there has been an increasing awareness, sensitivity, and response to the effects of traumatic losses and traumatic biological and interpersonal events, including abortion.

For a society driven by data, the effects of abortion on women had been disturbingly under-recognized. After an abortion, many women often dealt silently with many interior struggles including grief, mourning, and regret—experiences that could hardly be shared with an industry that touted their "decision" as "empowering." The effects—which often could surface immediately or even years after the abortion itself, sometimes triggered by an anniversary, dreams, seeing children born around the same time as their own unborn child was aborted—can have even more dire consequences, including depression, drug use, contemplated suicide, and relationship difficulties, as well as spiritual outcomes such as feelings of being unforgiveable and a depressed spiritual life.

In the 1980s, women who had undergone an abortion received a great friend, advocate, and healer in a women who would become a great friend of ours, Vicki Thorn, when she founded Project Rachel, a ministry for post-abortion healing; she was inspired by the experience of a friend who, having had one abortion and placed one child for adoption, said she could live with the adoption, but not with the abortion. Project Rachel was truly the pioneer in ministering to women post-abortion, including confidential hotlines with trained counselors and, for those seeking spiritual healing, connection with priests trained to deal with the unique trauma with sensitivity and gentleness. Given on September 18, 2009 in Milwaukee, Wisconsin, on the occasion of celebrating Project Rachel's twenty-fifth anniversary, this address celebrated one of the most important and necessary Catholic ministries in the United States.

It is necessary to state what is for all of us, I am sure, an obvious reality. Vicki Thorn—and all of those working with Project Rachel—have done truly pioneering work for the often silent walking wounded: those who have suffered as a result of their abortions.

In the often shrill debate over abortion, the work of post-abortion ministry is vital. It brings healing to those survivors of abortion that are so often ignored: the parents of the aborted child.

For several years now, the Knights of Columbus has worked closely with Project Rachel on a variety of projects. We have helped sustain the work of Project Rachel, and have co-sponsored two conferences on the effects of abortion on men. We have been pleased to have had Vicki speak on the effects of abortion on parents at a conference at the Pontifical John Paul II Institute for Studies on Marriage and Family in Rome.

Speaking to participants of the conference, Pope Benedict XVI pointed out the need for such post-abortion ministry, saying:

> In the often purely ideological debate, a sort of conspiracy of silence is created in their regard. Only by assuming an attitude of merciful love is it possible to approach in order to bring help and enable victims to pick themselves up and resume their journey through life.[109]

It is undeniable that every abortion produces multiple victims. Certainly there is the child, but also there are the parents, the siblings, and the medical staff who are all affected as well.

All of us who are pro-life learn from the example of Vicki's leadership in Project Rachel.

Her work is pioneering and international, and it follows the vision of another pioneering figure in the pro-life movement with whom I am sure we are all familiar: Pope John Paul II. Before becoming pope, the young Father Karol Wojtyła's experience as a pastor led him to a deep understanding of the trauma that takes place after abortion. In 1960 in *Love and Responsibility*, he discussed a woman's complex emotional response:

> Apart from its physical effects, artificial abortion causes an anxiety neurosis with guilt feelings at its core, and sometimes even a profound psychotic reaction. In this context we may note the significance of statements by women suffering from depression . . . who sometimes a decade or so after the event remember the terminated pregnancy with regret and feel a belated sense of guilt on this account."[110]

These are the people that Project Rachel has helped to heal: the women—and men—whose pain from abortion lingers for years. They aren't an abstraction or a faceless demographic: they are our neighbors, our family members, and our fellow parishioners. We find them in every walk of life and in every socio-economic group, in every ethnic group and working in every profession.

Anyone who knows Vicki, knows that she often cites the statistics from the Guttmacher Institute that show that between one-third and 40 percent of U.S. women have had an abortion. And thus, an equivalent number of men have been involved as well.

Because of widespread abortion experience, we must consider carefully the words that we use in this debate. With so many walking wounded, Project Rachel has been the face of the Church's healing message.

Pope John Paul II's understanding of post-abortion trauma found an articulate voice in *Evangelium Vitae*. Speaking directly to post-abortive women, he said:

> [D]o not give in to discouragement and do not lose hope . . . If you have not already done so, give yourselves over with humility and trust to repentance. The Father of Mercies is ready to give you his forgiveness and his peace in the Sacrament of Reconciliation. You will come to understand that nothing is definitively lost and you will also be able to ask forgiveness from your child, who is now living with the Lord. With the friendly and expert help and advice of other people, and as a result of your own painful experience, you can be among the most eloquent defenders of everyone's right to life.[111]

John Paul also wrote of the pressures that often drive people to have an abortion, pressures we must understand in dealing with those who have had abortion affect their lives. We also need to consider these pressures for those who are considering or might consider abortion. He wrote:

> Then there are all kinds of existential and interpersonal difficulties, made worse by the complexity of a society in which

individuals, couples, and families are often left alone with their problems. There are situations of acute poverty, anxiety, or frustration in which the struggle to make ends meet, the presence of unbearable pain, or instances of violence, especially against women, make the choice to defend and promote life so demanding as sometimes to reach the point of heroism.[112]

At the Cathedral in Los Angeles, I thought about the pain, the causes, and the importance of the Church's role in forgiveness and healing.

I was at the Cathedral of Our Lady of Angels in Los Angeles. And there, hanging in the alcove where confessions are heard is a print of Rembrandt's beautiful painting of the return of the prodigal son.

In that painting, we see the loving embrace that the father gives his son upon his return. He doesn't pass judgment. He simply loves and forgives. And in that tender moment, love overcomes the wounds of sin and weakness, and healing begins.

In looking at this painting and thinking about this gathering tonight, I was struck by how differently we might approach the abortion debate if we put front and center in our mind this spirit of forgiveness and healing, this spirit at work in Project Rachel.

There are little things. How we discuss abortion with someone we don't know or in public might change if we consider that there is a 33-percent chance that they have been involved in an abortion.

How we craft our Mass petitions on abortion might be different if we stop to think that as many as one in three parishioners may have had direct experience with abortion.

How we think about the issue, and our face to the world, might be different if we started from the standpoint of loving and caring for the survivors, while working to protect those at risk—the unborn and their parents alike.

The pain of these parents is also not an abstraction, but very real. And it is up to us to be the loving embrace of Christ and his Church to those suffering this pain.

And the message that abortion causes pain and is not a good choice for a woman is increasingly understood.

Polling makes clear that something is changing in the minds and hearts of Americans.

The American people no longer support the regime of *Roe v. Wade.* That's not a controversial statement; it's simply true.

Roe v. Wade, which has been interpreted to allow abortion without restriction throughout pregnancy, is at odds with the overwhelming majority of Americans according to several recent public opinion polls, including a comprehensive poll commissioned by the Knights of Columbus this summer.

Two other polls in the last few months—one by Pew, the other by Gallup—show far more consensus on the issue than the continued divisive political rhetoric would lead us to believe.

Pew found that only 18 percent favored legalized abortion "in all cases." While 28 percent said it should be legal in "most cases," 28 percent said it should be "illegal in most cases," and 16 percent said it should be illegal in all cases.[113]

In other words, even when polled with broadly worded questions, 72 percent of Americans are against the unrestricted abortion regime that followed *Roe v. Wade,* while only 18 percent are in favor of it.

An even more recent Gallup survey grabbed headlines by finding that a majority of Americans now identify as "pro-life."

Furthermore, it found that while 22 percent of Americans believe abortion should be legal in any circumstance, most do not. The survey found that 23 percent believe it should be illegal in every circumstance, and 53 percent believe it should be legal "only under certain circumstances."

The totals: 75 pecent of Americans don't agree with the Roe regime, while only 22 percent of those polled do agree.

But neither of these polls gives the full picture. A poll commissioned by the Knights of Columbus and conducted by the Marist Poll showed among the key findings that:

- 86 percent of Americans would significantly restrict abortion.

- 60 percent of Americans would limit abortion to cases of rape, incest, or to save the life of a mother—or would not allow it at all.

- 79 percent of Americans support conscience exemptions on abortion for health-care workers. This includes 64 percent of those who identify as strongly pro-choice.

- 69 percent of Americans think that it is appropriate for religious leaders to speak out on abortion.

- 59 percent say religious leaders have a key role to play in the abortion debate.

- 80 percent of Americans believe that laws can protect both the health of the woman and the life of the unborn. This includes 68 percent of those who identified as strongly pro-choice.

Additionally, the data showed that since October, nearly every demographic sub-group had moved toward the pro-life position except for non-practicing Catholics and men under forty-five years of age.

Independents and liberals showed the greatest shift to the pro-life position since October, while Democrats were slightly less likely to be pro-life now than they were in October.

The data show that the American people are placing an ever-increasing value on human life. Far from the great divide that most people think exists when it comes to the abortion debate, there is actually a great deal of common ground.

Americans are overwhelmingly unhappy with the unrestricted access to abortion that is the legacy of *Roe v. Wade*, and pundits and elected leaders should take note of the fact that agreement on abortion need not be limited to the fringes of the debate and issues like adoption or pre-natal care. The American people have reached a basic consensus, and that consensus is at odds with the unrestricted access to abortion that is the legacy of *Roe*.

Why is this happening? Why this sudden shift in public opinion toward the pro-life position? I believe that the work Vicki and Project Rachel have done provides a great part of the answer.

With one-third of Americans directly touched by abortion, it's safe to say that people know people who have been hurt by abortion.

Two statistics from our most recent polling is very telling on this issue. First: of all, 53 percent of Americans believe abortion does more harm than good to a woman in the long term. The second statistic—which we have not released until this evening—is that, in thinking about abortion, that same number (53 percent), *want to hear from women who have had abortions.* Only doctors, at 64 percent, had their opinions more in demand.

So the tide is turning, and the abortion's aftermath on parents has no small role in this. We saw this at the conferences the Knights of Columbus sponsored on men and abortion in San Francisco and Chicago. Even reporters from hostile publications broke down sobbing when confronted with the stories of abortion's legacy on parents.

Abortion has been sold to our country with the lie that it was a necessary choice for women. What all of you who have worked with Project Rachel know is that it is a tragic choice. There are no winners in an abortion. There are simply the dead and the wounded.

I believe that there is no more effective argument against abortion than this, and that no organization has done more to make this clear and change our understanding of the many victims of abortion than Project Rachel.

In its great work in dioceses throughout the world—and in the many other post-abortion ministries that have emulated various aspects of Project Rachel since 1984—the pioneering work of Vicki Thorn and Project Rachel stands out as a great model of healing and forgiveness that is at the core of the theology of the Catholic Church.

Each of us must work to also be that face of Christ's healing love. We must work to include recognition of the too often invisible walking wounded among us. We must be sensitive to the fact that so many who hear us speak out on the issue of abortion have been hurt by it themselves. We must seek to heal—not condemn—those who have experienced such pain. In short, we must answer our own call to love and to sharing that love with those who need it most.

Mother Teresa said that Christ comes to us in the distressing disguise of the poor. She also said that it is a terrible poverty that a child must die so that people might live as they wished.

Taken together, the poorest of the poor includes those whose poverty lies in the loss of a child. We should consider them the face of Christ in our life, and following the example of Project Rachel, we should help them with a kind word, a listening ear, a healing embrace.

Only love can overcome the tragedy of abortion, and that love must begin with each of us.

You know, we sometimes hear from politicians and others that *Roe v. Wade* is settled law. Last year, at the Knights of Columbus' annual convention, which we held in Quebec, I told our members that the Knights of Columbus will never consider *Roe v. Wade* to be settled law. And as with any civil rights issue of the past, if we, the people, don't consider an issue of this magnitude settled law, then it's not settled law, and it will continue to be legally contested.

As we work to legally protect the unborn, we must also work to help those living with us, wounded by abortion. I think a good model for us in this work is the homily that Paul VI gave at the conclusion of the Second Vatican Council. He said this:

> The old story of the Samaritan has been the model of the spirituality of the council. A feeling of boundless sympathy has permeated the whole of it. The attention of our council has been absorbed by the discovery of human needs. . . . But we call upon those who term themselves modern humanists, and who have renounced the transcendent value of the highest realities, to give the council credit at least for one quality and to recognize our own new type of humanism: We, too, in fact, we more than any others, honor mankind.

Vicki Thorn and the work of Project Rachel over the past twenty-five years have brought that message of the Good Samaritan to those most in need of the healing message of the Catholic Church. Twenty-five years ago, Vicki led Project Rachel to work that others dared not do. And as more and more people and organizations model the various aspects of her work, may they all, and may each of us here tonight, keep in mind as the model for our work the parable of the Good Samaritan.

16.

The HHS Mandate, Conscience and the Law

SPEECH

Upon receiving the *Evangelium Vitae* Award from
the Notre Dame Center for Ethics and Culture
April 26, 2015, Notre Dame, Indiana

Saint John Paul II's commitment to the life and dignity of every person was well known, and nowhere did he make the case more clearly than in his famous 1995 encyclical letter on the *Gospel of Life*—known by its Latin title *Evangelium Vitae*. That encyclical letter stated the Church's position clearly in relation to the threats to life of the modern era including—and especially—abortion. The following speech was delivered at the Notre Dame Center for Ethics and Culture on April 26, 2015, when I was given the *Evangelium Vitae* Award named after Saint John Paul II's lucid encyclical. Contextually, at the time this award was received, many Catholics and Catholic institutions were also continuing to oppose the HHS Mandate, which embodied government coercion in actions that undermined life.

The Promise of Conscience Protection

The University of Notre Dame has been a place where six presidents of the United States and many governors and senators have spoken—and now you are willing to listen to a supreme knight.

As Governor Adlai Stevenson used to say, it is now my job to speak and your job to listen; if you finish before I do, please feel free to leave.

I would like to offer some reflections concerning the challenges we face at the intersection of ethics and culture in working to see that our nation embraces a culture of life.

The last President of the United States to speak on this campus, President Obama, told the graduating class of 2009 that in a time of increasing diversity, especially "diversity of thought, diversity of culture, and diversity of belief," it was incumbent upon us to "find a way to live together as one human family."[114]

He specifically addressed the issue of abortion and said that we must work together to "discover at least the possibility of common ground." One of the ways we could do that, he said, was to "honor the conscience of those who disagree with abortion, and draft a sensible conscience clause." That is something, he promised, "we can do."

The HHS Mandate: a History of Intransigence

Six years later, however, that goal of drafting a sensible conscience clause has still not been achieved. The history of the Department of Health and Human Services contraceptive mandate makes clear why this is so.

Since it was announced in August 2011, the mandate has undergone several phases—all of them related to its failure to protect conscience. Consider the following events:

First, the original language provided only a very narrow exemption for religious organizations, so narrow in fact, that our nation's bishops observed, "Jesus and the early Christian Church would not qualify."

Then—facing backlash from religious organizations—it began a period of attempting band aid fixes to a systemic problem. After six months, the Administration delayed enforcement through a temporary safe harbor for religious non-profit organizations. Then, when that was proven inadequate, shortly before the 2012 presidential election, the Administration expanded this "safe harbor" to include more non-profits. That still was insufficient.

In February 2013, the Administration proposed another change: it removed the provision that exempted only those charities that serve only their own religious members. It took a remarkable eighteen months to modify the provision that had been objected to by nearly every church and religious organization in the country.

At the Knights of Columbus, our objection remained because the fundamental problem remained: those who object to paying for abortion-inducing drugs, contraceptives, and sterilization were still required to pay for them either directly or indirectly. And they were still required to initiate coverage for them.

In July 2014, the Administration announced final regulations that extended the safe harbor for an additional six months while exempting religious non-profits as long as they "self-certify" that they meet the exemption criteria.

But after losing the Supreme Court cases of *Hobby Lobby*, *Little Sisters of the Poor*, and *Wheaton College*, the Administration stated it would again revise the mandate.

And last August [2014], the Administration announced its new rule: organizations eligible for exemption may notify HHS of their objection to the mandate and the government will then arrange with their insurer to provide coverage at no cost to the organization.

Thus, after nearly four years of controversy, the Administration's goal will be achieved: contraceptives and abortifacients will be provided by religious employers notwithstanding their objection. But now the coverage will be provided by means of a subterfuge—services will be provided at "no cost" by government decree.

The Administration insists that "no-cost" coverage is possible because preventing births is less expensive than providing childbirth and infant care.

The National Right to Life Committee objected to the Administration's plan because in the future the same rationalization could mandate "no cost" coverage of abortion. The State of California has done just that: mandated that private employer's health plans include abortion coverage while denying conscience clause protection to religious organizations. Whether this Administration or a future one will follow California's lead on the abortion mandate cannot be predicted.

As the eminent Supreme Court Justice Oliver Wendell Holmes once observed, the life of the law has not been logic.[115]

But the direction of the Administration's logic is clear.

The history of the HHS mandate shows an administration grudgingly walking back its proposal only by the smallest steps and only when ultimately forced to do so by judicial action.

And in the end, not really walking it back at all.

By and large, Catholic organizations have treated the HHS mandate as they would most other regulations: they commented formally during the rule-making process, they met with Administration officials in the hopes of reaching a compromise, and, finally, they brought legal actions in federal court.

All during this time, the Administration has been stubbornly intransigent. Amazingly, even discussions between the president and bishops, cardinals, and the Vatican secretary of state have apparently made no discernable difference.

There is a lesson to be learned here about the future of Catholic institutions in America.

Their Catholic identity is now linked with the Affordable Care Act. It is the context in which the HHS mandate exists today and how it will be applied in the future.

An Anti-Democratic Search for Legitimacy

During a time when the search for common ground and consensus received heighten rhetoric in Washington, the [Affordable Care] Act itself has become an example of the way in which Washington is becoming *less* democratic and *less* capable of consensus.

The Act passed Congress on a schedule that denied legislators a realistic opportunity to read its provisions—and many of them admitted to being ignorant of them.

The bill's sponsors denied that the legislation was an exercise of the taxing power of Congress. But when its constitutionality was challenged, the Administration defended the law before the Supreme Court precisely on the grounds that it was an exercise of the taxing authority of Congress.

Furthermore, it is significant that mandated contraceptive services for religious entities were not an issue during consideration of the Affordable Care Act. Had they been, the bill would never have passed Congress.

Admittedly, free market delivery of health care has been less than perfect. But whatever its problems, it did one thing very well. It provided something absolutely necessary to the sustainability of Catholic health-care institutions: it provided freedom. Free markets provided an environment where pluralism and diversity allowed Catholic institutions to define and maintain their identity.

Absent Supreme Court intervention, the Affordable Care Act signals that those days of freedom—whether economic or religious—are over.

Some Catholics have considered this question primarily from the standpoint of whether complying with the mandate constitutes an impermissible material cooperation with evil.

But Catholic identity involves considerably more than that.

Saint Thomas More presents the issue when in Robert Bolt's play *A Man for All Seasons*, he says this about his refusal to take the oath mandated by the Act of Supremacy: "When a man takes an oath, he's holding his own self in his own hands like water, and if he opens his fingers then, he needn't hope to find himself again."

Catholic institutions in America today face something similar—and no less devastating to the soul of Catholicism.

The message of the HHS mandate is clear about how it values Catholic institutions' commitment to their faith: Catholic institutions remain free to fashion their own identity *as long as that identity conforms to the dictates of government.*

In the future, we may still choose to speak of Catholic institutions as being "counter-cultural" and "prophetic." But in what ways do we think this will remain true?

One of the important aspects of "American Exceptionalism" is that in America, religion is expected, at times, to be "counter-cultural." But that only really matters when religion can be counter-cultural when it counts.

The mutual respect President Obama promised during his commencement address at this university can now be understood through the HHS mandate. As he said on that occasion: "no matter how much we may want to fudge it . . . the fact is that at some level, the views of the two camps are irreconcilable." Perhaps that is all the more reason why the president, at that time, called for a "sensible" conscience clause to "honor the conscience" of those who disagree.

In preparing these remarks I found myself reflecting on a book by Henry Kissinger—*A World Restored.*[116] It was Dr. Kissinger's study of the Congress of Vienna and the diplomacy that followed the Napoleonic Wars.

Kissinger analyzed what drove Napoleon for almost twenty years to embroil Europe in wars that cost millions of lives. He concluded that Napoleon was in search of legitimacy. As long as there was one kingdom or one country free of his rule, Napoleon considered his legitimacy threatened.

Kissinger put it this way:

The distinguishing feature of a revolutionary power is not that it feels threatened . . . *but that nothing can reassure it.* Only absolute security—the neutralization of the opponent—is considered a sufficient guarantee, and thus the desire of one power for absolute security means absolute insecurity for all the others.

I will presume to add to Kissinger's hypothesis. It applies as well to the proponents of slavery in the 1850s. Like Napoleon, they too needed constant reinforcement of their legitimacy. That is why they ultimately concluded, along with Chief Justice Taney, that slavery could not be completely banned anywhere in the Union.

It seems to me that this is helpful in understanding our own situation today.

There is a tyrannical impulse within the pro-choice movement to mandate conformity by everyone in America—whether it's through the HHS mandate, state exchanges under the Affordable Care Act offering only providers that include abortion services, or the D.C. City Council repealing conscience clause protection for religious organizations regarding abortion.

Again, if we listen to Kissinger, "It is the essence of revolutionary power that it possesses the courage of its convictions, that it is willing, indeed eager, to push its principles to their ultimate conclusion."

What drives that impulse to a large extent is a deep-seated sense of illegitimacy.

That is why whenever there's a vacancy on the Supreme Court, the pro-choice lobby insists that *Roe v. Wade* is settled law.

But *Roe v. Wade* will never be settled law because *Roe v. Wade* is founded upon the falsehood that we do not know a living human being is at stake.

In America, constitutional law decisions that are founded upon such untruths are, in the long run, simply unsustainable. That is the lesson to be learned from the Supreme Court's shameful decision in the "separate but equal" segregation case of *Plessy v. Ferguson*. Such will be the lesson one day of *Roe v. Wade*.

The Supreme Court may have created a new right in what Justice Byron White called "an exercise of raw judicial power." But even this judicial power has not convinced America that what the judges did was *right* regarding legalized abortion. Consider the following:

- Our Knights of Columbus-Marist polling this year [2015] shows that 84 percent of Americans would limit abortion to the first three months of pregnancy. Almost six in ten would limit it to cases of rape or incest or to save the life of the mother, and that includes the majority of those who describe themselves as "pro-choice."

- 84 percent say our laws can protect both the life of the mother and the life of the child.

- Almost two-thirds say our abortion rate is too high.

- And 60 percent say abortion is morally wrong.

- And the youngest voting Americans hold these same opinions at about the same rate as older Americans. The Supreme Court has not convinced them either.

And so, we have reason for hope.

In spite of media bias and judicial intransigence, the American people have nonetheless reached a sort of consensus on abortion.

As I suggested several years ago in my book *Beyond a House Divided*, there is common ground on abortion and we should seek ways to build upon it.

The Federal Enforcement of Key Moral Myths

But today we face a new challenge.

With enactment of the Affordable Care Act, government now controls America's health care—approximately one-sixth of the U.S. economy.

Are we entering a time of such government control of the economy that the historical role of what Michael Novak called "mediating structures" to influence society will be less and less possible?[117]

Have we reached a new tipping point?

Does the expanding power of government to tax and regulate pose a new threat to the sustainability of our religious institutions?

Last month, an article in *Foreign Affairs* magazine entitled "Dark Days for Civil Society" quoted the president of the International Center for Not-for-Profit Law that "since 2012, more than ninety laws constraining the freedom of association or assembly have been proposed or enacted" around the world.[118]

"The shrinking space for civil society," the article says, "is a global problem."

Obviously, this problem is most acute in societies with emerging democracies. But it would be naïve to assume that this is not also a problem in established democracies.

It would be more accurate to describe the situation this way: "dark days for civil society" in emerging democracies and "shrinking space for civil society" in established democracies.

A November report by Europe's Organization for Economic Cooperation and Development suggests just how fast the space is shrinking. It finds that social spending among European nations remains at record levels: an average of 20 percent of gross domestic product.[119]

France leads Europe with 32 percent. In comparison, the United States spends 19 percent.

But Robert Samuelson, writing in the *Washington Post*, observes that this is not the most accurate way to view the situation.[120] He states that when the benefits provided by private companies are included—benefits that are often subsidized and regulated by government—the figure in the United States moves from 19 to 30 percent.

Thus, the potential for government control of the U.S. economy through HHS mandate-style regulation goes far beyond what we may have imagined just a few years ago.

In Europe, Catholic institutions have found it difficult to resist the steady pressure of socialist governments during the past four decades as they dismantled the legal structures protecting the sanctity of life, marriage, and the family.

Again, Kissinger's analysis is helpful in understanding this "revolutionary" dynamic and why responses to it have been inadequate. He writes:

> The defenders of the status quo . . . begin by treating the revolutionary power as if its (demands) were merely tactical; as if it really accepted the existing legitimacy . . . (and can) be assuaged by limited concessions. Those who warn against the danger in time are considered alarmists; those who counsel adaptation to circumstance are considered balanced and sane, for they have all the good "reasons" on their side.[121]

The inevitable failure of the balanced, tactical approach results, Kissinger observes, from its "inability to come to grips with a policy of unlimited objectives."

And so has been the recent history of family law in Europe.

It would be unrealistic to think that this "revolutionary" pressure has had no effect on the catastrophic collapse of Christianity on that continent during our lifetime—a collapse that necessitated repeated calls by Saint John Paul II for a new evangelization.

He realized that the problem we face is more than political. It is ideological. And therefore, an adequate response must be more than tactical.

In the United States and Europe—in fact, throughout the declining West—persons of faith confront an ideology based on a false concept of personhood.

Because this ideology does not understand the human person, it understands neither men nor women. It makes all of them—all of us—isolated beings, disconnected, living for ourselves.

It purports to take us back to the Garden of Eden. In reality, it leaves each of us stranded in our own Sahara of the spirit.

This has led to a perverse form of personal freedom, which in turn has led to perverse forms of liberation—one in particular is the liberation of men from the responsibilities of fatherhood.

There is a reason why most public opinion polls over the years have shown greater support for abortion among men than among women.

So now our country faces the emergence of a "new normal," children without a father in the house.

What does this have to do with the HHS mandate? Everything.

The mandate rests upon the myth that women's social and economic equality depends upon universal availability of contraception, sterilization, and abortion—imposed, if necessary, by government.

That myth is foundational to a political ideology that has been ascendant for some time in Europe and more recently in various degrees throughout the United States.

But that myth also provides something more: the justification—the cover, if you prefer—for all the afflictions consequent upon the sexual revolution.

In this light, the HHS mandate is not necessary to protect women's rights.

Rather, it is necessary to further secure the emancipation of men from the responsibilities of fatherhood. It does this by maintaining a socio-cultural status quo in which the deck is stacked against both women and children. It is rooted in an ideology divorced from the real needs of American women and alien to the realities of America's children.

Historically, the first principles of any ideology are non-negotiable. This is why the HHS mandate cannot be compromised.

Napoleon could not accept a multi-polar Europe. And the White House is not likely to back off its mandate.

So we must ask ourselves: How is it possible to preserve the liberty of our *institutions* when the authentic freedom of *individuals* is so badly misunderstood?

Of course, we hope that the Supreme Court will uphold our free exercise of religion with regard to the HHS mandate. Religious institutions cannot be allowed to become either the political or the policy servants of the state.

The Irreplaceable Role of Religious People

But even if successful, litigation is only part of the answer. The observation of Yale Law Professor Stephen Carter on this point is important. He writes in *The Culture of Disbelief*:

> At times the Supreme Court has been the great protector of the autonomy of religions as faith communities. . . . But American society should not depend on its courts as the sole or even the most important protectors of religious autonomy. Judicial authority extends to the bounds of, but not beyond, the Constitution. The nation's need for autonomous religions stands outside of that document; it is a need that flows from the nature . . . of popular democracy as a form of governance. To try to make the religions, in their internal organization, conform to the state's vision of a properly ordered society is not simply a corruption of the constitutional tradition of religious freedom; it is also an assault on the autonomy of religions as bulwarks against state authority.[122]

And so, how are we to engage this issue as Professor Carter suggests, that is, beyond the bounds of the Constitution?

This brings us to the mission of the Notre Dame Center for Ethics and Culture and its belief that "the truth the Church affirms about the human person is the foundation for freedom, justice, human dignity, and the common good."[123]

If we take this as our starting point, then the recent address of Pope Francis to the European Parliament should be our road map because it does not bother with tactical suggestions.[124] Instead, he gives us something more fundamental and enduring.

In his address, the Holy Father asserts that "at the heart" of Europe's democratic institutions is the "confidence" that men and women are "persons endowed with *transcendent dignity.*" And that this dignity requires government to recognize that each of us "possesses inalienable rights."

The pope then says that, "To speak of *transcendent human dignity* thus means appealing to human nature, to our innate capacity to distinguish good from evil, to that 'compass' deep within our hearts, which God has impressed upon all creation. Above all," he continued, "its means regarding human beings not as absolutes, but as *beings in relation.*"

And toward the end of his address he calls upon Europe to appreciate its "religious roots" and that these roots are still capable of "fruitfulness."

With these principles, Pope Francis has pointed out a constellation—a North Star, if you will, to guide our future path.

In going forward, let us remember the wisdom of the Second Vatican Council that "authentic freedom is an exceptional sign of the divine image within man."[125]

Early in these remarks, I quoted the last president to have spoken on this campus.

Permit me to close by quoting the first president to have done so.

In 1935, Franklin Delano Roosevelt said, "There can be no true national life . . . unless there be the specific acknowledgment of . . . the rights of man. Supreme among those rights we . . . hold to be . . . freedom of religious worship."[126]

He then observed, "George Mason in the Virginia Declaration of Rights, voiced what has become one of the deepest convictions of the American people: Religion, or the duty which we owe to our Creator, and the manner of discharging it, can be directed only by reason and conviction, not by force or violence; and therefore all men are equally entitled to the free exercise of religion according to the dictates of conscience."

The founders of our nation, those who pledged their lives and their sacred honor to the cause of liberty in Philadelphia—whether Deist or Catholic, Baptist or Anglican—all would have agreed with us that "freedom is an exceptional sign of the divine image within man."

If there is at the core of the American understanding of freedom a principle that can neither be negotiated nor compromised away, it is this recognition that freedom is a reflection of the divine image in every human being.

The time has come for bold action. For Catholics, it is time to take up a new evangelization of American freedom. And this year—on the fiftieth anniversary of the Second Vatican Council's Declaration on Religious Freedom, *Dignitatis Humanae*—is a good time to begin.

In doing this, we will affirm what is fundamental to the American character.

Pope Francis, in his apostolic exhortation *Evangelium Gaudium* calls for a new missionary spirit among Catholics. The great Catholic institutions of our country were built by men and women filled with a great missionary spirit. They seized an opportunity offered by our nation's commitment to the free exercise of religion—an opportunity offered nowhere else on earth.

And with that opportunity, they constructed an unprecedented network of institutions to help provide for the health, education, and welfare of millions—Catholics and non-Catholics alike—for whom government did not provide an answer.

But these institutions were not intended to simply fill a gap left by the limitation of government. They were not, as Pope Francis has reminded us, merely NGOs.

Their mission was greater. These institutions opened a window on the transcendent dignity of each human being and especially those whose dignity government neglected.

And these institutions offered something that government cannot offer—the promise of the Gospel of Life, of *Evangelium Vitae*.

This was not a promise spoken about only on Sunday mornings. It was a promise lived out in the hard realities of the day-to-day life of the poor and suffering.

You and I are called not only to sustain these institutions; we are called to sustain this promise.

We must preserve the free exercise of religion, which allows us not only to make this promise, but also to keep it. The autonomy of our religious institutions is not *extrinsic* to the missionary nature of Christianity, rather it is essential to it.

We must be missionaries of the Gospel of Life.

Today this means we must also be missionaries of authentic freedom.

17.

"Adam, Where Are You?" Bioethics and the Unique Dignity of a Human Person

SPEECH

Given at the Pontifical Academy of Theology
October 20, 2007, Krakow, Poland

Less than twenty years after communism collapsed in Poland and democracy returned, this speech, given in Poland, raised important threats to human life and drew on the thoughts and poetry of Saint John Paul II to find the answer to these thorny issues. The issues related to life and the human person—especially the unborn—have been mishandled and even avoided in the West. The speech detailed the U.S. Supreme Court's avoidance of the "Byrn" case, which would have provided the scientific answers about the unique life of the unborn child that *Roe v. Wade* declared beyond the competence of the court as it made abortion legal in the United States. The speech dealt also with the British government's 2007 move to allow human-animal hybrid embryos to be created and experimented on. For a world so "off track," the speech proposed that John Paul II's thought—and particularly his poetry—contained a viable response to a confusion that was threating human life and dignity.

Crossing the Threshold of Dehumanization

On September 5, 2007, the British government's Human Fertilization and Embryology Authority agreed in principle to allow human-animal hybrid embryos to be created and used for research. The Authority stated, "Having looked at all the evidence the Authority has decided that there is no fundamental reason to prevent cytoplasmic hybrid research." It continued, "This is not a total green light for cytoplasmic hybrid research, but recognition that this area of research can, with caution and careful scrutiny, be permitted."[127] In theory, a human-animal hybrid embryo would be made by: (1) removing DNA from the nucleus of a cow's egg; (2) injecting the nucleus of a human cell into the cow's egg; (3) applying electric shock to cause cells in the embryo to divide; and finally (4) removing stems cells from the hybrid embryo for further research.[128] Under British law such embryos must be destroyed after fourteen days and cannot be implanted into the womb.

The decision appeared to meet with broad public approval with the Authority releasing a public opinion poll showing that 61 percent of the public supports the creation of hybrid embryos to improve scientific understanding of disease.[129] The *Times* of London reported that two teams of scientists are expected to be granted licenses in November to create the first human-animal embryos by year's end.[130]

Bishop Elio Sgreccia, president of the Pontifical Academy for Life, criticized the decision as "a monstrous act against human dignity," pointing out that the "frontier, of the crossroads of distinct species, has been overstepped today."[131] Undoubtedly, Bishop Sgreccia is correct. It is nonsense to claim that, having crossed the momentous threshold of creating human-animal hybrids, it will be somehow possible to control it with "caution and careful scrutiny."

In the United States there is currently no federal law that regulates or bans human-animal hybrid cloning, or any other kind of human cloning for that matter. Neither has the U.S. Supreme Court ruled on its legality. In the absence of federal guidelines, some states have enacted total or partial bans on human cloning, while others allow it and even provide state funds for cloning research. In Massachusetts in 1998, a prominent biotech firm named Advanced Cell Technology produced human embryonic stem cells by inserting human somatic cells into a cow egg from which the nucleus had been removed.[132]

These techniques are driven by a crass utilitarian ethic that has become known as the technological imperative. Its principal dictate is simple: that which *can* be done *should* be done. We have begun a fearful descent toward the "brave new world" of which British author Aldous Huxley warned us.

Nearly forty years ago, Princeton University professor Paul Ramsey discussed the ethics of genetic manipulation and the technological alteration of parenthood. In his classic study of the ethics of genetic control entitled *Fabricated Man*, Professor Ramsey wrote, "It is a special form of suicide we have been talking about: suicide of the species. . . . Making radical changes in human mankind can only be described as the death of the species and its replacement by a species of life deemed more desirable."[133] Then he warned, "All this adds up to man's limitless dominion over man. Who will be the Creator and who the creatures, who the masters and who the slaves, who the miracle workers and who the things, at the end of these converging lines of development?"[134]

We have indeed crossed a fearful threshold. But we should recognize that it is a threshold we have reached in Anglo-American society by crossing another, related threshold nearly four decades ago: the threshold of legalized abortion.

In Great Britain this was accomplished by an act of Parliament; in America by a decision of the Supreme Court. The United States Supreme Court's abortion decision, *Roe v. Wade*, is, of course, famous. It is remarkable for many reasons, not the least of which is the court's contention that we need not resolve the difficult question of when human life begins. Notwithstanding this conclusion, the court went on to rule that it could resolve the question of when *potential* human life begins. It held that human life before birth was only *potential* human life. Then the court legalized abortion throughout pregnancy saying the procedure was protected by a constitutional right to privacy.[135]

Roe v. Wade: Willful Ignorance?

This abortion threshold really has two parts. The first part is that government may consider what we know to be a human being and define it by law as something *less* than fully human—in the Supreme Court's language, as "potential" human life. The second part is that this less than fully human being may be intentionally killed.

Much has been written about the *Roe v. Wade* decision. But little mention has been made of the fact that had the Supreme Court selected a different case to review, its abortion decision might have been entirely different.

In the United States, abortion laws are under the jurisdiction of the fifty states. During the 1960s and the early 1970s, many abortion laws were being re-examined by legislatures and courts. By 1972, the *Roe v. Wade* case was one of several cases the Supreme Court could have considered. But the *Roe v. Wade* case was in one way special: *it was a case in which the trial record contained very little evidence regarding the humanity of the unborn child.*

In 1972, a different case coming on appeal to the Supreme Court had a very different trial record. That case, entitled *Byrn v. New York City Health & Hospital Corporation,*[136] presented the question of the legalization of abortion in an entirely different way from *Roe v. Wade* in that it provided substantial evidence of the humanity of the unborn child.

In 1970, New York State enacted legislation similar to that enacted in Great Britain. It permitted abortion without restriction within the first twenty-four weeks of pregnancy. Fordham University law professor Robert Byrn obtained appointment as legal guardian for all unborn children under twenty-four weeks' gestation in New York State. He then sought to have the law declared unconstitutional as a violation of the unborn child's constitutionally protected right to life.

During the trial, Professor Byrn presented extensive expert testimony on the biological humanity of the unborn child. In fact, the trial record in this case was so comprehensive that the New York court concluded: "It is not effectively contradicted, if it is contradicted at all, that modern biological disciplines accept that upon conception a fetus has an independent genetic 'package' with potential to become a full-fledged human being and that it has autonomy of development and character. . . . It is human . . . and it is unquestionably alive."

But then the court made a distinction between biology and law. It said, "It is not true . . . that the legal order necessarily corresponds to the natural order." The court stated that "what is a legal person is for the law . . . to say." In its view, "whether the law should accord legal personality is a policy question." The court rejected the argument that abortion violated the unborn child's right to life, because the court concluded: "The point is that it is a policy determination whether legal personality should attach and not a question of biological or 'natural' correspondence."

If this language disturbs you, it also disturbed dissenting judge Adrian Burke. He wrote that, "This argument was not only made by Nazi lawyers and judges at Nuremberg, but also is advanced today by the Soviets in Eastern Europe. It was and is rejected by most western world lawyers and judges because it conflicts with natural justice and is, in essence, irrational." In effect, Burke accused his fellow judges on the New York court of accepting exactly the same argument that was rejected at the Nuremberg trials.

The *Byrn* case was appealed to the Supreme Court as *Roe v. Wade* was being scheduled for rehearing. We do not know whether members of the Supreme Court studied the *Byrn* case or the issues presented by it. All we know for certain is that the court ignored the

Byrn case and that the case was superseded by the Supreme Court's decision in *Roe v. Wade*.

But this case is important historically because it makes clear why *Roe v. Wade* is so problematic. First, the New York case raises the question of the adequacy of the trial record in *Roe v. Wade*. If the *Roe v. Wade* case had included the evidence presented in the *Byrn* case, the Supreme Court would have found it very difficult to claim that it could not decide when the life of a human being begins. Second, in light of Judge Burke's dissent, it is obvious why it was important that the abortion case had only a certain type of trial record. A trial record that convincingly demonstrated the humanity of the unborn child would make it difficult for the Supreme Court to fashion a right to abortion without sounding like the New York court, that is, without sounding like the judges who were condemned at Nuremberg.

The solution was to hide the reality of human life before birth and then deal with abortion as one type of medical procedure.

Obviously, we should avoid any simplistic equation between the Nazi exterminations and today's abortions. But a society that begins to regard certain of its members as dispensable or outside the protection of the law soon may find itself sliding down a slippery slope. It has been said that the two law cases we have discussed present two jurisprudences in conflict.[137]

But because every jurisprudence rests upon an anthropological foundation, we may say more than that. We may say also that these cases present two anthropologies in conflict; two very different views of the human person in conflict.

A Poetic Response

It has become commonplace in the United States to speak of the John Paul II generation. In general, this reference is made regarding those seminarians and newly ordained priests who exemplify a distinct enthusiasm for the Catholic Faith and its proclamation. They have a clear understanding of why they are entering a life of priestly ministry. Many have attended one or more World Youth Days. They look to John Paul II as a spiritual father.

But there is another way in which we might speak of the John Paul II generation. This way applies more directly to Poland. We may speak of our late Holy Father as John Paul the Great for what he accomplished for the liberation of Eastern Europe and the nations of the former Soviet Union—for the miracle of 1989. Since that time, Poland has been on the path of democracy—taking its first steps and seeking to ground its path upon a solid foundation that will last and will lead to increasing respect for human dignity.

As you know, I had the privilege of serving at the White House during the presidency of Ronald Reagan. On one occasion, I remember him speaking about the American experience of democracy. He said, "We are all Jefferson's children." Indeed, the principles articulated by Thomas Jefferson and his colleagues in the U.S. Declaration of Independence and the vision of the person underlying it have served American democracy well for more than two hundred years. Yet, in America, Catholics have come to understand that there are limitations to the Enlightenment philosophy of man that Jefferson championed.

At Aparecida in Brazil this summer, Pope Benedict XVI reminded us that our ethical decision-making should be guided by a simple rule. Place "everything," he said, "at the service of the human person, created in the image and likeness of God."

But who is this person? And what is this image and this likeness?

In order to answer these questions, Karol Wojtyła dedicated his life as a scholar, as a priest, and as pope. We might even say he dedicated the Church entrusted to his care with revealing this reality more fully to humanity.

We could look throughout John Paul II's pontificate for evidence of this legacy. But let us look instead to the end to what is regarded as his spiritual last testament: his *Roman Triptych*. In Meditation II, the Holy Father recalled the words of the Creator from *Genesis*:

"Adam, do you remember?" In the beginning He asked, "Where are you?"

Today, in a strange way society is asking this same question: "Adam, where are you?" Society is asking, "Where is the human being that the Lord has made? Where is the man who is the image and the likeness of the God who is love?" Let us recall the answer from *Roman Triptych*:

"Male and female He created them."
God bestowed on them a gift and a task.
They accepted—in a human way—the mutual self-giving, which is in Him.

And then further:

Existence itself is the outward sign of eternal love.
And when they become "one flesh"
    that wondrous union—
on the horizon there appears the mystery of
    fatherhood and motherhood.
They return to the source of life within them.
They return to the Beginning. . . .
They know that they have crossed the threshold
of the greatest responsibility![138]

In presenting *Roman Triptych* in March, 2003, Joseph Cardinal Ratzinger said this about the meaning of the poem:

the way of looking that Christ has opened for us directs our gaze far beyond this and shows . . . who the human person really is. The Creator—the beginning—is . . . "a communion of persons, a mutual exchange" . . . [W]e now learn to see the human person starting with God: a reciprocal gift of self—the human person is destined for this—if he manages to find the way to achieve this, his is a mirror of the essence of God.[139]

Is it too much to hope that some day this vision of the human person will be the one that supports the life of a truly Catholic culture? That what will emerge from the crucible of the twentieth century will be a wiser, more humane society; a society in which solidarity and communion of persons are fundamental; a society in which the dignity of the person is respected as a true reflection of the Creator?

Is it possible that such a vision of the human person could be the one that one day sustains democracy in Poland?

Could it be that a future president of Poland will one day celebrate the "Miracle of '89" by saying, "We are all Wojtyła's children"?

Perhaps in some countries it is too much to ask that those in government remember the words of a poet. But perhaps in some countries it is not.

I dare to think it is not too much to hope for in Poland because of what you have already accomplished and what you will accomplish in the future.

18.

The Meaning of the Suffering of John Paul II for the Church and the World

SPEECH

Given at the XVIII World Day of the Sick,
Pontifical Council for Health Care Ministry
February 9, 2010, Rome

One of the great consolations of being a Catholic is that—not only does our faith urge us to alleviate suffering—our faith also claims some answer, some Divine companionship, and eternal worth of our life no matter how horribly or debilitatingly a person suffers. The Catholic Church brings this to the world's attention each year, celebrating the World Day of the Sick, and for the 2010 event, this address highlighted John Paul II's personal witness on the matter.

As God would have it, around this time, other tremendous witnesses to faith in the face of suffering touched my life. The devastating earthquake in Haiti not only wreaked havoc a month before, but brought the Knights and me personally to its soil, where the spiritual resilience of those we met and assisted made an impression on us. And a key man in the K of C response there was my close friend Emilio Moure, who simultaneously fought his own battle with terminal cancer even while serving as supreme secretary. He embodied a profound spiritual faith throughout his battle with cancer that was not only constant but generous, praying for others like most people only pray for themselves. An eternal view of life and afterlife animated his day, conversations, and judgements on events, and his sense of his own life as both a gift from God and a gift he could give to God and, through God, to all God's children—would be, like John Paul, one of those examples of holiness amid and through suffering that one can never shake from memory or heart.

A Persistent Witness

In 1979, the first secretary of the Polish Communist Party, Edward Gierek, made a decision that would change the world. Gierek agreed to let John Paul II visit Poland.

The recently elected John Paul was a young, healthy, vibrant man in his fifties. Millions of Poles were thrilled; but the Communist establishment was furious. After all, John Paul was a known critic of communism, as well as a man of great personality. So when the Soviet Premier Brezhnev heard the news, he lambasted Gierek and ordered him to rescind the invitation, saying, "Just tell the pope, who is a wise man, to say publicly that he is ill and can't make the trip."[140]

How little did they know John Paul!

In 2002, after years of Parkinson's disease, after two assassination attempts, after several serious health events, at a time when living and breathing and eating and speaking were laborious for him, John Paul's doctors forbade him to travel to Mexico City for the canonization of Saint Juan Diego. But after the consultation, John Paul turned to his doctors and said, "I'll see you in Mexico." Infirm as he was, he went.

This was how John Paul was. He understood that sickness was not what mattered most. He understood that, in sickness and in health, what mattered most was the Gospel, and that being present to others, he could be a living witness and true evangelist.

Throughout his life, I found it remarkable how he constantly preached the Gospel using every gift God had given him, whatever his condition might be. He used every means of communicating the Gospel that was at his disposal. He used his gift for writing poetry and plays. He used his baritone voice and sang. And as life went on, we saw him communicate the Gospel using what he also called "a gift."

That is, we saw him use his own suffering.

The Humility to Suffer

In this, I see that Brezhnev was right about something. John Paul was indeed a "wise man." But John Paul's wisdom was not Brezhnev's wisdom. John Paul's wisdom was not fear of the State, but humility before God.

He had the humility to see that suffering had a power that could only come from a God who is Love. His life, despite suffering and debilitation, had a dignity and worth, which also could only come from a God who is Love, and should not be suppressed.

As Pope Benedict said on Epiphany, "the Magi not only had zeal and the humility to see the star of Bethlehem but also to recognize and follow Christ in the surprising form of a defenseless child. Their humility enabled them to see that God's "greatness and power are not expressed in the logic of the world, but in the logic of a defenseless child, whose strength is only that of love entrusted to us."[141]

It took another type of humility as well: humility before people. Sometimes, people fear such sickness and suffering. Often, people even avoid keeping company with other people because they are afraid of appearing infirm before them. But John Paul suffered boldly before millions. He was willing to have the humility to do this before the world. And in his humility, John Paul II was a witness to suffering like few had seen before.

Through this, John Paul showed exactly what human dignity is all about. People followed his decline of health with interest, especially those attributes affecting human dignity—a decline of autonomy, weakness, inescapable pain, or diminished mobility. In the world's eyes, someone couldn't possibly lead a meaningful life this way. But this was what John Paul II did. And he accepted his afflictions with humility. In this way, John Paul showed that life can be lived as deeply in a wheelchair as on the ski slopes.

The Gospel of Suffering and the Sign of Contradiction

Of course, it did not begin that way.

At the beginning of his pontificate, John Paul was a Colossus: he was a dynamic person, an actor, a skier. The world soon saw him face to face as he became a world traveler, like no pope before him. Throughout the world, he captured attention and was incredibly influential.

People marveled at just how influential he was, and ascribed it to his personality. Before John Paul's first visit to Poland, the Communist regime told teachers in training that "Because he is unusually talented and has a great sense of humor, he is dangerous, since he can charm everybody."[142] Indeed, people constantly spoke of his dynamism, his endearing humor, his athleticism, his artistic creativity—characteristics that were not in themselves exclusively Christian, nor particularly holy. They were simply human.

At the end of his pontificate, these characteristics were subsumed beneath the veil of his illnesses and suffering. And yet, even with none of his past vitality, his impact grew. In this way, he was an enigma for the world. He was truly "a sign of contradiction," causing people to still wonder.

What then was his influence? What drew people to him? Why did people place their trust in him, and respect him?

For the world, it's often about sickness, not about the man. But in both states, as a strong healthy man and as an old, frail man, John Paul revealed more about the man—and mankind—than the world expected. He showed that it's not about the sickness. Nor is it even about the man at all. It's about the other man. It's about Christ.

Unity with the Suffering Christ

Thirty years ago, in his encyclical *Redemptor Hominis*, John Paul wrote "through the incarnation, Christ unites himself with every man." In a special way, this is intensified in the Cross: in the Cross, Christ unites himself with all who suffer, which enables us to be united with Christ, who suffered. As he said, "Precisely through this sacrifice, he *joined suffering to love once and for all, and in this way redeemed it.*"[143]

In an unparalleled way, John Paul testified to this at the end of his life. He became a worldwide example of what Saint Paul wrote: "yet I live, no longer I, but Christ lives in me."[144] These words were rooted in John Paul throughout his pontificate—as a man of prayer and finally toward the end of his life through his suffering. During his last Good Friday observance, it was clear to all that John Paul was not only holding the cross, but he was truly united to it.

Today, suffering is not understood, because the human person is not understood. Yes, of course, medicine and science daily make new discoveries. But the meaning of suffering is often lost because the human person is seen as a physical being with spiritual desires, not as a physical and spiritual being desired and loved by God.

The fact is, without love, without Christ, suffering cannot make sense. For this reason, suffering is one of the last and perennial questions that immediately propel people to consider whether there is a God, and who this God is. Suffering is a challenge that cannot be answered satisfactorily by atheism and by non-Christian belief systems. Only Christianity reveals the truth that "God so loves each person, that not even suffering sets one apart from him. He suffered for each of us, so that when you suffer, you may suffer with him."

John Paul once said that "without Christ's suffering and death, God's love for humanity would not have been manifested in all its depth and immensity."[145] In John Paul's life, we see the same blessing. While John Paul was blessed with long life, we were doubly blessed to see his transformation. Without his long pontificate and suffering, we would not have seen his many faces of humility, of holiness, of dedication. We would not have seen his many faces of Christ: Christ the healer, Christ the preacher, Christ the one spending fellowship with his disciples on a stormy sea, Christ the man of prayer suffering in a garden, Christ the incapacitated, immobile victim in pain raised high in plain sight of those watching him below. And just as a resurrected Christ would have been less marvelous without his suffering, so John Paul's holiness achieved greater depth because it preached not only the Gospel of love, but the Gospel of suffering wholeheartedly.

The Sick and the Suffering: The New Evangelists

Of course, through Christ, the sufferer not only gains a companion in Christ and suffering gains meaning, but suffering gains a purpose. And perhaps at no moment was John Paul more eloquent about this than at the times when he himself suffered most.

On May 17, 1981, as people gathered in St. Peter's Square at the usual time for the pope's Angelus address, John Paul did not appear on the balcony. Only his voice was heard in a message he had recorded from the Gemelli Hospital, where he was recovering from the bullet wounds from the assassination attempt against his life just four days before. The message was the briefest of his pontificate, and he concluded with these words:

"United to Christ, Priest, and Victim, I offer my suffering for the Church and the world. To you, Mary, I say: '*Totus Tuus ego sum.*' ('I am entirely yours.')"[146]

Not only, then, is suffering a method of growing close to God, but it is a participation in his suffering, and thus a participation in redemption.

The next week, he expounded on this further:

Suffering, accepted in union with the suffering Christ, has its unparalleled effectiveness in the implementation of the divine plan of salvation. May I repeat with Saint Paul: "I rejoice in my sufferings for you, and in my flesh I fill up what is lacking in the sufferings of Christ for his body, the Church" *(Col 1:24)*. I invite all the sick to join me in offering to Christ their sufferings for the good of the Church and humanity.[147]

For him, suffering truly was not simply a hurdle that individuals could overcome and benefit from personally, but he truly understood and valued suffering, which, through Christ, could "unleash love."

In an "Address to the Sick and Disabled" in 1989, John Paul II expounded further, and proposed a radical strategy for the new evangelization. He said:

The evangelizing strength, which suffering has, cannot be measured. So when I call all the Christian faithful to the great missionary task of carrying out a new evangelization, I have in mind that in the front line will be, as exceptional spreaders of the Gospel, the sick, young sick people.[148]

In 1994, after John Paul fell and had to have hip surgery, he once again reflected on his suffering in an Angelus address. He said:

I meditated on all this and thought it over again during my hospital stay. . . . I understood that I have to lead Christ's Church into this third millennium by prayer, by various programs, but I saw that this is not enough: she must be led by suffering, by the attack thirteen years ago, by this new sacrifice. Why now, why this, why in this Year of the Family? Precisely because the family is under attack. The pope has to be attacked; the pope has to suffer, so that every family and the world may see that there is . . . a higher Gospel: the Gospel of suffering, by which the future is prepared, the third millennium of families, of every family and of all families.

[. . .] I understand that it was important to have this argument before the powerful of this world. Again I must see these powerful of the world and I must speak. What arguments? I have left this matter of suffering.[149]

The crucifixion, it can be said, is the wedding of Christ and the Church. And for the Church throughout the world, for every suffering is an invitation to love. For the Church, engaging suffering then becomes a renewal of the Church's marriage vows to Christ, an opportunity to recommit ourselves. In the words of John Paul: "Suffering man belongs to us."

Mary and Suffering

This ecclesial dimension of suffering brings us to another dimension of suffering close to John Paul's heart: the Marian dimension of suffering. As he said in one Angelus address, "The first and foremost to be *associated with Jesus* in this mystery of suffering and love is *his Mother Mary.*"[150]

On Calvary, Mary was unable to remove his physical suffering, but she was able to change it. She stayed with him, she looked at him, and she listened to what he had to say. She also heard him suffer from feeling abandoned by God the Father, and undoubtedly, she prayed to the Father as well. John Paul was deeply aware of how this role, her Motherhood beside the Cross, was also given to all Christians when Christ entrusted Mary to John at the foot of the Cross.

This was, in part, why John Paul's visit to Mexico in 2002 was so important. He came to canonize someone who had heard from the lips of Mary the reason why we can face suffering and say even then "Do not be afraid." When Saint Juan Diego's uncle was sick, Our Lady of Guadalupe came to Saint Juan Diego, and said, "Listen, put it into your heart . . . that what frightened you . . . is nothing. . . . Do not fear this sickness or any other sickness. . . . Am I not here, I who have the honor to be your mother? Are you not in my shadow and under my protection? Am I not the source of your joy?"

These words capture what was true in John Paul's own life. Just as Mary had stayed with Christ on Calvary, so Mary was always close to John Paul in his suffering. And at the time of his assassination attempt, the world caught a glimpse of exactly how much. There is the connection to Our Lady of Fatima, in that he was shot on her feast day, fulfilling the third message of Fatima. And as he was shot, he saw Mary with him. Today, if we need a reminder of this, we can stand in St. Peter's Square facing the Basilica and look up to the right. You will see the mosaic of Our Lady, which he had placed there after his assassination attempt, so that all might look up and see the woman who had come to him, to save him, in his most dangerous moment.

In this, Mary expressed personally what Pope Benedict, as cardinal, described as three aspects of how love is expressed in how we live out our humanity. Being human, we are created in God's image in that we are a being from someone, a being for someone, and a being with someone. To live our humanity fully requires a total gift of self.

The Compassion of John Paul II

John Paul II understood that suffering is a time for closeness with those who suffer. In Lent of 1969, when Cardinal Wojtyła made his canonical visitation to the Corpus Christi Parish in Krakow, he desired to visit the sick of the parish who were in private homes. We have a beautiful account of his visits from Sister Irena Odoy, who was the parish's caretaker of the sick. She recounts:

> His Eminence the Cardinal planned two days of visits. . . . We went by car from house to house, street by street. The Cardinal was alone, without his chaplain, with only his driver. We visited all the houses whose addresses I knew; many were

humble, neglected, some not prepared for such a visit; we went into courtyards, basement apartments, upper stories, garrets, wherever there were sick people who were bedridden or otherwise unable to leave their homes.

The Cardinal would sit very close to the bed of each sick person and talked to them with paternal kindness. The sick, I noticed, were not flustered; they spoke freely of things which were close to their hearts. The Cardinal carefully listened to everything, sometimes wrote down an address, asked questions, kissed them on the head or the forehead, blessed them, and asked for their prayers for the intention of the Church. One sick woman asked with great simplicity for intervention in arranging summer convalescence outside of the city. . . . Thanks to his intervention, the sick woman spent a vacation at a convent near the mountains.

Sister Irena then recounts one particularly difficult visit to the house of a forty-two-year-old woman who had had an operation for a brain tumor and was so weak that she couldn't sit up:

The Cardinal leaned over her bed and with great compassion listened as she told him of her suffering. The situation was very grim. Her husband was an addicted alcoholic, her younger daughter mentally retarded and crippled by polio. Throughout her married life, and even now, she said, she often had to run away from her husband with her children and mother, afraid for their lives. She also talked about her brain operation. The Cardinal was extremely concerned and moved by the suffering and the situation of this woman. I noticed that his brow was covered with beads of sweat and his veins bulged. With his hand, he wiped the tears from her face, and kissed her several times on the forehead. He also spoke with the crippled daughter. . . .

Every person was important to him, for everyone he had a kind word or some gesture of compassion.[151]

For John Paul II, this gift of self was not an abstraction; nor was it only possible for clergy. Young Karol Wojtyła saw it in his own brother Edmund, a dedicated doctor, who gave his life attending patients during a scarlet fever epidemic when many doctors were afraid to administer. It is also seen in ten-year-old Karol Wojtyła visiting his physician brother working at the hospital, and entertaining patients with little plays.[152] Indeed, throughout his life, he lived this extreme love, loving others "in our human condition, with our weaknesses and our needs."[153]

Final Witness

At the last Angelus address delivered before he died, John Paul was so weak he could not deliver it himself, but entreated Archbishop Sandri to read it for him. In this address, John Paul wrote these words: "*joy united to the Cross*, which in itself sums up the Christian mystery."[154] Looking back at his life, I believe we can say that joy united to the Cross summed up the mystery of his holiness.

Certainly, all people will wish to claim John Paul as their patron saint. Dramatists, parish priests, workers—the list is endless. But when you look at the end of his life, you see how clearly, how courageously, how unequivocally he lived through his suffering. Because of the dignity of human suffering shown through him, we know that he will always be especially, even first and foremost, the patron of the suffering—a group that will at some point include every one of us.

SECTION 4

Transcending Partisanship

In the early twenty-first century, as tensions on the national and international level often exploded into the public eye, sometimes with words and sometimes with violent actions, the need seemed ever greater for a better civilization. Deeply ingrained hostilities daily made clear that only love could answer the root causes of this deep angst.

Against this backdrop, the ideal and practical goal of building the antidote—"a civilization of love"—has been an important theme during my tenure as supreme knight. The phrase—promoted first by Pope Paul VI briefly, and extensively by Pope John Paul II as well as by his successors—also featured prominently in the themes of my speeches, columns, and books (two of which bore the phrase in their titles).[155] Exemplifying this, the Knights of Columbus undertook numerous initiatives worldwide, which added to the already robust record of charity performed on the council level in communities and parishes.

For Catholics in particular, I thought it very important to stress the spiritual answers to these problems. In particular, Divine Mercy—a concept and devotion popularized by Saint John Paul II and embraced also by Pope Francis—is essential to founding such a civilization. Only mercy can break a cycle of recrimination or violence. Only mercy—based on authentic love—can heal deep divides and mistrust.

Facing some of the most partisan moments in the past century, this series of speeches and columns sought to provide a path by which Catholics—and indeed all people of faith—could move forward with principled action in a way that transcended political considerations. An example of one specific instance where I have personally advocated an approach which transcends partisanship is in the way that we as citizens vote for candidates. My position has been that Catholics should not vote for any candidate, from any political party, who supported the de facto abortion-on-demand regime ushered in by the Supreme Court in *Roe v. Wade* in 1973. It seemed clear that only by solving this gravest issue (qualitatively and quantitatively more serious and deadly than any other) could Americans move on to the discussion that was so urgently needed on so many other issues of great importance.

This seemed to be a natural position to take if authentic commitment to Christian faith informed politics, and not the other way around.

And if faith were to be the driver for political positions, many of the seemingly insurmountable "partisan" issues of the day could give way to fraternal solidarity. Indeed, in urging Catholics to live out their faith in the political as well as the personal spheres, I have explicitly urged that this include their entire faith—including forgiveness and love of one's enemies, lest hatred beget hatred and not be responded to with love.

For that reason, I frequently shared a prayer offered by Saint Thomas More, written during the pinnacle of his personal suffering, while he awaited execution in the Tower of London. He wrote:

> Almighty God, have mercy . . . on all that bear me evil will, and would me harm, and their faults and mine together . . . vouchsafe to amend and redress and make us saved souls in heaven together, where we may ever live and love together with Thee and Thy blessed saints. . . . Amen.

Expressing both regret for all our common failures as human beings as well as a common hope of heaven for himself as well as for his enemies, this prayer provides a roadmap for political differences in a big-picture, Christian context, whose relevance has grown rather than diminished.

19.

MLK's Example Holds the Answers to Both Racism and Political Violence

OP-ED

Co-authored with Reverend Eugene F. Rivers, III
Time Magazine, October 18, 2017

In 2017, the United States was convulsed by racist attacks from white supremacists and by political violence from the leftist Antifa movement. In a *Time Magazine* opinion piece that I coauthored with Pentecostal Pastor Eugene Rivers (founder and president of the Seymour Institute for Black Church and Policy Studies), we argued that violence based on race or politics had no place in our country, and urged the adoption of the models of Christian forgiveness advocated by Reverend Dr. Martin Luther King, Jr. and put into practice by the members of Mother Emanuel Church in Charleston, South Carolina, as an antidote to the culture of hatred and violence that had taken root in some quarters.

In the current climate, our country desperately needs to rediscover the moral example of Reverend Dr. Martin Luther King, Jr. His commitment to loving nonviolent struggle and protest was a principled response to the verifiable injustices committed against defenseless black people in our society.

From King's conception of love and non-violence sprang the equally weighty duty of confronting those responsible with the call to end a system of racial subjugation.

In his essay "Nonviolence and Racial Justice," published in the *Christian Century* in 1957, King laid out a path forward for the country modeled on a love-based, nonviolent resistance. He wrote:

> At the center of nonviolence stands the principle of love. In struggling for human dignity, the oppressed people of the world must not allow themselves to become bitter or indulge in hate campaigns. To retaliate with hate and bitterness would do nothing but intensify the hate in the world. Along the way of life, someone must have sense enough and morality enough to cut off the chain of hate. This can be done only by projecting the ethics of love to the center of our lives.

If King were here today, we know from the historical record that he would have condemned in the most explicit terms, any form of violent political protest.

He would have condemned both the program and the violence of neo-Nazis, white supremacists, and other racist hate groups. While even these—like all Americans—have the constitutional right to speak and protest, they have neither a constitutional nor a moral right to violence. King would have spoken up clearly on all of that. In fact, his entire program was designed to show the moral and political bankruptcy of those who traded in racism.

But King would not have sanctioned the violent actions of extremists such as Antifa either. If they seek to resist racism, they should adopt him as the exemplar of legitimate opposition.

For King, nonviolence did not mean staying silent, it meant speaking and acting against racism while avoiding the violent tactics of the racists.

Six decades after Dr. King wrote, we—and other religious leaders from throughout this country—have added our voices to his, signing a letter embracing the principles that he laid out in that essay. We understand that trying to justify violence based from any political viewpoint is a recipe for coming apart at the very moment we need to come together.

Now as then, we must choose whether this country will overcome deep racial and political divisions with justice and forgiveness, or deepen them with hatred and violence.

Concrete examples of the power of forgiveness continue to show the importance of heeding the better angels of our nature. In Charleston, South Carolina, in 2015, the congregation of Mother Emanuel AME Church reacted with love and forgiveness to an act of domestic terrorism. The pastor and eight members of the congregation were murdered immediately following a prayer meeting that the killer had attended with them. Their reaction stood in sharp contrast to the urge to retaliate that has met violence elsewhere. Dylann Roof had wanted to launch a race war, but the forgiveness expressed by the families of the victims and the congregation affected meant that love stopped that outbreak of racist violence from going any further.

That church community reminded us of the truth of Reverend King's words fifty years ago in his book *Where Do We Go from Here: Chaos or Community*, where he wrote:

> Returning violence for violence multiplies violence, adding deeper darkness to a night already devoid of stars. Darkness cannot drive out darkness; only light can do that. Hate cannot drive out hate; only love can do that.[156]

The actions of the community of Mother Emanuel captured the attention of the country because hatred and revenge are often easier paths to follow than love, nonviolence, and forgiveness. When wronged, "an eye for an eye" is often more appealing to us mortals than the tougher admonition "love your enemies."

For that reason—among others—love and nonviolence are all

the more powerful. Especially in a democracy, nonviolent principles do not enable evil or violence to triumph, rather they break their hold and show a better path forward by staking out a moral high ground that is indisputable. Acting on these standards underlines the deficiencies of the opposite path while also showing a better way to our antagonists.

The better path, the only path to our salvation as a country, was made clear by Reverend King in 1967: "The beauty of nonviolence is that in its own way and in its own time it seeks to break the chain reaction of evil."[157] We can again break that chain reaction, and the prescription is the same one given by Reverend King. Now as then, religious leaders have taken the first step. For their own sake—and that of future generations—the rest of the country should do so as well.

20.

What Every Catholic Can Do to Transcend Partisanship

SPEECH

Given to the Catholic Press Association
June 22, 2012, Indianapolis, Indiana

Speaking to the assembled journalists of the Catholic Press Association, in the midst of serious tensions between the Obama Administration and the Catholic Church over the HHS Mandate, this speech laid out the steps every Catholic could take to begin to transform American politics into something with a moral rather than partisan compass. With the Mario Cuomo model of "personally opposed to abortion, but supportive of it legally" increasingly the mantra of some Catholic politicians, this speech presented a different model, that of Sargent Shriver, the founder of the Peace Corps and Democratic presidential candidate in the 1976 primary. Shriver, who was both pro-life and a Democrat, stood as a prime example of the fact that the abortion issue need not be a partisan issue, and that Catholics could lead on the issue from both sides of the aisle, not by abandoning their conscience, but by embracing it.

Catholics' Unique Role

I would like to begin by thanking you for the service Catholic journalists provide to the vitality of the Catholic faith in our country. At a time when information sources seem to be growing at an exponential rate and much of the media coverage of our Church is inaccurate or unfair, you are needed today more than ever to accurately inform our fellow Catholics.

All of us have at one time or another lamented the sad state of today's political environment: the intransigence and partisanship that disfigure nearly every national policy debate and make the search for solutions virtually impossible. It is an environment that drives away from national leadership many persons of intelligence and integrity.

But I believe we can find a way out of the present politics of gridlock and politics of destruction if we think beyond the next election and if we sincerely work together.

Catholics are uniquely positioned to offer a solution to our current dilemma. We have an extraordinarily rich tradition of social teaching and the experience that much of American history has been shaped by Catholics.

If we are faithful to the social teaching of our Church, I believe Catholics can truly transcend partisanship and transform our nation's politics. I would propose four steps by which we may do so.

Civility in America's National Discourse

Writing in *The City of God*, Saint Augustine observed, "let this city bear in mind, that among her enemies lie hidden those who are destined to be fellow citizens, that she may not think it a fruitless labor to bear what they inflict as enemies until they become confessors of the truth."[158] Augustine reminds us that as Christians we must hope that even our most strident adversaries may one day join us as saved souls together in heaven.

This perspective obliges us to insist on a more respectful civil discourse. Our approach ought to be one of seeking the conversion, not the destruction of our political opponents.

In my recent book *Beyond a House Divided*, I observed that as a nation we adopt this insight in times of national crisis, for example, in the days following the terrorist attack on 9/11 or after the murder of the Reverend Martin Luther King, Jr.

I concluded *Beyond a House Divided* by quoting from Robert Kennedy's speech following the announcement of Dr. King's death: "What we need in the United States is not division; what we need in the United States is not hatred; what we need in the United States is not violence or lawlessness, but is love and wisdom and compassion toward one another. . . ."[159]

We need to embrace this attitude not only after a national tragedy. This attitude should be normative of our national life.

Our first step as Catholics must be a firm commitment to civility in America's national discourse.

Charity as a Distinctive Catholic Contribution to National Life

You may notice that the title of these remarks is similar to the title of my book *A Civilization of Love: What Every Catholic Can Do to Transform the World*. That book grew out of my experience with the Knights of Columbus on the role of charity and solidarity in society, and ethics and sustainability in business.

In both areas Catholics can make a unique contribution to American life.

This is the lesson we should learn from the religious brothers and sisters and other Catholics who by their sacrifice built our schools and hospitals, orphanages, and universities. They did so much to make America a more humane society.

Catholic charity is not simply a mechanism for the more efficient or cost-effective delivery of social services.

As Pope Benedict XVI reminded us in *Deus Caritas Est*, Catholic charity arises from "a heart that sees where love is needed" and responds appropriately. It arises from a religious tradition that understands that *caritas* is the prerequisite of justice. And as Pope

Benedict observed, there is no society so perfect as to have escaped the need for love.

Catholic charity, grounded in the Christian vision that we are our brother's keeper, provides an irreplaceable contribution to society since it introduces the reality of fraternal brotherhood as a source of national unity.

The personal relationship of giving something of one's self to another creates a bond and a solidarity that can unite society in profound ways. I saw this first hand in Haiti, when we provided wheelchairs and prosthetics to children and adults who had lost legs in that country's terrible earthquake.

My experience with the Knights of Columbus convinces me that every Catholic is capable of a charity that can change countless lives.

Thus, our second step must be to build up the fabric of American society through a fraternal solidarity based on personal works of charity.

Consistent Commitment to the Church's Social Teaching

The candid observer must admit that when it comes to a consistent commitment to the social teaching of our Church, Catholics in America still have a long way to go. We have made considerable progress, but in the words of Robert Frost, we have "miles to go before we sleep."

In 1976, I had the opportunity to go to Washington, DC to work as a legislative assistant in the United States Senate. For the next five years I spent almost all of my time working on the pro-life cause: promoting legislation to prevent funding abortion as part of U.S. foreign aid; helping to pass the Hyde Amendment restrictions of abortion funding; as one of the attorneys successfully defending the Hyde Amendment before the U.S. Supreme Court; and organizing the bi-partisan Congressional Pro-life Caucus.

Later, I joined the Secretary of Health and Human Services in the Reagan Administration, where one of my principal responsibilities was working to provide new federal protections to stop discrimination against handicapped newborn infants. Two years later, I joined the White House staff of President Reagan and helped draft the Mexico City Policy to cut off U.S. foreign aid to organizations that perform or promote abortion overseas.

In 1987, I left the White House staff to join the Knights of Columbus. As I told President Reagan then, I left politics in order to serve a higher calling and to promote key elements of Catholic social teaching beyond the political realm. I believed these issues could not simply be limited to—or dismissed as—the domain of a political party.

Since 2008, the Knights of Columbus has worked with the Marist Institute for Public Opinion on a series of surveys on the ethical attitudes of Americans that we have termed our Moral Compass Project.

Our polling—as illustrated in my book *Beyond a House Divided*—has shown that Americans' attraction to Catholic social teaching transcends party lines. Americans share a broad moral and even spiritual consensus that often tracks closely with Catholic social teaching.

Over the years, it has become clear to many that if Catholics in both political parties had evidenced a consistent commitment to Catholic social teaching and if they had been able to overcome partisan rigidity and hostility, we would have been able to significantly restrict abortion.

We were not able to do this because of a failure of our elected Catholic officials.

But there was also a failure by Catholic voters who were led to believe that their choice was between candidates who were only partly committed to a consistent ethic of life.

However, if Catholic voters had insisted that this choice was not acceptable, we might have been able to solve the abortion issue decades ago.

One of the great obstacles to the formation of a successful Catholic coalition on the life issue was the position Governor Mario Cuomo articulated in a 1984 speech at the University of Notre Dame. There, he defended his position of being personally opposed to abortion but unwilling to take a position in opposition to abortion because this would mean imposing his beliefs on his fellow citizens.

Those of us who disagreed saw a fatal flaw in his argument.

We understood Catholic teaching on abortion to have nothing to do with faith per se. Medical science has concluded that the being alive in a mother's womb is a human being irrespective of one's religious conviction. Therefore, the protection of innocent human life that is a fundamental legal principle of every civilized society should apply to protect unborn children.

Those of us who criticized the so-called "Cuomo Doctrine" saw the issue not as a question of Catholic faith, but as a matter of social justice and human rights.

Yet, the force with which Governor Cuomo made his argument and its widespread acceptance effectively inoculated a generation of "pro-choice" Catholic politicians. The result has been a political stalemate on the abortion issue for nearly three decades.

But there was also another effect.

Governor Cuomo's rationale created an environment in which it became easier for candidates to dismiss other principles of Catholic social teaching.

So every election year, many Catholic voters see their choice as between the lesser of two evils. They face candidates who argue that while they may not be consistent with Catholic values on all issues, they are consistent on some and that should be good enough.

But it is not good enough.

And as bad as this situation is, it has produced an even worse result.

It has blocked the potential of Catholic social teaching to transform our politics.

But must it always be this way?

Can we find a way that both political parties may come into alignment with the fundamental principles of Catholic social teaching?

If so, future Catholic voters may one day freely choose between political parties based upon their prudential judgment of which candidate is more likely to advance the common good.

As Catholics, we must stop picking and choosing which parts of Catholic social teaching we will accept.

And we must insist that our politicians stop doing this as well.

So our third step must be to build a consistent commitment to Catholic social teaching among Catholic voters in America.

Transforming Politics by Transcending Partisanship

We can find a solution if we learn from the Civil Rights Movement of the 1950s and 1960s.

The most important thing we need to do is to take the long view.

Consider, for example, the situation of the Democratic Party when the Supreme Court overturned the legal doctrine of "separate but equal" in its 1954 decision in *Brown versus Board of Education.*

The Democrats had integrated their national convention in 1948, causing Senator Strom Thurmond to run for president that year as a Dixiecrat. But throughout the 1950s and into the 1960s, the Democratic stronghold of the South remained in the hands of entrenched segregationists. Yet, in little more than two decades, the segregationist base of the Democratic Party was gone and a Democratic governor from the Deep South committed to civil rights was elected president.

Who could have possibly foreseen this outcome on the day the Supreme Court announced its decision in *Brown versus Board of Education?*

But if such transformation in American politics was possible within two decades, why can it not happen regarding Catholic social teaching?

Do we really think that African Americans had more influence in the 1950s and 1960s than Catholics in America have today?

Yet recent events suggest that we may have little choice but to act boldly.

During the 1980s, some Catholics came to regard the "Cuomo Doctrine" as a kind of "truce" in the culture wars. Catholics would be free to practice their faith while not taking positions consistent with fundamental Catholic teaching because this would be imposing their morality on others.

But today, many Catholics sense that this "peaceful co-existence" with secular culture has ended as a result of the HHS mandate on contraception.

Catholic public officials, who for years maintained that they would not impose their religious morality on others, now appear entirely comfortable with imposing secular values on their fellow Catholics and Catholic institutions.

Our bishops tell us that, if implemented, the HHS mandate will affect the autonomy and integrity of our Church and its institutions—that it will dramatically change the mission of the Catholic Church in the United States.

Therefore, the HHS mandate confronts us with a challenge that is very different from that of social issues such as legal abortion. It is different because it is a challenge to the integrity of our Catholic institutions and our own lives as Catholics.

It seems that it is no longer acceptable for Catholics to be "counter-cultural" on the life issues since the HHS mandate makes conformity the new rule of the day.

The HHS mandate has profoundly raised the stakes for our political choices.

The question is not primarily about a public policy choice. Instead, the question now concerns the sustainability of the mission and integrity of Catholic institutions.

In these circumstances Catholics can no longer accept politics as usual.

Today, Catholic voters must have the courage to act boldly and insist that every candidate for public office respect the autonomy, integrity, and mission of the Catholic Church and its institutions.

Catholic voters must have the courage to tell candidates that if they want Catholic votes, they will have to respect the fundamental principles of Catholic social teaching, such as the sanctity of human life before birth as well as the institutions of marriage and family.

Catholic voters should insist that candidates measure their political platforms by Catholic social teaching—especially if they are Catholics.

Catholic voters should have the courage to settle for nothing less than this.

And they should have the courage to withhold their vote from candidates who fail this test—even if it means at times that they will withhold their vote for both candidates for a particular office.

The bishops' document, "Faithful Citizenship," tells us that some actions are intrinsically evil and must always be opposed. As Catholics, we wish we could debate and vote on the full range of Catholic social teaching—including prudential issues that raise serious moral questions. But to be able to effectively do that, we must first refuse to support candidates who advocate policies that are intrinsically evil.

Withholding a vote may at times be the most effective vote.

In 2005, an Italian referendum that would have removed Italy's restrictions on in vitro fertilization and embryonic research failed because of low voter turnout. The Italian Bishops Conference had urged Catholics to boycott the referendum. Political pundits in Italy were convinced that the referendum would easily pass, but what the bishops had described as the "double no" of a Catholic voter boycott reversed the expected result in a dramatic fashion.

And it was an election strategy that only days before the vote, Pope Benedict XVI appeared to bless saying that in their actions "involved in enlightening and motivating the decisions of Catholics and of all citizens concerning the upcoming referendum. . . . I am close to you with my words and my prayers."

Obviously, there is a difference between a national referendum and the election of candidates for public office, but consider what we could achieve over the next decade if we insist that politicians seek our vote on our terms—that is to say, on the terms of an authentic appreciation of Catholic social teaching.

Consider one example from recent history.

In the 1976 Iowa Caucus, Jimmy Carter and Sargent Shriver were both seeking the Democratic presidential nomination. As we know, Jimmy Carter won in Iowa and went on to win the nomination and become president. But what if Shriver had won in Iowa and he had gone on to become president?

Is it likely that four years later, Ronald Reagan would have been able to build a winning coalition of so-called "Reagan Democrats" composed primarily of blue-collar Catholics to defeat an incumbent pro-life Catholic President Shriver?

How would American politics have been different after eight years of a Shriver Administration rather than a Reagan Administration?

Shouldn't our goal as Catholics be a political environment where Catholic voters can choose between candidates who are in agreement on the fundamental social teaching of the Church?

And if so, how would that new reality change the platforms of both our major political parties regarding other principles of Catholic social teaching?

I cannot predict the answers to these questions, nor can I say which political party would benefit. I cannot say how our political parties may change during the next decade if politicians take seriously Catholic social teaching.

But the outcome could be a new political coalition in which Catholics would play an irreplaceable role. This is not promoting partisan politics—it is the opposite of partisanship.

Our fourth step must be to transform our national politics by transcending partisanship on the basis of Catholic social teaching.

It was in our grasp to transform American politics in 1976.

And it can be again.

No political party in America can be successful and at the same time lose a majority of Catholic voters.

The solution is as simple as this: We should exercise our right to vote on our own terms and not on the terms of others.

If we do, America will be a better place.

I believe that as Americans and as Catholics, you and I have a responsibility to make this happen.

There may be those who say that now is not the right time. But we must look not to the next election, but to the next decade.

Dr. King had the courage to dream a great dream.

I believe that Catholics can dream great dreams as well.

21.

The "Catholic Vote" Should Matter After the Election Too

OP-ED

Crux, November 8, 2016

In the run up to the 2016 election, it became clear that some persons of influence had sought to specifically manipulate the doctrine of the Catholic Church for political gain. In response, I advocated that Catholic voters had a responsibility that continued even after the election, and laid out a series of prescriptions that could inform Catholics and help them be a "source of reconciliation" and leaven in society, not just on election day, but every day. When originally printed, this article was entitled "After Today, the 'Catholic Vote' Should Matter More, Not Less."

It has been the strangest election season any of us can remember. And among the many surprises was the disclosure by WikiLeaks of emails from within a presidential campaign organization that caused great concern among many Catholics for the disparaging language used to describe Catholics.

The disclosure prompted the president of the United States Conference of Catholics Bishops, Archbishop Joseph Kurtz, to issue an unprecedented public statement about what he described as an attempt "to interfere in the internal life of the Church for short-term political gain" and to urge "public officials to respect the rights of people to live their faith without interference from the state."

While the fact that these disclosures came from within a political campaign was troubling, more troubling still was the fact that they were made by Catholics about other Catholics.

The episode points to a serious challenge for Catholics: regardless of the outcome of tomorrow's election, America will remain a deeply divided country and those divisions are, to a very real extent, reflected within our own Catholic faith community.

The question that we as Catholics should ask ourselves is in what way Catholics in America can in the future be a source of unity and reconciliation, or whether we will be a cause of further division.

The answer to that question will depend largely on what we think it means today to be a Catholic in America. In other words, what is fundamental to our identity as Catholics?

Pope Francis, in his book *On Heaven and Earth*, written while he was Archbishop of Buenos Aires, stated: "There are those that seek to compromise their faith for political alliances or for a worldly spirituality. . . . Henri de Lubac says that the worst that can happen to those that are anointed and called to service is that they live with the criteria of the world instead of the criteria that the Lord commands from the tablets of the law and the Gospel."

While the pope was specifically writing about the clergy, I think what he says applies to all Catholics.

Speaking about this to my brother Knights of Columbus, I have said that as an organization dedicated to the principles of charity, unity, fraternity, and patriotism, we must strive to be a source of unity in our church and society, and to do this in a way consistent with our commitment to charity, fraternity, and patriotism.

Many Americans, and many Catholics among them, are disheartened and frustrated about what has happened during this political season. But this is precisely the time that Catholics need to step up and more fully exercise their responsibilities as citizens for the common good.

It is time for more—not less—Catholic involvement in the life of our nation.

But how are Catholics to do this? Pope Francis has already suggested the answer: to live more fully by the criteria that the Lord commands rather than by the criteria of the world.

In other words, we need to continue the renewal of our own faith community as Catholics if we hope to influence more effectively our national life as Americans.

I would suggest six areas.

First, continue the renewal of parish life as a true Eucharistic community with a fuller appreciation of how the "the source and summit of the Christian life" is also the source and summit of our unity and charity as Catholics.

Second, the evangelization of Catholic families as a domestic church, which, like the universal church, is called to reach out in solidarity to other families as a source of unity, charity, mercy, and reconciliation.

Third, a renewed devotion to the Blessed Virgin Mary, not only as the perfect model of the Christian life, but also as an unsurpassed model for understanding our responsibilities as citizens for the common good.

Fourth, a deeper understanding of those moral principles and issues that have "absolute value" (as Pope Francis has said the Fifth Commandment does) for us as a faith community and that are the basis for a more adequate engagement with the social doctrine of our church.

Fifth, a heightened commitment to Catholic education that is not simply abstract, but one that seeks to form the entire person.

Sixth, a greater appreciation of the office of bishop as the source of unity for the local church—a unity that promotes a deeper communion among bishops, priests, religious, and laity.

Other considerations could be added to this list. But if we begin thinking in this way, then whoever wins the election, a greater unity among Catholics may provide a roadmap for greater unity for our entire country.

And that would be a "Catholic vote" that would endure far beyond tomorrow's balloting.

22.

The Pope of Mercy
The Role of Blessed John Paul II in the Lives of the Laity

SPEECH

Given at the Divine Mercy Center
October 4, 2011, Krakow, Poland

In this 2011 speech given in Poland, the Catholic concept of mercy was explored as an antidote to the tendency of secular culture, and human nature generally, to put a premium on dominance far more than on forgiveness. Using Saint John Paul II's words and actions—including forgiving his would-be assassin—and citing the forgiveness of other great witnesses to this virtue, including Saint Maximilian Kolbe, this speech presented Catholics with models of personal life filled with love of God and love of neighbor, and on that basis, with mercy as well—models that, if magnified by imitation and adoption by many today, could have not only profound religious effects, but also profound societal ones. Imagine the effect on our politics if mercy rather than revenge was normative.

Pope of Mercy

One of the beautiful things about this year's celebration of Divine Mercy is its attention to Blessed John Paul II.

For me personally, when reflecting on Divine Mercy, it is also natural to remember Blessed John Paul. Like Saint Faustina, he lived with complete trust in Christ. Like Christ, he expressed the urgent need to turn toward the "Father of Mercies." This was at the center of Blessed John Paul II's life and at the center of his spirituality.

In 2003, when John Paul celebrated his twenty-fifth anniversary as pope, the Knights of Columbus sought to honor him by devoting a year to spreading devotion to Divine Mercy.

Two other events influenced this. First, John Paul had recently canonized Saint Faustina. And second, the United States had recently suffered its greatest act of violent hatred of recent memory: the terrorist attacks of September 11, 2001.

It is said that those terrorists attacked for religious reasons. But if God is love, then there is nothing so God-less as an act of hate-filled violence. At that time, as always, we recognized a great need to remember who God is, in whose image all of us are made.

It became our most popular prayer program. Councils arranged over 28,000 Divine Mercy events for their parishes, and the image of Divine Mercy, entrusted to us by Saint Faustina's Sisters, was brought to cathedrals throughout the United States, Canada, Mexico, and the Philippines. The affection for the devotion was striking—over 2 million people attended.

When Pope John Paul personally blessed that image for us, I had the added grace of speaking with him about Divine Mercy. In that meeting, it became clear to me that God's mercy had captured the gaze of John Paul's saintly heart.

Some of you may know that in the past several days, the Knights of Columbus has purchased the Pope John Paul II Cultural Center in Washington, DC. Our intention is to transform the Center into the Shrine of Blessed John Paul II. I am grateful to the Archbishop of Washington, His Eminence Donald Wuerl, who has recently designated the Center as a Diocesan Shrine, and it is our intention at the earliest practical date to request that the Center be named the National Shrine of the United States devoted to Blessed John Paul II.

I am also very grateful for the cooperation and support of our beloved Archbishop of Krakow, His Eminence Stanislaw Dziwisz, for making available to us a precious relic of blood of Blessed John Paul II.

I mention this to you today in order to say that my first action upon taking over the Center was to have the beautiful painting of Divine Mercy, which was personally blessed by the Holy Father in 2003, placed prominently in the chapel of his new shrine in Washington, DC.

John Paul II: Model of the Depth and Breadth of Catholic Mercy

Some people might deride our devotion to Divine Mercy as another Catholic "obsession" with sin. In the United States, jokes about "Catholic guilt" abound, implying that the Church teaching on sin makes people "feel bad" about themselves for no apparent reason.

Indeed, this negativity is a significant obstacle to evangelization.

But the Church's unique message is *not* that human beings sin. You don't need a church to tell you that people do bad things—just look at history. The world may disagree about some behaviors and whether those behaviors are morally wrong or not, but no one believes that everyone does the right thing all the time.

The Church's real message is that mercy exists. Reconciliation is both possible and worthwhile because God is Love, and God is abundant in mercy.

Thus, the Church's message is one of hope. No sin is greater than God's love. But only mercy—God's infinite mercy—can transform the deserts that man creates.

God's mercy is the love that heals. And because God's mercy exists, we can say with confidence "Love conquers all."

Thus, in a real way, mercy needs to be at the forefront of the new evangelization.

And by mercy, I do not only mean "forgiveness." Mercy is, generally speaking, also the generous response to the needs of man. As Cardinal Wojtyła said in 1958 to a meeting of physicians: "[T]he scope of the need for mercy is much wider than we think. . . ."[160]

He went on to describe Christian mercy as the very basis for the *reality* of Christianity.

> Each man stands at a point where he is needed by someone. And each man stands at a point where there are people all around him who need his help. Each one of us stands at such a point of always being needed by someone and being surrounded by those who need. This is why Christianity is real.[161]

If mercy is what makes what we believe real, then if mercy is taken away, we are left with something *unreal*. But only a real Christianity can evangelize culture and transform real lives.

When I think of Blessed John Paul's death on the eve of Divine Mercy Sunday, it seemed so appropriate for him to enter new life on the day Christ established as a generous outpouring of graces, a day Blessed John Paul embraced. The prayers, promises, and tasks associated with that feast day mirrored his life so well. Besides his trust in Christ, one of Christ's commands for that day stands out:

> [T]he first Sunday after Easter is the Feast of Mercy, but there must also be deeds of mercy, which are to arise out of love for Me. You are to show mercy to our neighbors always and everywhere. You must not shrink from this or try to absolve yourself from it.[162]

Blessed John Paul II brought out the effect that God's mercy has in our interactions with others. He communicated the *interpersonal* expression of God's mercy—the mercy we share with our brothers and sisters.

As a priest, and as human being loved by God, Blessed John Paul saw himself as an instrument of God's mercy.

Beginning with his first two encyclicals—*Redemptor Hominis* and *Dives in Misericordia*—Blessed John Paul revealed the essentials of Christianity before the world.

On the issue of abortion, Blessed John Paul maintained a perfect sense of justice and mercy, defending the lives of the unborn while also extending Christ's invitation to reconciliation to parents who suffered from abortion. Recognizing that many women after abortion feel as if God would never forgive them, Blessed John Paul encouraged these women to approach Our Lord's superabundant mercy:

> But do not give in to discouragement and do not lose hope. Try rather to understand what happened and face it honestly. If you have not already done so, give yourselves over with humility and trust to repentance. The Father of mercies is ready to give you his forgiveness and his peace in the Sacrament of Reconciliation. To the same Father and his mercy, you can with sure hope entrust your child."[163]

His sense of mercy went beyond forgiving others or inviting others to welcome God's grace into their lives. Sometimes, asking forgiveness from each other can be harder and more humiliating.

And yet, in the Jubilee year, he surprised Catholics and non-Catholics alike by confronting history and publicly apologizing for various offences done by Catholics over the centuries.

He made this personal as well. Who can forget his example of forgiveness after the assassination attempt? Mehmet Ali Ağca tried to kill him, and his wounds from that assassination attempt continued to be a source of suffering for him throughout the rest of his life. But John Paul forgave him more readily than many people forgive minor offenses.

In preparation for John Paul's beatification, the Knights of

Columbus collected notes of thanks from young people of the "John Paul II generation." Several notes recalled the 1981 assassination attempt, and for some, the real hallmark moment was afterward: when he left the Vatican and sat down in a prison to speak with and forgive the man who tried to kill him.

That act of forgiveness was a "sign of contradiction."

As one girl wrote: "You are a great hero. . . . I still wonder, how did you so easily forgive the person who shot you? Honestly, it takes a kind, understanding, loving, and faith-filled person. I may not know everything about you, but I know that you are the closest thing to our Lord I have ever witnessed."[164]

Had John Paul been alive, he might have answered: I forgave "following the teaching and example of Jesus."[165] "Christians hold that to show mercy is to live out the truth of our lives: we can and must be merciful because mercy has been shown us by a God who is Love."[166]

Mercy: A Timely Antidote

Looking at the twentieth century, it seems as if, through Saint Faustina, God was preparing Poland spiritually to face the horrors of the following decades—the oppression of World War II, the oppression of workers, and most of all, the movement to suppress the strong Catholic faith of the people of Poland.

Although Saint Faustina died before these events, John Paul II lived through these events. His experience brought him to the conclusion that forgiveness is a fundamental requirement of peace.[167]

As he said in his message for the World Day of Peace for 2002: "No peace without justice," and "no justice without forgiveness."[168]

In a similar way, it seems that Saint Faustina was canonized at a pivotal time.

As John Paul wrote in his encyclical on mercy, "The more the human conscience succumbs to secularization, loses its sense of the very meaning of the word 'mercy,' moves away from God, and distances itself from the mystery of mercy, the more the Church has the right and the duty to appeal to the God of mercy 'with loud cries.'"[169]

For one thing, secularism seems to encourage forgiveness only insofar as it foresees a tangible benefit for forgiveness. The problem is, "Forgiveness in fact always involves an apparent short-term loss for a real long-term gain. Violence is the exact opposite; opting . . . for an apparent shortterm gain, it involves a real and permanent loss."[170]

Without the truth, forgiveness and justice can become arbitrary and, eventually, dispensable.

The long-term gain of forgiveness is authentic love. This is one reason why I believe Blessed John Paul's Catechesis on the Theology of the Body has already made a profound difference in the lives of Catholics. In his words, we discover the beauty of authentic love, and become aware of how we are "wonderfully made" in the image of God to love and serve one another.

By the grace of God, that vision of authentic love can lead many to embrace their vocation with joy and hope. As one young man of the John Paul II generation wrote: "Pope John Paul II's Theology of the Body changed my life, and, led me back to the Catholic faith!"[171]

In our families, communities, and world, we need to be not only the heart of Christ, which bleeds for man, but the arms of Christ, which stretch out between heaven and earth. Every difficulty, by us or against us, is an opportunity for mercy and therefore an opportunity for love.

The family, as John Paul frequently said, is "the school of love," that first place where children encounter God, witness love, and learn to love God and each other. As the Parable of the Prodigal Son teaches, we also see in the family the occasion for Divine Mercy and reconciliation.

Christian families should be the leading examples of forgiveness. Christ says at the last supper, "I give you a new commandment: love one another. As I have loved you, so you also should love one another. This is how all will know that you are my disciples, if you have love for one another." (John 13:34–35)

Each Catholic marriage can be a saintly witness to the beauty and reality of authentic love.

A perfect example of destructive nearsightedness is the prevalence of no-fault divorce, which encourages divorce even for minor offenses. The long-term result often includes depriving children of a parent and leaving a legacy of fear about marriage, lack of trust in resolving disagreement, and the feeling that one is unlovable.

One of the most urgent needs of Christian married couples and families today is to practice a spirituality of mercy and forgiveness after the example of Blessed John Paul II.

In this way, may we see more clearly the joy, pride, and love found in couples and families who learn to reconcile, growing closer in authentic love!

Loving one another goes beyond family and marriage—relationships that even non-Christians see as relationships built on love. It extends to every place where man goes—even to those places that are darkest.

Mercy: Not Easy, But a Grace

During my first visit to Krakow, I had the opportunity to visit also the Nazi death camp at Auschwitz. While we were there, we found the cell of Saint Maximilian Kolbe in the basement of Building 11, known as the Death Block.

I do not need here to recount the extraordinary life and heroic death of this Polish priest and saint. As I stood at the doorway of his cell and prayed, I asked myself how many times this saint would have prayed the Lord's Prayer in that room, and whether the Lord's Prayer had ever been prayed more intensely than it had been by the victims in those camps.

But especially I asked myself how was it humanly possible in those circumstances, without God's special grace, to be able to say,

"Forgive us our trespasses as we forgive those who trespass against us."

Surely Saint Maximilian Kolbe did just that: prayed to forgive those who intended to kill him. His life and death will be an example for the ages—but it should be an example especially for *our* age.

Blessed John Paul's "recipe" for peace in the world—justice and forgiveness—is also the recipe for peace in our communities and nations.

The message of merciful love needs to resound forcefully anew," Blessed John Paul reminded us in Krakow in 2002. And he continued:

> The world needs this love. The hour has come to bring Christ's message to everyone: to rulers and the oppressed, to those whose humanity and dignity seem lost in the *mysterium iniquitatis [The mystery of evil]*.[172]

Blessed John Paul's hope was grounded in realism. Again in 1958, he answered an unspoken question: *If mercy is so good, then why is forgiving and seeking forgiveness so difficult?* He said:

> Basically, man carries within himself a resistance to mercy. However, since he recognizes mercy, he must acknowledge that he himself needs at least the help of other men. Meanwhile, each person carries within himself a strong need of self-sufficiency: not to need! Not to find oneself in a situation of need! And from this aspect, mercy and a religion of mercy are not looked favorably upon by people. On the other hand, man needs mercy—herein lies the paradox."[173]

This paradox is answered by the truth of Christianity. Every person feels the tension between self-sufficiency and mercy. This tension also exists in one's culture.

Forgiveness often begets forgiveness, even if not immediately. On the other hand, violence, resentment, or indifference to God can capitalize on our need for self-protection, and leads many to believe that revenge is just.

How do we take up John Paul's exhortation: to "Help modern men and women to experience God's merciful love"—a love that, "in its splendor and warmth, will save humanity?"

For is it possible to have any human community without a love that extends mercy and makes reconciliation possible?

But we cannot do this alone. We can only do it with Him, Christ the redeemer. And so we turn, always, to Christ.

The famous *Diary of a Country Priest* ends with a touching line: "Everything is grace." Grace is, in a sense mercy, God's action in our life. If in the end everything is grace, then in the end everything is mercy and everything is love.

This grace, this mercy, this love is at the center of charity, unity, and solidarity.

This is at the center of Christian life. This is at the center of the spiritual life of our blessed pope.

Let us with John Paul recognize this as "the hour . . . when the message of Divine Mercy is able to fill hearts with hope and to become the spark of a new civilization: the civilization of love."[174]

Let us bring our hearts, mind, and labors to the Father of Mercies.

Let our homes be eloquent with love, truth, and forgiveness.

Let us become new evangelists, bringing the good news of reconciliation and the promise of authentic love to our cultures.

And above all, let us, with Saint Faustina, place our trust in the one who never disappoints: *Jezu ufam Tobie* (Jesus, I trust in You).

Love in Society

One of the strongest, most complex, and pervasive networks in any country is the web of relationships made by love.

On the level of individuals, the power, generosity, and resilience of love can generate relationships unlike any other, as in the case of marriage. In other cases, the existence of a relationship—such as the grandparent/grandchild bond—ignites a unique type of love. Love and charity manifest also in the bonds of friendship, as well as to a different degree in activities such as advocacy and care. Considering the 330 million individuals in the United States, as well as how many relationships each person maintains, it becomes clear that the impact of love in shaping society arguably outstrips any other societal-shaping force.

But even as love and its relationships impact and shape society, society and civic entities create the landscape for love. For better or for worse, the law, too, impacts the relationships which engender love, and the interplay of families, society, and governments begins.

Governments and society in general also must contend with the religious element of love—an element which, like religious practice itself, puts love and love's relationships in some ways above the law, especially in the context of Christianity. For Christians, love exists as something preeminent, anchored in the divine, shaped by the fact that "God is Love." More than just another internal motivation, the love Christians bear others—as well as our ability and motivation for loving one another—are drawn equally from God: "Beloved, let us love one another, because love is of God; everyone who loves is begotten by God and knows God. . . . We love because he first loved us. . . . This is the commandment we have from him: whoever loves God must also love his brother."[175]

While our society rightly provides protection for religious belief (the first great commandment, to love God) through the recognition of the right of religious freedom, the second great commandment (to love your neighbor as yourself) is more complex in terms of civic life.[176] The law finds itself of more solid footing when it mandates justice than when it manages the generosity of love. This by default puts civic life up against its limits, reflected in the inadequacy of justice alone described by Saint John Paul II in his 2004 message for the World Day of Peace: *By itself, justice is not enough. Indeed, it can even betray itself, unless it is open to that deeper power which is love.*"[177]

The irreplaceable role of love in society and the need for government to yield ground and power to authentic love was articulated eloquently by Pope Benedict XVI in his encyclical on love, *Deus Caritas Est*:

> Love—*caritas*—will always prove necessary, even in the most just society. There is no ordering of the State so just that it can

eliminate the need for a service of love. Whoever wants to eliminate love is preparing to eliminate man as such. There will always be suffering which cries out for consolation and help. There will always be loneliness. There will always be situations of material need where help in the form of concrete love of neighbour is indispensable. The State which would provide everything, absorbing everything into itself, would ultimately become a mere bureaucracy incapable of guaranteeing the very thing which the suffering person—every person—needs: namely, loving personal concern. We do not need a State which regulates and controls everything, but a State which, in accordance with the principle of subsidiarity, generously acknowledges and supports initiatives arising from the different social forces and combines spontaneity with closeness to those in need. The Church is one of those living forces: she is alive with the love enkindled by the Spirit of Christ. This love does not simply offer people material help, but refreshment and care for their souls, something which often is even more necessary than material support. In the end, the claim that just social structures would make works of charity superfluous masks a materialist conception of man: the mistaken notion that man can live "by bread alone" (*Mt* 4:4; cf. *Dt* 8:3)—a conviction that demeans man and ultimately disregards all that is specifically human.[178]

One institution stands at the exact intersection of faith, love, and civil life: the family.

Rightly, the family has been called simultaneously "the first school of love,"[179] "the first school of faith,"[180] as well as "the cornerstone of all society and government."[181]

As the first—and in most cases, the most lasting—arena of personal love, the family earns unique respect as a force providing the essential element of love. In terms of society and civic life, the family performs a unique role, animating society with its people and principles, as well as nurturing the next generation of citizens and teaching freedom and responsibility—even as it bears unique vulnerability to threats from civil society.

And although much ink is spilled in noting markers of the decline of the nuclear family, facts still evidence a continued—if delayed—interest in marriage and family formation, including the fact that the vast majority of children and youth (about two out of three) currently live with two married parents.[182] The family is now and for a while more, still very much a formative building block of the future.

At the same time, the family, as a natural institution with a divinely-inspired and religiously-supported mandate and structure, can claim a certain independence from the legal systems which ultimately offer little more than a supporting role. Like religious belief itself, the family's ability to function with a certain degree of independence from civic life in many areas, has caused some ideologically-motivated regimes to paint a target on the family, and on the structure of marriage especially. Even in less-oppressive civic environments, it is imperative to consider the downstream effects on society if its very model, the family, is undermined. With such broad consequences, that concern transcends any single religious tradition.

One specific area illustrating the complex relationship of faith and civic life as it plays out in the family, is the experience and legalization of divorce. Through the legalization of especially no-fault divorce, the legal definition of marriage fundamentally changed. This created a distinct parting of the way in terms of the traditional religious definition of marriage and legal definition in our country. For many citizens of faith, especially Catholics who continue to adhere to the belief that sacramentally joined marriages cannot be broken, the chasm proves complicated to say the least. The societal consequences, explored here, manifested particularly in the next generation, on the effect divorce has on children.

In the Catholic Church in the last half century, the disruptions to the natural family structure—which at times coincided with threats to religious freedom—accentuated the need for nurturing marriages and families in concrete ways. Even as the Catholic Church—and especially Saint John Paul II—gave fresh insights into the beauty of such vocations, they were put in context of the broader underlying foundation, summarized in shorthand as the "vocation to love." This phrase captures the idea that God created each person in his image as someone who loves, and that he calls each person to the mission of loving throughout life. Lived out with particular visibility in the family, the vocation to love provides an essential building block and transmission of values in society. The possibility and results of embracing that idea as the foundation of society merits attention. So too does an honest assessment of whether our society grows out of such a foundation of love, and whether social and civic structures help nurture the vocation to love of those who live in it.

The positive experience of wise and nurturing love frequently drew well-merited attention in my years at the Knights of Columbus as well as in my roles serving on the Pontifical Council for the Family and as vice president of the Washington Session of the Pontifical John Paul II Institute for Studies on Marriage and Family; the selected addresses here are the tip of the iceberg of my work in this area. Among the diverse audiences addressed—from students to leaders in the Catholic Church to international and interreligious groups—I found the pervasive interest in the unique beauty of the family relationships a constant hope in the power of love to form the future.

Whether the future of this country will follow the lead of such hearts eager to embrace their vocations to love, is yet to be seen.

23.

Which Society?
The Love that Generates
the Common Good

SPEECH

Given at the International Seminar of Professors
entitled "The Future of a Way: the Fruitfulness
of *Familiaris Consortio* 30 Years Later"
May 14, 2011, Rome

One of the pivotal writings of Saint John Paul II was his apostolic exhortation on the family, *Familiaris Consortio*. It provided a thorough framework for Catholic teaching on the family, in many ways providing a lasting presentation of the continued relevance of Biblical teaching on marriage and family in context of modernity's societal shifts and personal family challenges. Although early in his pontificate (1981), it was scarcely his first major treatment of the issue, and another pivotal, although much briefer, text from much early in his life, showed similar attentiveness and insight into the goodness of marriage and family through Catholic understanding. Another work, raised here, *Bellezza e spiritualita dell'Amore Coniugale* ("The Beauty and Spirituality of Married Love"), was, at the time of this speech of mine in Rome, neither widely known and, in fact, had no published English language translation. The latter problem would be one of several straws that would compel the Knights of Columbus to broker the rights for the pope's entire body of written work to be published in English. The reason for this focus was simple.

Teaching True Love: An Eminent Form of Love

Some years before writing *Familiaris Consortio*, Karol Wojtyła warned in a collection of reflections upon marriage published recently in Italian under the title *Bellezza e Spiritualita dell'Amore Coniugale*, that society was approaching a "dead-end" regarding marriage and family.[183]

In the decades since, we have observed in many different ways this dramatic and self-destructive development in family life. The beautiful mosaic of the family has been reduced to a network of separated actions where familial bonds—and even the lives born of those actions—are attenuated and diminished. Love is separated from sexuality, sexuality from bearing children, children from parents, parents from being spouses, and spouses from authentic conjugal love. And all of this is usually justified in the name of individual autonomy.

In the past, the family was described as "the first and vital cell of society" and as the building block of society.[184] This was because the family was understood as a natural institution that served as the first school in which the common good was lived out and taught to future generations, prompting *Familiaris Consortio* to describe the family as "the first and irreplaceable school of social life."[185]

But today this masterfully composed mosaic has been deconstructed—the shards of glass intended to be together in intricate relationships to create a beautiful composition have been set out, sorted into autonomous piles of blue glass, red glass, and so on, until the entire picture is missing. We know all too well the social, philosophical, legal, and scientific trends that have led to this deconstruction of the family.

But while we generally understand these trends as occurring outside the Church and in contrast to its teaching, in the same essays mentioned above, Karol Wojtyła recognized that there were also tendencies *within* the Church, which, if not contributing directly to this deconstruction of family life, nonetheless weakened the ability of the People of God to withstand it.

Years before he became pope, Karol Wojtyła understood that the Church would be incapable of successfully defending the family unless it was able theologically and pastorally to support families by showing the beauty of family life and of demonstrating the possibility of actually living life in this way.

It was this pastoral attitude—reflected in the pages of *Bellezza e Spiritualita dell'Amore Coniugale*—which guides the approach of *Familiaris Consortio*.

As John Paul II notes in *Familiaris Consortio*, at a time when

> the modern Christian family is often tempted to be discouraged and is distressed at the growth of its difficulties, it is an eminent form of love to give it back its reasons for confidence in itself, in the riches that it possesses by nature and grace, and in the mission that God has entrusted to it.[186]

But how are we to approach the "riches" that the Christian family "possesses" by grace? How are we to approach the "mission that God has entrusted to it?"

The Implications of Reputation

In *Bellezza e Spiritualita dell'Amore Coniugale*, Wojtyła notes that the Church must move beyond the impression that its view of the family is essentially legalistic. "It will not succeed," he writes, "if right from the start it supports a negative norm, that is a certain 'one must not.'"[187]

He also recognizes that in the past, a negative view of the sacrament of marriage has prevailed in which marriage was viewed as a "thing of the flesh" in opposition to the things of the spirit.

The negative or "glass half-empty" view of marriage, he suggests, probably comes from one of several tendencies. One is that the sinfulness of spouses overwhelms our sense of the beauty of marriage. In this view, marriage is indeed a path of salvation for the spouses—but in the sense that the spouses are fundamentally a "cross" for one another to bear in this vale of tears.[188]

Another tendency, he suggests, is this: "Probably there is a certain prejudice against the body within us, a trace of Manichaeism such that we fail to imagine the achievement of perfection (spiritual and supernatural) in a state of life in which body issues are presented as a factor so important and essential of the life of two people."[189] This tendency leads to a way of looking at marriage that is essentially negative. He writes that "the suggestion that marriage should be treated from 'the sin point of view' is so strong and overpowering that very few people consider marriage 'in a dimension of perfection.'"[190]

If we are to defend marriage and family, our first question must be: "What concept of marriage and family are we defending?" Are we capable of defending an institution in society that we see primarily and essentially in a legalistic, "negative" way from "the sin point of view?"

Thus, the first step in our defense of family would seem to be a reconstruction of our own understanding of these institutions—to rediscover the plan of God for marriage and family. One of the fundamental tasks of *Familiaris Consortio* is precisely to set forth an adequate understanding of the Christian family.

Love-Based Society

We are also presented with the question of whether it is possible in our present cultural situation to think of building an authentic human society, that is, one that recognizes both the good of the individual and the common good according to these ideas?

In other words, if it is possible to defend the Christian family, is it still possible to think of building a Christian society?

In his essay *The Idea of a Christian Society*, T.S. Eliot offered a useful guide to these questions. According to Eliot, a "Christian" society should not be measured according to the degree to which it professes aspects of the Christian faith or of Christian practice. Instead, Eliot's concern is with another question: "what—if any—is the 'idea' of the society in which we live?" And even more important: "To what end is it arranged?"[191]

In his 1988 book, *Whose Justice? Which Rationality?*, Alasdair Macintyre explored different types of rationality falling under different philosophical traditions. Today, from a cultural perspective, we might put the question somewhat differently. We might ask instead, "What Love? Which society?" This in turn poses for the Christian a set of fundamental questions:

What is the "idea" of love in the society in which we live?

Is this "idea" of love a value around which our society ought to be arranged?

Is it possible to take seriously the idea of building a civilization of love without at the same time promoting an authentic idea of love as the "end" toward which society ought to be directed?

In a society where the concept of love is a love that is directed to others—that is to say, a selfless love and, therefore, inherently a familial love—this idea of love may generate the common good. It is also easy to understand that if the concept of love around which society is arranged has been distorted into a form of self-love, love instead becomes an obstacle to the realization of the common good.

Looking at our society, we no longer have a clear idea of what idea of love around which is it arranged. And if society no longer treasures the selfless love upon which the family is built, it is unclear whether society may sustain a commitment to the common good.

The Family's Pedagogical Role in Shaping Society with Love

As we know, *Familiaris Consortio* finds the plan of God for the family in an anthropology of the human person grounded in love. The human person has been called "to existence through love" and called "for love."[192] Moreover, "God inscribed in the humanity of man and woman the vocation, and thus the capacity and responsibility, of love and communion. Love is, therefore, the fundamental and innate vocation of every human being."[193]

The family has a fundamental role in promoting this vocation of love through its "complex of interpersonal relationships . . . through which each human person is introduced into the 'human family.'"[194] Thus, the family "as an intimate community of life and love" is grounded in its own vocation of love.[195] *Familiaris Consortio* observes that "the essence and role of the family are in the final analysis specified by love."[196] Therefore, the task of the family is to strive continually "to develop an authentic community of persons" and the "inner principle of that task, its permanent power and its final goal is love."[197]

In this sense, the family becomes "a school of deeper humanity" in which the community of persons within the family provides for the "care and love" for those of its members in need.[198] *Familiaris Consortio* concludes that "the Christian family places itself at the service of the human person and the world, really bringing about the 'human advancement.'"[199] And it goes on to quote the Synod's message to families: "Another task for the family is to form persons in love and also to practice love in all its relationships, so that it does not live closed in on itself, but remains open to the community, moved by a sense of justice and concern for others, as well as by a consciousness of its responsibility towards the whole of society."[200]

The essential elements of the family, which make it "the first and irreplaceable school of social life"[201]—elements such as being "sincere gift of self" and "communion of persons," and the personal disposition to self-giving, reconciliation, sacrifice and unity—are also essential elements in realizing the common good of society—elements that are present in a distinctive way only in the family.

If we are to understand the teaching of *Familiaris Consortio* that these elements are essential to our "idea" of the family and that the family is "the first and vital cell of society,"[202] then the question arises to what extent these concepts are also essential to our "idea" of society and the goals to which society is directed.

Alternative Voices: A Foundation of Selfishness

Other voices, presenting other interpretations of love or alternatives to love, should also be considered.

Recently in the United States, the film adaptation of Ayn Rand's book *Atlas Shrugged* appeared. Although perhaps not well known in Europe, the book is so popular in the United States that it was named by American readers as second only to the Bible as the most influential book they had read. Coming from an admired novelist with a ready readership, the book advocated the author's philosophy of "Objectivism." Rand declared the absoluteness of truth, of the necessity to conform one's conscience to virtue and of the importance of a true understanding of the self through her self-styled philosophy of "selfishness." Some have even seen in her philosophy a sort of atheist's "Golden Rule" when she states that man "must live for his own sake, neither sacrificing himself to others nor sacrificing others to himself."[203] Among Americans, Rand and her Objectivism philosophy present one of the most complete voices of opposition to the Christian anthropology of *Familiaris Consortio*.

In a 1960 speech at Yale University, Rand professed "the concept of man as a heroic being, with his own happiness as the moral purpose of his life, with productive achievement as his noblest activity and reason as his only absolute."[204]

In her book, *The Virtue of Selfishness*, Rand proposes that "man is an end in himself."[205] Since self-interest is the means for self-preservation, and life is the ultimate good, selfishness is a virtue. Man is by nature a selfish creature. In contrast, "the basic principle of altruism is that man has no right to live for his own sake, that service to others is the only justification of his existence, and that self-sacrifice is his highest moral duty, virtue, and value."[206] Altruism must be rejected, she contends, because it makes "the self as a standard of evil, the selfless as the standard of the good" with the result that man is made "a sacrificial animal serving anyone's need."[207] Thus altruism is evil because, "altruism permits no concept of a self-respecting, self-supporting man—a man who supports his own life by his own effort and neither sacrifices himself nor others." And for her, love is simply "an expression of self-esteem."[208]

Obviously, there are many parallels between Rand's philosophy of Objectivism and corporate behavior on Wall Street and other social indicators in the United States, which provide stark examples of the "crisis of truth" Pope John Paul II spoke of in his *Letter to Families:*

> Who can deny that our age is one marked by a great crisis, which appears above all as "crisis of truth"? A crisis of truth means, in the first place, a *crisis of concepts*. Do the words "love," "freedom," "sincere gift," and even "person" and "rights of the person," really convey their essential meaning?[209]

A crisis of concepts about human action cannot be separated from a crisis in the concrete reality of human relationships.

In *Caritas in Veritate,* Pope Benedict warned about the effects of not knowing the truth about love, saying, "Without truth, charity degenerates into sentimentality. Love becomes an empty shell, to be filled in an arbitrary way. In a culture without truth, this is the fatal risk facing love."[210]

If we are to bring society out of its dead end, I think we should begin by taking to heart the conclusion of *Familiaris Consortio,* in which John Paul II made a particular plea to us. After entreating every person of good will to "endeavor to save and foster the values and requirements of the family," he said:

> I feel that I must ask for a particular effort in this field from the sons and daughters of the church. Faith gives them full knowledge of God's wonderful plan; they therefore have an

extra reason for caring for the reality that is the family in this time of trial and of grace. They must show the family special love. This is an injunction that calls for concrete action.[211]

This "concrete action" includes loving the family, proclaiming the good news about the family, and collaborating with all people of good will to serve the family.

If we are to love the family as John Paul II requested, we must also defend the "family" in society. But in order to do this, first a sense of authentic love must be restored, which, in turn, requires the restoration of our understanding of an adequate anthropology of the human person.

Witnesses to the Spiritual Dignity of the Human Person

The beatification of Blessed John Paul II was a privileged time to reflect on aspects of his life and papacy that touched us in so many ways. Many of us were able to watch in the early years of his papacy his remarkable strength and vigor and especially his courage during the dramatic confrontation with the Soviet Union. As Pope Benedict observed during his beatification homily, Blessed John Paul II had "the strength of a titan" who by "his witness of faith, love, and apostolic courage . . . gave us the strength to believe in Christ."[212]

It was conventional wisdom that Blessed John Paul II's achievements during the early years of his papacy were the result of physical characteristics: his experience in the theater, his energy, athleticism, and stamina. But in the later years of his life, when none of these were left, conventional wisdom questioned whether he should resign the papacy. The pope indirectly addressed this concern during his beatification homily when he mentioned Blessed John Paul's "witness in suffering" and further observed that while "the Lord gradually stripped him of everything, yet he remained ever a 'rock' as Christ desired."[213]

And in this we may say that Blessed John Paul II gave us one of his greatest gifts: his spiritual triumph over suffering. Blessed John Paul II's final gift was to testify during the last days of his life to the truth that the dignity of the human person does not rely upon his physical qualities or material possessions, but upon his spiritual greatness and willingness to make a sincere gift of self to others. In this final testament, he provided one of the most remarkable testimonies to the indispensable foundation of the civilization of love—the spiritual dignity of the human person. With the final days of his life, Blessed John Paul II wrote more eloquently than any words possibly could that man can never be reduced to simply the sum of his physical qualities or material possessions.

To attempt to reduce man to merely the physical, that is, to deny his spiritual dignity, is one of the great crimes against humanity.

If we wish to know the love that generates the common good, we only have to recall the final days in the life of Blessed John Paul II.

Not long ago, I had the opportunity to travel to Haiti on a Knights of Columbus mission to provide 1,000 wheelchairs to Haitians who had lost legs as a result of the terrible earthquake there. During the wheelchair distribution, I met a young Haitian woman who had received one of our wheelchairs. She had lost her entire family: her father and mother and her five brothers were gone and she was now alone. And yet she, like the other Haitians that we helped, was not angry or bitter. In fact, they were the opposite— they were grateful and friendly. Many of these Haitians said that they could never thank us enough for our help and that they would pray for *us*. When we asked one man what was the first thing he intended to do when he left the hospital, he said he wanted to go to Church and thank God for saving his life and for the help he had received since losing his leg.

It seems to me that these poor Haitians—like Blessed John Paul II before them—made with their lives an eloquent testimony to the spiritual greatness of the human person. These people radiated a spiritual dignity that is completely independent of their physical capacities or their material possessions.

What we experienced in Haiti was much more than a distribution of aid. It was an exchange of gifts between members of an affluent society and a poor society—an exchange of material gifts on the one hand and of spiritual gifts on the other. Both are necessary for generating the common good. Both are indispensable in building the civilization of love. And this is one reason why Christians must have a strong and persistent preferential option for the poor, not only as a matter of the common good, but also as a matter of concrete personal commitment. Perhaps it is the mission of the poor in so many places to show us how it is possible to make a sincere gift of self, since in so many instances their self is the only "possession" that they possess.

In *The Letter to Families*, John Paul reminds us:

> The family is indeed—more than any other human reality—the place where an individual can exist "for himself" through the sincere gift of self. This is why it remains a social institution which neither can nor should be replaced: it is the "sanctuary of life."[214]

This mission of the family as the "the place where an individual can exist 'for himself' through the sincere gift of gift," itself does not depend upon the material possessions of the family or of its affluence. This mission is equally present in both poor and rich families—indeed it may be even more present in poor families.

We are accustomed to speaking of the family as both the object and the subject of evangelization. But we might also speak of the poor themselves and of poor families as both the subject and the object of evangelization. This is not to say that we need to maintain the presence of the poor in order for them to fulfill their evangelizing role in society. But it is to say that the poor have a role in defending the spiritual greatness of the human person which is absolutely necessary in building the civilization of love.

Moreover, this role of the poor is not to be seen primarily in how they may evangelize themselves, but how they may transmit to the more affluent members of society the truth about the dignity of the human person. But this can only happen if our understanding of "communion of persons" is strong enough to bridge the economic gap between the poor and the affluent. The poor cannot remain an abstraction. They must become in the words of Karol Wojtyła's play, *Our God's Brother.*

The temptation in such an individualistic society as the United States is to succumb to the self-centeredness of the type of world view expressed by Ayn Rand. But in a society with a greater social services tradition such as found in the socialist influenced nations of Europe, a different temptation exists—the temptation to indifference.

In *Deus Caritas Est*, Pope Benedict reminded of the need for personal involvement, writing:

> Love—*caritas*—will always prove necessary, even in the most just society. There is no ordering of the State so just that it can eliminate the need for a service of love. Whoever wants to eliminate love is preparing to eliminate man as such. . . . The State which would provide everything, absorbing everything into itself, would ultimately become a mere bureaucracy incapable of guaranteeing the very thing which the suffering person—every person—needs: namely, loving personal concern.[215]

Consequently, the recent popes have encouraged Christians toward building, not a specific political system, but a civilization of love.

Christianity is not a way of government, but a way of love.

New Evangelization and Theology of the Body

The negative trends that Karol Wojtyła had discussed in *Bellezza e Spiritualita dell'Amore Coniugale* have also been taken up in Pope

Benedict's writings, specifically as such negativity relates to the family. In his address to the attendees of our conference on the consequences of abortion and divorce he said: ". . . the "No," which the Church pronounces in her moral directives on which public opinion sometimes unilaterally focuses, is in fact a great "Yes" to the dignity of the human person, to human life, and to the person's capacity to love."[216]

And speaking earlier to the Irish bishops, the pope stated: "Even though it is necessary to speak out strongly against the evils that threaten us, we must correct the idea that Catholicism is *merely* a collection of prohibitions." Sound catechesis and careful "formation of the heart" are needed here. . . ."[217]

Formation of the heart is synonymous with discovering this "great yes." It is about illuminating the greatest vocation each person has: the vocation to love. And this in turn brings us back again to the vocation to love made explicit in *Familiaris Consortio*.

What the pope has called "formation of the heart" is at the center of the New Evangelization, which, as we know, is an approach to evangelization "new in ardor, methods, and expression."[218] *Familiaris Consortio* presents a form of evangelization as personal witness inseparable from the realities of family life—realities such as communion of persons and nuptial mystery. In other words, *Familiaris Consortio* envisions a dynamic Christian witness grounded upon a dynamic Christian anthropology.

The New Evangelization seeks to address a new situation. It is the situation in Western societies where the decisive question is not "What do Christians believe?" But it is the question: "Is it possible to live in the way Christians believe?" Thus, the New Evangelization is premised on Paul VI's recognition that "contemporary man listens more willingly to witnesses than to teachers, and if he listens to teachers it is because they are witnesses."[219]

As we know, approximately, two decades before John Paul II founded our Pontifical Institute in Rome, Karol Wojtyła had founded an Institute for the Family in Krakow. In a document outlining the

Polish institute's purpose, he stressed a concrete practical approach, in particular by providing resources to the laity and by promoting family parish ministry. "It will probably need to always maintain this character [of parish ministry], since that points it in the direction of the ministry to the lay apostolate, which, simply stated, means a direction towards real life, and not merely knowledge about life."[220]

This distinction—direction towards real life witness on the part of the laity and "not merely knowledge about life"—is the key to understanding the fundamental "newness" of the New Evangelization.

The "newness" of expression in the New Evangelization is also grounded upon the centrality of Christian anthropology. John Paul II's *theology of the body* is an important and we might even say an irreplaceable presentation of this anthropology in that it re-proposes a Christian anthropology to our contemporary sensibilities, re-presenting at the same time a vision of mankind as a unity created by God.

The theology of the body not only advances our understanding of what it means to be a *human* person with a vocation to love. By also restoring a sense of unity between man and woman, the theology of the body also makes possible a re-proposal of the common good. As an expression of Christian anthropology, the theology of the body provides an opportunity for us live more fully the full truth about love, and in so doing to appreciate in new ways the "riches" and "mission" of the family.

Training a Heart that Sees

Pope Benedict XVI has written in *Deus Caritas Est* about the necessity of possessing "a heart [that] sees where love is needed."[221] This is the first lesson that Christian spouses learn within their marriage and the first lesson Christian parents learn within their family.

Artists speak of "training your eye" to see reality accurately. Only by seeing reality as it is can the artist bring out the truth about the reality that he has "learned" to see.

It is the same with the love that generates the common good. Each of us needs to develop more fully "a heart that sees where love is needed." We need to train our eyes to see reality as it "really" is—as it has been made and intended by God.

And how does a good art teacher train a student to see? By sitting side-by-side with the student, so that together they experience a common image, its details and the relationship of those details.

If we hope to recover the concept of a love that generates the common good, we must do something similar—we must train our eyes and hearts to see the reality of a sincere gift of self. We must make the "gift of self" our own gift and we must do so in a way that others may see it and in seeing it also train their hearts.

Training the eyes of people to the beautiful truth about love cannot depend solely on academic institutions, lectures, writings, and rules. It requires personal witness.

Recently, the Knights of Columbus was able see the deep and personal impact of one such teaching witness. In preparation for John Paul II's beatification, the Knights collected testimonies of gratitude from members of the "John Paul II Generation." The testimonies spanned hundreds of memories, as Catholics thanked him for his many gifts to them.

It was interesting to see how often their families—and his contributions to families—were singled out for special mention by young Catholics. People thanked him for blessing family members; for changing their understanding of responsible parenthood; for his intercession in pregnancies; for peaceful, dignified, Catholic deaths of their parents; for his theology of the body and his attention to the vocation of the laity.

One of the most moving was from a man named Kenneth. He wrote:

I was lost in darkness. I didn't believe in God. When I was eighteen, I came to the Catholic Church. After having lost my father when he was murdered (I was two [years old]), and having been abused physically (in many ways) by my "step" father, I had little faith in Fatherly love.

However, seeing His Holiness JPII be a true father to the whole world changed my perspective. Learning to call a man father, and not then have to fear him hurting me, healed me greatly.

JPII's homilies and teachings have taught me over and over that love and forgiveness are always the answers.

I now feel like a whole person because his example allowed me to have faith in a Father God, and his Son, and their Spirit. Amen!! Halleluja!![222]

The inherent vocation of love may be obscured in a person. And when it is obscured, it is usually because of the selfish action of another person and not by the influence of a philosophical or political argument. But if the vocation of love may be obscured, it may also be uncovered, by making people aware of the dignity and value they see in themselves and in the ones they love.

The Place of God in a Love-Generating Society

In his address to educators at The Catholic University of America in 2008, Pope Benedict stated that "The Church's primary mission of evangelization . . . is consonant with a nation's fundamental aspiration to develop a society truly worthy of a human person's dignity."[223] This brings us back again to the question: "Which society? The love that generates the common good." But it brings us back with a more radical perspective. As John Paul II wrote in his *Letter to Families:*

there is no true love without an awareness that God "is Love". . . . Created in the image and likeness of God, man cannot fully "find himself" except through the sincere gift of self. Without such a concept of man, of the person, and of the "communion of persons" in the family, there can be no civilization of love; similarly, without the civilization of love, it is impossible to have such a concept of person and the communion of persons."[224]

In *Spe Salvi*, Pope Benedict wrote about "the joy of entering into Christ's 'being for others.'"[225] We might say that the civilization of love is just such a society—a society informed by the "idea" that we are to enter into "Christ's being for others."[226] Of course, it is absurd to think that such an "idea" can be legislated or formally enacted by a society in its pursuit of the common good. But it is not absurd to think that Christians could in sufficient numbers actually witness to this type of love. And if they did so, it is possible to imagine that "being for others" and "the sincere gift of self" might actually become the "ideas" around which a society might be built.

At the same time, as Blessed John Paul warned, while there exists a civilization of love, there also exists a destructive, anti-civilization opposed to it. By now, it is evident that, for whatever reason, argumentation alone has been insufficient to stop the advance of the destructive anti-civilization throughout much of Western society. Our disputations have been necessary and they will continue to be necessary. But something more is also necessary. It is not enough to speak to others about how Jesus Christ reveals his transforming love and truth. Non-believers must be able to experience for themselves this transforming power in the lives of believers and especially in the witness of the laity.

During his address at The Catholic University of America in 2008, Pope Benedict asserted that, "The dynamic between personal encounter, knowledge, and Christian witness is integral" to the mission of the Church.[227] In no academic community is this dynamic of which the pope speaks more evident than in our Institute, the Pontifical John Paul II Institute for Studies on Marriage and Family. And this reality gives to us both a tremendous opportunity and a tremendous responsibility.

Both this opportunity and this responsibility is entirely consistent with the pope's message this week when he told the faithful
that they have the mission of "witnessing to the love of God for
humanity, above all, through acts of love and life choices made in
favor of actual persons, beginning with the most vulnerable, fragile,
and defenseless . . . such as the poor, the elderly, the ill, and the
disabled."[228]

Faced with today's challenges that are aggravated by a number
of elements, including "the often exacerbated search for economic
well-being in a period of serious economic and financial crisis,
the practical materialism, the prevailing subjectivism,"[229] families
can take heart in the mission entrusted to them in the daily living
of their lives, a timeless mission of being evangelists of authentic
Christian love described so well by Pope Benedict:

> [Y]ou must promote the Christian meaning of life through
> the explicit proclamation of the Gospel. . . . From faith lived
> courageously arises, today as in the past, a fertile culture of
> love for life, from its conception to its natural end, for the pro-
> motion of human dignity, for the exaltation of the importance
> of the family based on faithful marriage and openness to life,
> and for a commitment to justice and solidarity.[230]

24.

The Family Beyond Ideology

ADDRESS

Fifth World Meeting of Families
July 6, 2006, Valencia, Spain

The kernel of the idea of this piece was a concept that I had begun to develop at the 1986 Ninth International Congress for the Family in Paris. Two decades later, at the time of the 2006 World Meeting of Families, the prevailing atheistic ideologies of the previous two centuries seemed to have grown rather than to have diminished; so had their impact upon marriage and family at a macro level. This remains especially true in terms of both how those ideas have spread to other countries, and the degree to which the effects of those large-scale social experiments had matured from their twentieth-century petri dishes.

The Fate of the Family in the Age of Ideology

History will surely regard the twentieth century as the "Age of Ideology." During the Holy Father's recent visit to Auschwitz, the world was again reminded of the many victims of modern ideology. This modern ideology was built upon a view of government in which the power of the state is the only legitimate authority. The Italian dictator Benito Mussolini summarized the claim of this modern ideology: "Everything *in* the State, nothing *outside* the State, nothing *against* the state" (emphasis added).[231]

But this modern ideology has another victim—one that we do not often recognize as a victim. But it is a real victim, a victim that continues to suffer even today. Even in our present day, the family continues to be a real victim of modern ideology. As the British historian Paul Johnson has written, "The power of the Fascists, of the Nazis and of the Communists was built on the smoking ruins of family loyalty and affection."[232] During the last century, the family was made the victim of both Fascist *national* socialism and Communist *international* socialism. For the sake of the future, we must place the family beyond ideology.

We know that the Industrial Revolution that began in the eighteenth century brought tremendous suffering to many families as many economies in Europe began the transformation from agriculture to manufacturing. But it also brought a transformation of living standards.

In England, for example, the nineteenth century (precisely 1830 to 1890) experienced the longest sustained period of rising living standards in that nation's history. This was an unprecedented economic achievement. But this was paid for by the suffering of women and children who were forced by financial necessity into the new manufacturing and textile industries. At one time, 58 percent of the 420,000 workers in Britain's textile industry were female, and 46 percent were under age eighteen; only 23 percent of the labor force was made up of adult males.[233]

Clearly, the social and economic role of the family was being weakened by the demands of the new industrial economy. This was the harsh reality—especially that affecting women and children—that Karl Marx and Friedrich Engels knew when they developed their socialist critique of capitalism. In 1845, Engels wrote that when married women and children enter the industrial labor force, "family life is destroyed (and) its dissolution has the most demoralizing consequences both for parents and children."[234]

In writing *The Origin of the Family, Private Property and the State*, Engels placed the family at the center of socialist theory. He maintained that the evolution of the family was directly related to the evolution of the means of production. In other words, the evolution of the family was inseparable from the evolution of the economy toward socialism.

Engels wrote that the first *division of labor* in history occurred between man and woman within the family. Therefore, he also concluded that the first *class conflict* in history occurred between man and woman within marriage. He wrote, "Monogamy does not by any means make its appearance in history as the reconciliation of man and woman. . . . On the contrary, it appears as the subjection of one sex by the other, as a proclamation of a conflict between the sexes."[235] For Engels, the family is an unjust society based upon the enslavement of the wife—she represents the proletariat and her husband represents the capitalist.[236]

Marx and Engels were justified in their view that the economics of the Industrial Age had invaded the life of the family and threatened its existence. Unfortunately, the socialist solution to the evils of economic exploitation of family life that Marx and Engels presented only intensified the assault of economics on the family.

Ironically, what they said was a solution to the problems of family life instead threatened the very existence of the family based upon marriage. Although Engels observed (in 1845) that the introduction of married women into the industrial work force made healthy family life impossible for themselves and for their children,[237] he later insisted that "the first premise for the emancipation of women" is the introduction of all women into public industry.[238]

During the nineteenth century, capitalism assaulted the family by treating it only in economic terms and then only as a source for laborers. But the socialist response of Marx and Engels greatly increased the assault by insisting that *all* men and *all* women should be in the labor force. In this way, Marx and Engels sought to destroy the family as a social and economic reality in society.

But to realize the goal of total participation of women in the workforce requires a condition. Women must have total control of their fertility. Therefore, all women must have access to contraception and when contraception fails, they must have access to legal sterilization and legal abortion.

This condition leads to another misguided conclusion: The economic, social, and legal distinctions between marriage and civil unions must be eliminated since marriage no longer is regarded as a unique and valuable social institution.

First, the family is emptied of its economic content by moving women into the workforce. Second, the family is emptied of its social content by eliminating childbearing as a primary goal of marriage. Third, since the family has been emptied of its economic content and then its social content, the final step is to remove from the family its unique status as a protected institution by the law.

From this conclusion it follows that divorce at the will of either spouse for any reason or none at all should be recognized. Since marriage is no longer seen as a unique and important legal institution in society, civil unions and childbearing outside of marriage can be given the same legal status as marriage.

Emptied in this way of its social, economic, and legal status, the traditional family as a unique institution of society no longer has a unique function in society; it can be expected to wither away.

Thus, socialist theory seeks an "evolution" of marriage and the family to the point where they are no longer necessary and therefore disappear. The disappearance of the family is the necessary condition for the emergence of something entirely new in history: the free and equal socialist person.

Differing Understandings of Personal Equality

This attack on the family results from an internal logic tied to the Marxist understanding of equality. This understanding of equality precludes the possibility that this "new person" can emerge from within the traditional individual family.

Today, many of us think that equality means that people who are similarly situated in morally relevant respects should be treated similarly. People should have the same legal and political rights and they should have the same opportunities for social and economic advancement. All people are entitled to the same respect and we should not discriminate on the basis of race, religion, sex, or national origin.

Igor Schafaravich, a member of the former Soviet Academy of Sciences, suggests that the socialist understanding of equality is different. He writes, "In socialist ideology, the understanding of equality is akin to that used in mathematics (when one speaks of equal numbers or equal triangles)." Equality means "the abolition of differences in behavior, as well as in the inner world of the individuals constituting society. . . . The equality proclaimed in socialist ideology means identity of individualities."[239]

According to Marxist socialism, the state first *alienates* the person by means of the radical individualism of the capitalist economic system. Then the state transcends this alienation by abolishing individualism and totally absorbing each person into the collective life of socialist society by applying its view of *equality*.

The Marxist view of marriage and the family found legal expression within weeks of the Russian Revolution. The *first* general decree of the new Soviet government concerned the repeal of traditional marriage laws. It was frequently stated at the time that the absolute right of divorce was one of the great achievements of the October Revolution. The more comprehensive Soviet Family Code of 1919 entirely rejected the religious character of Russian marriage by providing only for civil marriage, and the Soviet Family Code of 1926 granted legal recognition to civil unions with full rights.

It is remarkable that during the same time, Marx and Engels were developing classical socialist theory, the greatest British philosopher of the nineteenth century and the father of classical liberal economics and political theory, John Stuart Mill, had a view of marriage similar in many respects to that of Marx and Engels.

Mill is best known for his work *On Liberty* (1859) in which he argued that people must be free to realize their own individual potential in their own way. He argued that in this way individual liberty makes possible the individual creativity that is the pre-requisite for social progress.

Mill carried forward this theme in his later essay, "The Subjection of Women" (1869). In it, Mill argued for "a principle of perfect equality" between women and men. He insisted that women be given "the free use of their facilities" and "free choice of their employment."[240]

But it was Mill's view of marriage that has had a lasting effect on the classical liberal treatment of marriage. "Now that negro slavery has been abolished," Mill wrote, "Marriage is the only actual bondage known to our law. There remain no legal slaves, except the mistress of every house."[241]

Once again, marriage is seen as an institution of oppression and an institution that prevents individual development and attainment.

In Mill's view, this applies also to men. He writes, "We see that young men of the greatest promise generally cease to improve as soon as they marry and, not improving, inevitably degenerate."[242]

Thus, for Mill's classical Liberal theory, marriage and family are barriers to the attainment of individual liberty and equality. Here too, escape from marriage and family and entry into the workforce is understood as a principle means of liberation.[243] He writes, "opening to them the free choice of employments, and opening to them the same field of occupation and the same prizes and encouragements as to other human beings, would be that of doubling the mass of mental faculties available for the higher service of humanity."[244]

Liberal Western democracies that have followed Mill's view have also found divorce, sterilization, and abortion as necessary to guarantee liberation and happiness. We see examples of both socialist and liberal societies where the laws have been changed to accommodate divorce, abortion, sterilization, and civil unions.

In both type of societies, economic life has become dependent upon women abandoning their traditional role as mother and their introduction into the workforce outside the home. Where economies become dependent upon this model, it becomes increasingly difficult and often impossible to choose the traditional role of full-time wife and mother within a family of many children because of the shift in economic, tax, and labor policies.

Ironically, classical socialism and classical liberalism find agreement in their rejection of traditional marriage and family.

In these traditions, the family remains the central barrier to the realization of the socialist, egalitarian society. Within the Western tradition, "It is the family that takes each man and woman out of anonymity and makes them conscious of their personal dignity, enriching them with deep human experiences and actively placing them in their uniqueness within the fabric of society."[245]

As Professor Paul Ramsey has written, "The notion that an individual human life is absolutely unique, inviolable, irreplaceable, non-interchangeable, (and) not substitutable . . . with other lives is a notion that exists in our civilization because it is Christian; and that idea is so fundamental in the edifice of Western law and morals that it cannot be removed without bringing the whole house down." [246]

But this understanding of the individual should not be confused with the classical liberal understanding of *radical* individualism.

As Pope John Paul II has reminded us in *Familiaris Consortio*, the unique, irreplaceable, individual person becomes so, precisely through the unique, irreplaceable relationships within the family.

The family is "a community of persons" premised upon the equal dignity of each member of this community. It is "community of life and love" in which husband and wife, brother and sister, parent and child, all realize their true potential and their true happiness precisely within their relationships with one another.

It is precisely through the community relationships of marriage and family that each person becomes more fully human and more fully a person.

Within the Western tradition, the family stands as a mediating institution between the person and the state. The family protects the vulnerable individual from the power of the state.

Marriage and family are natural institutions. They arise from the concrete reality of the nature of man and woman who become husband and wife and then parents. These relationships possess their own inherent and inalienable rights because these relationships arise from concrete human reality, not abstract economic or social ideologies.

No government can rightfully treat these concrete human realities in an arbitrary or artificial manner. Because of the inherent dignity and nature of the family, the family stands as the basis of free and just government.

In his encyclical *Centesimus Annus*, Pope John Paul II wrote that "the fundamental error of socialism is anthropological in nature. Socialism considers the individual person simply as an element, a molecule within the social organism" (no. 13). In this view, there is no room for "natural" institutions such as marriage and family.

We might say that the fundamental error of liberalism is also anthropological in nature. Its "error consists in an understanding of human freedom, which detaches it from obedience to the truth."[247] In this case, liberalism has detached liberty from the truth of the natural institutions of marriage and family.

As the *Compendium of the Social Doctrine of the Catholic Church* states, "A society built on a family scale is the best guarantee against drifting off course into individualism or collectivism, because within the family the person is always at the center of attention as an end and never as a means."[248]

Voice of the Church

This understanding of the person as an "end" and never as a "means" in turn requires a realistic vision of the present economic and social situation. The real problem, according to John Paul II, "is a growing inability to situate particular interests within the framework of a coherent vision of the common good," which "is not simply the sum total of particular interests; rather it involves an assessment and integration of those interests on the basis of a balanced hierarchy of values; ultimately, it demands a correct understanding of the dignity and the rights of the person."[249]

The Social Doctrine of the Catholic Church presents precisely this coherent vision of the common good. It situates the dignity of the person with the context of his and her everyday reality. That is to say, it situates the dignity of each person within the reality of marriage and family life.

In this regard, the encyclical *Sollicitudo Rei Socialis* states, "The Church's social doctrine is not a 'third way' between liberal capitalism and Marxist collectivism . . . rather it constitutes a category of its own." The Social Doctrine of the Church "belongs to the field, not of ideology, but of theology."[250]

In other words, the importance of marriage and family in the eyes of the Church is not a matter of abstract ideology, but of the most profound reality affecting the life of every person.

In 1981, Pope John Paul II proposed in *Familiaris Consortio* a new Charter of the Rights of the Family. At that time, he said such a charter was necessary because

> The situation experienced by many families in various countries is highly problematical, if not entirely negative: institutions and laws unjustly ignore the inviolable rights of the family and of the human person; and society, far from putting itself at the service of the family, attacks it violently in its values and fundamental requirements.

The pope concluded, that the family "finds itself the victim of society . . . and even of its blatant injustice."[251]

The pope stated that the charter should include the following principles:

- The right to exist and progress as a family;

- The right of the family to exercise its responsibility regarding the transmission of life and to educate children;

- The right to the stability of the bond and of the institution of marriage;

- The right to believe in and profess one's faith and to propagate it; and

- The right to bring up children in accordance with the family's own traditions and religious and cultural values.

Because these rights must be recognized by the state in its public responsibilities, the pope stated that families are "called upon to find expression also in the form of *political intervention:* families should be the first to take steps to see that the laws and institutions of the state not only do not offend but support and positively defend the rights and duties of the family." He called upon families to be "protagonists" of a new "family politics" and to "assume responsibility for transforming society" (no. 44).

For Europe, the last century was the century of ideology. However, the present century may be known by historians as the century that bears the bitter fruit of ideology's effect upon family life—that is to say, the present century may be regarded as the century of Europe's demographic winter.

It should surprise no one that the lasting attacks upon marriage and family life that we have experienced during the last century and that we continue to experience today have had a disastrous effect upon a principal goal of marriage—that is, the welcoming of children within the family.

According to the United Nations, the population of Europe has already passed through its peak period and has entered a state of steady and steep decline. Europe has begun a decline, which the United Nations predicts will fall from a total of more than 727 million in 2000 to 603 million in 2050. In less than fifty years, Europe will lose a portion of its population greater than the current combined populations of Italy and France.[252]

However, the country that will suffer the most devastating loss of population will be the country that first and consistently implemented the socialist ideology regarding marriage and the family. For example, if current trends continue, the population of Russia could decline from its current 148 million to only 58 million by 2050—a decline of 60 percent. In other words, the effect of socialist ideology on the family will impact Russia's population more dramatically than the impact of the Second World War and more dramatically than anything seen in Europe since the Black Plague of the fourteenth century.[253]

The most accurate measure of society's ability to support itself is what the United Nations has described as the "dependency ratio." This ratio is obtained by first adding the number of people under age fifteen to the number of people sixty-five and older. This total is then compared with the number of people of working age, that is, between the ages of fifteen and sixty-four.

This ratio is the most accurate way to predict future economic viability. According to the United Nations projections, the trend in Europe is astounding. In 2000, the dependency ratio was 48 percent, comprised of 26 percent children and 22 percent elderly. However, by 2020 the total of children and elderly will become the new majority of the population at 51 percent. By 2050 the dependency ratio will reach 75 percent, that is, three persons of dependent age for every one person of working age.

Familiaris Consortio reminds us that "the future of humanity passes by way of the family" (no. 86). This truth is clearly evident in the demographic crisis that faces Europe today. Europe's crisis is a crisis of marriage and the family. It is a crisis that has been brought about by the assault of ideology upon the family. The solution can only be one that respects the reality and the dignity of marriage and family—a solution that places the family beyond ideology.

It is up to us to live this reality faithfully and to courageously help everyone understand that the family must never be used as the tool of an ideology because the family is one of the most precious, universal values of humanity.

Nearly three decades ago, on his first trip to the United States, John Paul II stood between the Capitol and the White House in Washington, D.C., and he said this:

> We will stand up every time that human life is threatened. When the sacredness of life before birth is attacked, we will stand up and proclaim that no one ever has the right to destroy unborn life. When a child is described as a burden . . . we will stand up and insist that every child is a unique and unrepeatable gift of God. When the institution of marriage is abandoned to human selfishness . . . we will stand up and affirm the indissolubility of the marriage bond. When the value of the family is threatened . . . we will stand up and reaffirm that the family is necessary not only for the private good but also for the common good of every society.[254]

Today, our beloved pope watches us from his window in the Father's house. And in two days, his great successor will be with us. It is up to us to keep his great promise. Now is the time for the families of the world to stand up. Now is the time for us to stand up together.

25.

Divorce and the Future of Children

PAPER

Conference on John Paul II Institute for
Studies on Marriage & Family
February 12–16, 2007, Rome

Divorce—especially in terms of its larger society context—is often discussed largely as an issue affecting marriage. And that is true up to a point. However, divorce is also both deeply personal to the children involved and has a real effect on them. The breakdown of the fundamental building block of society also has real consequences far beyond the satisfaction of a particular marriage. Moreover, the health of families society-wide ought to consider the macro effects of such personal effects on the children, especially when the tragic event occurs with the frequency it does in our nation. What happens to the family affects our society, and what happens to children within the family can affect their view of institutions—both church and state. As such, divorce is relevant within this broader survey of rights in the United States.

Although psychologists, family members, and teachers certainly contend with the deep, lasting wounds children bear due to the marital choices the children have no part of, there is a kind of taboo on raising the issue, in no small part because the divorce's legality and reputation as a necessity. Pushing against the silence, the following was part of a lecture series on divorce, which included a consideration of its broader consequences. The topic, and this paper in particular, laid the foundation for another ground-breaking conference held the next year in Rome, which brought the issue to greater attention within the Vatican. Cosponsored by the Knights of Columbus, that conference, entitled "Oil on the Wounds," explored the effects of divorce on children and the effects of abortion on mothers and other family members, and was addressed by Pope Benedict XVI.

The Effects of Divorce on Children

The family has been rightfully called "the matrix of identity."[255] Outside the context of family, it is difficult, if not impossible, to understand the developing personality of the human person. For example, in *Childhood and Society*, Eric Erikson suggests that the unfolding of the human personality occurs in response to eight critical periods of development ("ages of man") involving basic trust versus basic mistrust, autonomy versus doubt, initiative versus guilt, industry versus inferiority, identity versus confusion, intimacy versus isolation, productivity versus stagnation and, finally integrity versus despair.[256] Yet each of these formative periods occur either in the context of family or in a context conditioned by family.

It has long been recognized that "the nuclear family has two irreducible functions: the primary socialization of the young and the stabilization of adult personalities."[257] Similarly, it is also clear that as Nichols and Everett point out, "the family is an integrative system because of its developmental role in the formation and functioning of persons both while they live within their nuclear family and long after they have left their family of origin . . . the family is integrative because of the family processes that work over several generations and that continue to operate long after one has physically 'left home'."[258]

If we consider approaches to personality development in terms of the structure of family life cycles, we may consider "the family as a system whose various members and subsystems interact much like the organism of the human body,"[259] and like the human person, each human family evolves in its own unique way."[260] Within the system of the nuclear family are three subsystems, each with its own interactions and relationships and each with its own influence on the development of the child: the marital subsystem, the parent-child subsystem, and the sibling subsystem. Yet within this system of subsystems, the primacy of the marital relationship must be recognized. As Nichols and Everett point out, "Inside the nuclear family, it seems necessary for the adult marital partners to form a solid coalition between themselves and to maintain the boundaries between the generations, that is, between themselves as marital partners and parents and their offspring, in order to provide maximally for the development of children."[261]

Thus, it should not come as a surprise that children who experience the destruction of their family and the transformation of their living patterns as their parents' divorce also experience profound and, in many cases, long-lasting emotional and developmental problems. It is important to mention here the most important American study of the emotional and psychological effects of divorce upon children, Judith Wallerstein and Joan Kelley's five-year study of divorced families entitled *Surviving the Breakup*. Upon learning of their parents' intention to divorce, the initial reaction of over 90 percent of the children was "an acute sense of shock, intense fears, and grieving, which the children found overwhelming." Following the divorce, "two-thirds of the children, especially the younger children, yearned for the absent parent . . . with an intensity (which the researchers described as) profoundly moving." Five years after the divorce, 37 percent of the children were moderately to severely depressed, were intensely unhappy and dissatisfied with their lives, and their unhappiness was greater at five years than it had been at one and a half years after the divorce. Ten years after the divorce, 41 percent of the children were doing poorly; "they were entering adulthood as worried, underachieving, self-deprecating, and sometimes angry young men and women. The rest were strikingly uneven in how they adjusted to the world; in the opinion of the researchers, "it is too early to say how they will turn out."[262]

Wallerstein and Kelly reported that: "For children and adolescents, the separation and its aftermath was the most stressful period of their lives. . . . Over one half of the entire group was distraught, with a sense that their lives had been completely disrupted. Less than 10 percent of the children were relieved by their parents' decision to divorce despite the high incidence of exposure to physical violence during the marriage."[263]

Permit me to relate several more brief excerpts from the Wallerstein and Kelly study: "Children were heavily burdened by their enormous sense of loss. Jay, age five, solemnly announced as he came into the consulting room, 'I have come to talk about death.' More than half of the youngsters were openly tearful, moody, and pervasively sad."[264]

"After his father left the home, Robert sat for many hours sobbing in his darkened room. The father visited infrequently and continued to disappoint the child. When seen by us, Robert offered smilingly, 'I have a grand time on his visits,' and added, unsolicited and cheerily, 'I see him enough.' Only later, in the context of our third interview, would he shamefacedly admit that he missed his father intensely and longed to see him daily and was profoundly hurt by his father's inconstancy."[265]

"Betty, age fourteen, began to sob, 'I am in the middle. It is my struggle. I am loyal to my father and I love my mother. I want to help my mother and I know she needs it."[266]

"Particularly striking in this age group was the yearning for the father. More than half of these children missed their father acutely. Many felt abandoned and rejected by him and expressed their longing in ways reminiscent of grief for a dead parent. Jack appeared unable to play without interrupting himself frequently and turning disconsolately from one activity to another. He told us 'Nothing feels right because daddy isn't home,' adding that before he goes to sleep nightly he prays for his father's return and that he cries in his sleep."[267]

"Jean began her sexual activity at age fourteen [and] continued on a course of sexual involvement with a succession of lovers in the year that followed the divorce. Her primary interest at school at the time of the separation seemed to be flirting with her male teachers. She was aimless, not motivated to develop plans for her own future, preoccupied with anger at her father and with her own sexual activities. Shortly thereafter, she became involved in drinking and drug abuse."[268]

Wallerstein and Kelly concluded: "There is considerable evidence in this study that divorce was highly beneficial for many of the adults. There is, however, no comparable evidence regarding the experience of the children. There is, in fact, no supporting evidence in this five-year study for the commonly made argument that divorce is overall better for children than an unhappy marriage."[269] Wallerstein and Kelly found that "only a few of the children in our study thought their parents were happily married, yet the overwhelming majority preferred the unhappy marriage to the divorce. As the children spoke with us, we found that although many of them had lived for years in an unhappy home, they did not experience the divorce as a solution to their unhappiness, nor did they greet it with relief at the time, or for several years thereafter. Many of the children, despite the unhappiness of their parents, were, in fact, relatively happy and considered their situation neither better nor worse than that of other families around them. They would, in fact, have been content to hobble along. The divorce was a bolt of lightning that struck them when they had not even been aware of the existence of a storm."[270]

While the emotional trauma of divorce for children is long-lasting, it is compounded by the emotional and developmental consequences for children of their losing contact with their fathers following divorce. The disappearance of the father following divorce has become epidemic in the United States with devastating frequency and consequences for children. The National Center for Health Statistics reports that only a little more than one-half of all fathers (55 percent) even receive visitation rights to see their children on a regular basis. But only a small minority of divorced fathers (approximately one-third) who live apart from their children saw them at least once each month. Among the remaining children, 15 percent said they saw their fathers less than once a month and 16 percent report only some contact within the past five years. Tragically, the largest category of children in the study were not those who reported seeing their father once a month, but those who reported not having seen their father in the past five years and many of whom stated that they did not even know where their fathers lived (36 percent).[271]

The father's nurturance, support, and attention are essential to the child's development, self-esteem, and competence. Many middle-aged men and women who continue highly dependent relationships with their mother, who are unable to establish close relationships with others and who encounter substantial difficulties in parenting their children are likely to have been paternally deprived in childhood.[272] "Gender difficulties or problems in later family and sexual functioning are much more common among individuals with childhood history of paternal deprivation."[273] Studies have found that "boys with strong father identifications scored higher on measures of internal moral judgment, moral values and conformity to rules than those with weak feelings of paternal similarity."[274] Boys with weak father identification were found to have less adequate conscience development than those boys with strong father identification. And those boys whose fathers were absent scored lower on a variety of moral indexes including internal moral judgment, guilt after wrongdoing, acceptance of blame, moral values and conformity to rules.[275] A strong father-son relationship enhances not only the moral development of the child, but also his intellectual development. Boys who experienced at least two hours of contact with their fathers each day generally received superior grades in school and performed approximately a year above their grade level on achievement tests. Boys with low levels of father contact generally scored below their grade level on achievement tests and performed at an average level or below in classwork.[276] Armand Nicholi's study of the case histories of hundreds of male students who left Harvard University for psychiatric reasons found a pervasive characteristic: "a marked isolation and alienation from their parents, especially their fathers."[277] Studies have found that as many as 50 percent of adolescents who attempted suicide and nearly as many who succeeded in killing themselves came from homes where the father was absent.[278]

However, the turn to violence by young men as a response to being abandoned by their fathers is not only self-directed, it is more often directed toward the community at large. A case in point was the CBS *60 Minutes* interview in 1993 with convicted Los Angeles gang leader Kody Scott in which he discussed his life of robbery and murder. In the interview, Scott, whose gang name is "Monster," praised his hardworking single mothe but had this to say about his natural but absent, father: "Dick never came . . . I hate him. I hate him because I think about what I could have been, you know. And . . . I can't dig that, man, running out on your kids . . . because I wouldn't have had to go to the street. . . ." How many of the 17 million children living in single-parent homes feel such anger and resentment against their fathers is impossible to say, but that there are countless numbers who do and who take out that anger in anti-social behavior or criminal activity in American cities is beyond question.

Studies of the long-term effects of divorce upon girls provide substantial evidence of profoundly negative effects related to low self-esteem and early sexual promiscuity. One 1972 study of thirteen- to seventeen-year-old girls from intact, divorced, and widowed families found that "all the daughters from divorced families showed more heterosexual patterns and lower self-esteem" as well as "more inappropriate receptiveness and seductiveness toward males, and earlier and more frequent dating and sexual intercourse."[279] The researchers concluded that for girls, the effect of the loss of a father following divorce manifested itself during adolescence "mainly as an inability to interact appropriately with males."[280] A later study of seventeen- to twenty-three-year-old college students who had experienced divorce found that "daughters experiencing early father absence were reported as being more accepting in their attitudes toward sexual intercourse."[281]

Already in some American cities a majority of children are growing up in single-parent homes and some researchers estimate that after the year 2000, approximately half of the young Americans will have grown up without the care and daily presence of their fathers.

A new study of 47,000 public school students in 121 communities throughout the United States found that children of single parents face greater risks to their health and welfare than did children in two-parent families. Among other findings, children in single-parent homes were found to be more than twice as likely to be sexually active and twice as likely to attempt suicide than those from two-parent families.[282] After reviewing the research evidence regarding single-parent households, Urie Bronfenbrenner concludes that the

> results indicate that, controlling for associated factors such as low income, children growing up in (father absent) households are at a greater risk for experiencing a variety of behavioral and educational problems, including extremes of hyperactivity or withdrawal, lack of attentiveness in the classroom, difficulty in deferring gratification, impaired academic achievement, school misbehavior, absenteeism, dropping out, involvement in socially alienated peer groups, and, especially, the so-called "teenage syndrome" of behaviors that tend to hang together—smoking, drinking, early and frequent sexual experience, a cynical attitude toward work, adolescent

pregnancy, and, in the more extreme cases, drugs, suicide, vandalism, violence, and criminal acts. Most of these effects are much more pronounced for boys than for girls."[283]

In early 1980, a survey of fifty-eight studies of parental absence and academic achievement found that "children in single-parent families receive lower grades and lower achievement ratings from teachers."[284] The analysis of these studies and others indicate that following divorce there is a "domino effect" producing definitive behavioral and intellectual deficits, including significant impairment of cognitive achievements.[285] These findings were consistent with those reached by Wallerstein and Kelly regarding the long-term effects of divorce. Wallerstein and Kelly presented "a grim picture" of these children and identified "a distinct subgroup of intensely angry adolescents" who "grew even angrier as they moved into adolescence." Among adolescent males this anger manifested itself in anti-social and self-destructive ways and even though fewer females were as disturbed and angry as were males, there were still significant numbers who were intensely angry five years after their parents' divorce. However, the anger of adolescent girls showed itself in "increased sexual activity and promiscuity" causing researchers to conclude that young females "perceive this type of acting-out as more hostile and more rejecting of parents than failure at school."[286]

In 1993, the National Commission on America's Urban Families reported, "The family trend of our time is the deinstitutionalization of marriage and the steady disintegration of the mother-father child-raising unit. This trend of family fragmentation is reflected primarily in the high rate of divorce among parents and the growing prevalence of parents who do not marry. No domestic trend is more threatening to the well-being of our children and to our long-term national security."

Although the developmental problems of children following divorce are profound and long-lasting, research undertaken in the

United States for the National Center for Health Statistics suggests that as bad as the situation in the single parent home following divorce may be, the situation of children living with their biological mother and a stepfather in what is currently termed "blended" or "reconstituted" families may be worse. Among children living with both biological parents 5.5 percent were found to have a learning disability; that figure rose to 7.5 percent for children living with their biological mother only; but it increased to 9.1 percent for children living with their biological mother and a stepfather. Among children living with both parents, 8.3 percent were found to have a significant emotional or behavioral problem; among children living with their biological mother only, the figure was 19.1 percent; and for children living in a "reconstituted" family, the number rose to 23.6 percent. Again, among children living with both biological parents, 14.6 percent were found to have had one or more developmental, learning, or emotional problems; among children living with their biological mother only, the figure increased to 24.8 percent; and for children living in a "reconstituted" family, the number increased to 29.6 percent.[287]

Significantly, the research found a variety of childhood pathologies occurring with two to three times more frequency in so-called "blended" families than they did in families in which both biological parents were present; and "blended" families consistently sustained higher frequencies of such pathologies than did homes in which only the biological mother was present. These results are consistent with the 1988 National Health Interview Survey on Child Health which assessed data from 17,110 American children nationwide.[288] This survey found "an excess risk of negative health and performance indicators among children who did not live with both biological parents,"[289] which in turn were consistent with the findings of the 1981 NHIS-CH survey.[290]

Earlier studies have also found negative indicators of child development linked with single parenthood or divorce, including lower levels of academic achievement, aggression, anxiety, stress, depression, and other behavior problems.[291] However, what is new in the more recent studies is that they have "found almost no statistically significant differences in terms of physical health, school performance, or behavioral problems among children living with formerly married mothers, never married mothers, or mothers and stepfathers."[292] Certainly emotional and behavioral difficulties among children were to be expected following the trauma and conflict of divorce. The findings that emotional risk for children appears relatively constant in all "alternative" living arrangements other than that of the traditional nuclear family of two biological parents, suggests a substantial correlation between the physical and emotional health of children and family structure.[293]

Certainly, as Gesell writes, "each child has a tempo and a style of growth, which are as characteristic of individuality as the lineaments of his countenance."[294] It is also true that each stage in the child's development has "its own individuality, its own growth task, its own climate, its own way of being."[295] Yet this individuality is not independent of family, but rather the product of the interaction between an absolute unique, unrepeatable human being and an equally unique, unrepeatable human family. As Gesell counsels us, we must think of the development of the human child "not as an empty abstraction but as a living process, just as genuine and as lawful as digestion, metabolism, or any physiological process. We must also think of 'the mind' as being part and parcel of a living organism. As such the mind has form, contour, tendency, and direction. It has 'architecture.' It is as configured as the body with which it is identified. It reveals this configuration in modes of reaction, in patterns of behavior."[296]

If the development of the child has 'architecture,' then it is an architecture profoundly dependent upon the joint pillars of two biological parents. The judgment of current scientific research to this effect as reflected by the literature in the field is overwhelming. As Wallerstein and Kelly point out, "the developmental needs of children do not change in accord with changes in the family structure." They continue that, "unfortunately, it appears clear that the divorced family is, in many ways, less adaptive economically, socially, and psychologically to the raising of children than the two-parent family."[297]

The Effects of Legalizing Divorce

What should be clear after nearly thirty years of this revolution in family law and policy is that differences in family structure are not merely harmless alternative lifestyle preferences. Moral choices do have real consequences. The moral harms resulting from so many in society abandoning marriage and the family responsibilities that go with it have had devastating economic, social, and emotional consequences for millions of women and children. Far from being a truly liberating experience, this revolution has instead resulted in economic and emotional dependency for millions of our most vulnerable citizens and neighbors. Society's treatment of marriage and the family based upon it should recognize a basic principle of social justice, which, during the past several decades has been largely neglected; marriage has been respected and given a privileged position in our society because of our longstanding experience that the stable, long-lasting marriage is the best way to nurture, educate, and bring up children. In short, strong marriages are in the best interest of children and society has every right and indeed a duty to ensure that families with children are supported and not burdened by governmental policies.

The legal tendencies we have been discussing have profound consequences for family law and society's view of the nature of marriage. First, recently enacted "no-fault" divorce legislation has radically changed the couple's expectations regarding marriage. A system of divorce at the will of either spouse does more than simply affect exit from marriage. It changes the social "rules" for entry into marriage. A system of "no-fault" divorce rewards the spouse's commitment to individuality and the individual's good. At the same time, "no-fault" divorce laws penalize a spouse's commitment to the common good of the marital community and couple. Because a commitment to the marital community is not protected by the "no-fault" legal environment, such a commitment is made solely at the spouse's own risk.

Thus, the new legal framework actually promotes tendencies that enhance individuality and separation of the marital couple rather than tendencies that support unity and mutuality. Since the "no-fault" legal structure tells the marital couple to invest less in the marital community, it is not surprising that they increasingly expect less from it. With fewer and fewer legal, economic, and social benefits or "returns" from marriage, it is not surprising that more and more couples find less reason to maintain the marital commitment.

Lenore Weitzman concludes that "no-fault" divorce laws actually shift the role of government. She maintains that "the divorce law reforms reflect an underlying shift in the role of the state from a position of protecting marriage (by restricting marital dissolution) to one of facilitating divorce. The new divorce laws," she continues, "adopt a laissez-faire attitude toward both marriage and divorce. They leave both the terms of the marriage contract—and the option to terminate it—squarely in the hands of individual parties." Yet, perhaps most importantly Weitzman argues that "the pure no-fault states also eliminate the traditional moral dimension from the divorce: guilt and innocence, fidelity and faithlessness, no longer affect the granting of the decree or its financial consequences."[298]

As we have seen with the report of the California Governor's Commission on the Family, one explicit goal of no-fault divorce laws was to remove the moral dimension from the decision of whether to grant a divorce. It was hoped that by so doing, the new legislation would avoid the scandal of collusion between the spouses and perjury regarding the very existence of the "fault" claimed in order to obtain the divorce. However, by banishing the moral dimension from the question of divorce, the new divorce laws have eliminated, in a sense, this moral dimension from marriage law itself. The traditional "fault" divorce laws, which recognized adultery as the only ground on which a divorce could be granted, sent a powerful message to those contemplating marriage that fidelity was a very important part of the marriage contract—indeed, from the legal point of view perhaps one of the most important parts. However, under the new divorce laws, this moral commitment has become totally irrelevant. This factor alone may be more responsible for the transformation of the institution of marriage than all the other social and economic factors combined. The new law sends a message to the married couple that is fundamentally unjust: there will be no punishment for the guilty spouse, whether or not his (or her) actions have amounted to desertion, cruelty, physical abuse, or infidelity and, at the same time, there will be no reward or even protection for the innocent spouse.

The weakening of the marital bond is also promoted by government's treatment of marriage, which essentially views marriage not as a unity of two persons or an institution, but essentially as a contractual relationship between two separate and distinct individuals. The conclusion is virtually inescapable that the new divorce laws have transformed marriage from a lifelong commitment to an optional, time-limited contract.[299] Considering the attitude of those who consider marriage to be nothing more than an optional, time-limited agreement, one can appreciate the consistency of their view that it deserves no special recognition under the law.

Clearly, for the U.S. Supreme Court, marriage and the family based upon it are not deserving of any special status, rights, or respect. Instead, the principle that the Court consistently applies to marriage and family issues—the right to privacy—is said to have equal application to the married and non-married alike, since both the married and non-married are interested in protecting their privacy. Thus, the right to privacy has become a powerful weapon to dismantle legal traditions that made important distinctions between the family based upon marriage and other living arrangements.

That tradition, based for the most part upon Christian and natural law presumptions, was marriage and family oriented. By discouraging divorce and making it difficult to obtain, the old system supported self-sacrifice, partnership, and mutual investment in the marital community. But the new family law system is directed away from the family; it promotes self-sufficiency, self-interest, and self-investment. The new system is no longer friendly to the family based upon marriage. It has shifted the legal and economic groundwork against the choice of marriage, childbearing, and motherhood. Under the new assumptions, the woman who makes the choice for marriage and motherhood now does so at great risk.

One law school textbook in the United States describes the shift in family law in these terms: "Perceived as neither a sacrament nor a status necessarily assumed for life, the relationship contemplated by parties is not dissimilar from that of other long-term contracts, such as partnership, cotenancy, and sometimes employment."[300]

In short, contemporary marriage has become something like a speculative joint venture for profit.

The new system has in effect a built-in mechanism for marital instability. Since under the new system the spouses' commitment to mutuality and the marital community is increasingly subordinated to self-interest, the "parties" tend to "invest" less in the marital community and hence derive less from it. The "joint venture" becomes increasingly "speculative" as its "profitability" diminishes.

One measure of this diminishing "profitability" can be seen in the changes regarding the median age of women who marry for the first time. That age has substantially risen since the 1970s from 20.8 years to 23.7 years. Another indication can be found in the fact that the labor force participation rate of married women with children under six years of age rose from 30 percent in 1970 to more than 60 percent by 2005.

Certainly not all labor force participation by women is a result of economic necessity, but most public opinion polls generally agree with a 1990 Gallup Poll, which found that 63 percent of Americans agreed with the statement that the "ideal family situation is one in which the father has a job and the mother stays home and cares for the children." In that same poll 73 percent of Americans thought that children were better off with a mother who is not employed outside the home.

One important aspect of this new feminization of poverty, which I think would more accurately be described as the "maternalization" of poverty, is that the economic consequences of divorce affect the spouses differently. A study conducted at the University of Michigan reported that while divorced men lost 11 percent in real income, divorced women lost 29 percent. More dramatic were results regarding the long-term consequences of divorce: among former spouses studied seven years after divorce, the economic position of former husbands improved by 17 percent while that of former wives decreased by nearly 30 percent.[301] The latest figures published by the Bureau of the Census indicate that families headed by never married or formerly married women account for more than 52 percent of the 13.4 million families with incomes below the poverty level.[302]

What should be clear after twenty years of this revolution in family law and policy is that differences in family structure are not merely harmless alternative lifestyle preferences. Moral choices do have real consequences. The moral harms resulting from so many in society abandoning marriage and the family responsibilities that go with it have had devastating economic, social, and emotional consequences for millions of women and children. Far from being a truly liberating experience, this revolution has instead resulted in economic and emotional dependency for millions of our most vulnerable neighbors.

In building up a culture that fully respects the institutions of marriage and family, it will not suffice to simply speak of the "sacred precincts of the marital bedroom" or to praise marriage as an institution that is "intimate to the degree of being sacred." To view sexual intimacy or one's expectation of privacy associated with it as the defining characteristic of marriage is to misunderstand the precise point on which the unique position of marriage has been based within Western culture.

This tradition views matrimony as a natural institution with one of its principal ends being the good of the offspring. Procreation concerns more than simply the decision to bear or beget a child. It is also a commitment to the upbringing, education, and development of the child. To reduce the procreative end of marriage to merely sexual activity is to fundamentally re-define the meaning of marriage. Having lost the connection between the unitive meaning and the procreative meaning of marriage many contemporary societies easily take the second step of equating sexual activity within marriage with that occurring outside of marriage.

The unique position of marriage in Western culture arose not only as a result of a more complete understanding of procreation, but also as a consequence of the Judeo-Christian insight that the commitment of the spouses to one another was faithful and exclusive until death. This irrevocable (in canon law) and nearly irrevocable (in civil law) gift of one person to another within marriage distinguished it from all other relationships. Yet, it is this commitment of the spouses to treat each other as irreplaceable and nonsubstitutable that is precisely denied by cohabitation outside of marriage. Sexual activity outside of marriage by its very nature communicates to the other that he or she is replaceable and that a substitute may be found in the near future. Outside the marriage bond or within a bond that may be easily dissolved, sexual activity ceases to be the unique gift of one person to another person.[303]

The Western tradition, in holding that one of the principal ends of marriage includes the good of the offspring, developed through time a comprehensive legal structure around the institution of marriage to protect not only the spouses themselves, but also their children. That structure was premised on the realization that there existed a profound connection among the begetting, nurturing and educating of children. To the degree that we are once again able to live according to these fundamental insights and impart them to others, we will be able to establish the foundation for a truly marriage- and family–centered society.

The United Nations is to be commended for the recognition in the Convention on the Rights of the Child that "the child, for the full and harmonious development of his or her personality, should grow up in a family environment" (Preamble), "that the States Parties shall ensure to the maximum extent possible the survival and development of the child" (Art. 6), and that "in all actions concerning children, whether undertaken by public or private social welfare institutions, courts of law, administrative authorities or legislative bodies, the best interests of the child shall be a primary consideration" (Art. 3).[304]

We must now have the courage to insist that those social, economic, and legal structures that encourage both men and women to disinvest in family life or abandon their children must be changed. In particular, we must re-examine laws that facilitate divorce, laws that undermine the institution of marriage as a partnership of mutuality, laws that promote self-sufficiency at the expense of the good of the marital and family community. Such laws cannot co-exist with an authentic cultural commitment to children's welfare.[305] These laws in many ways reflect a fundamental shift in society's priorities—a shift that no longer recognizes children at the highest level of priority. Such laws also reflect a national disinvestment in family life. Some have described this social trend as a national "parent deficit" in which both men and women are equally engaged in a "flight from the traditional nuclear family."[306] If so, then this "parent deficit" is, in turn, the product of a deficient view of what it means to be a person.

Christianity's efforts to understand the human person in light of the Incarnation—especially those efforts leading up to and following Chalcedon—have provided a vision of the human person that grounds both his integrity and autonomy not in isolation but within a community. The greatness of human personhood in the eyes of the Christian is that "a particular being is 'itself'—and not another one—because of its uniqueness, which is established in communion and which renders a particular being unrepeatable as it forms part of a relational existence in which it is indispensable and irreplaceable. That which, therefore, makes a particular personal being be itself—and thus be at all—is in the final analysis communion, freedom and love. . . ."[307]

The human person at the center of his or her personality possesses an "openness of being" constantly seeking to transcend itself in a movement towards communion with another.[308] The ultimate ground of this relational category of human existence is, in the Christian vision, the Trinity. In our world, its watermark is the human family—that cradle for the transcendental journey, which each of us has begun on the way towards a fully human existence— uniquely our own and yet radically dependent upon others. The sign that this journey may be made in a way that is faithful, caring, and enduring is to be found in the stable, monogamous communion of two persons in marriage. It is the responsibility of the law to ensure that this journey may be undertaken with the support and encouragement of the larger community, which, in doing so, makes possible the realization of a society that respects and promotes the true dignity of every human being.

26.

The Testimony and Presence of Grandparents in the Family

SPEECH

Given at the Plenary Assembly of Pontifical Council
for the Family
"Grandparents: Their Witness and Presence in the Family"
April 2008, Vatican City

Family—in a larger, generational view—provides a unique shape to culture. At this time, the cultural changes that spanned the years have created a fascinating point in history in which the experience of older generations differed greatly from those of younger generations. This is certainly true in terms of technological changes over the decades. But it is also true in terms of cultural norms, the experience of wars internationally, and the practice of formal religion, which has largely diminished with each passing generation. But the bond of love between grandparents and grandchildren still holds a uniquely powerful place in the family and, because of its place in the family, a uniquely powerful role in shaping culture and the future.

Creating a Human Context of Love

Not far from here in the Roman Forum, one of the oldest Latin church representations of Saint Anne appears in Santa Maria Antiqua. Devotion to this grandmother of Christ, we are told, was popular almost exclusively in the Eastern church until the fifteenth century, making the Latin work's subject an even more intriguing choice. Interestingly, the artist, unknown but skilled, digressed from the Byzantine styles of the Eastern church, and instead painted this mother and daughter standing beside one another with what scholars have called vivid faces with "astonishing lifelike appearances."[309]

When discussing the experience of grandparenting in the United States from a Catholic perspective, it is tempting, like the artist, to draw out the humanity of the grandmother of the divine babe or to speculate how Saint Joachim may have spoken to his daughter when, like the parents of a million and a half American women this year, he and his wife found an unmarried daughter pregnant and themselves unexpected grandparents.[310] And perhaps in these speculations some wisdom could be found. It might surprise us then that in the Middle Ages, Saint Peter Damian criticized those who popularized the cult of these Jewish grandparents of the Christ for ignoring the biblical genealogies in favor of the vividly personal stories found in the apocryphal gospels.[311] Since the Bible did not mention them, he argued, it was superfluous to draw attention to grandparents. Saint Peter Damian seems to have won the day.

But Saint Peter Damian, nonetheless, seems to suggest something important to evaluating the experience of grandparenting: grandparenting is a thoroughly human interest. However family-oriented the theology of God may be, there is no spiritual model and little theological development for grandparents in the tradition. However family-oriented the theology of God may be, the vocabulary of grandparenting is absent, deferring to the immediacy of the language of the nuclear family. We speak of the Father and the Son, of Mary our Mother, and of living with each other as brother and sisters of an unmarried Christ. All this language draws on the nuclear family in all its immediacy and intimacy. Grandparenting, in contrast, is explicitly defined by degrees of separation that come about not through one's own will and action, but from that of another. Something in the experience of the grandparent or grandchild is too indirect, too subordinate, and too dependent on temporality to express the full possibilities of an intimate relationship with a God who is Love itself.

This thoroughly human nature appears in a unique way, however, as crucial to supporting love within the family in the second creation account in Genesis. In that account, the foundations for grandparenthood are established or implied almost as soon as is human love. When Adam recognizes Eve as flesh of his flesh and names her woman, his search for—and God's gift of—a relationship is described only in words of companions and helpers. But when the moment comes to introduce their marital union, Scripture does not describe this first union of parentless being. Rather, it gives their union a historical view, as a union that is a participant in and icon of the progression of generations: "Wherefore a man shall *leave his father and mother*, and shall cleave to his wife."[312] There is the sense that a marriage without family is a marriage created out of nothing, out of a void. It is not an isolated relationship, but a living part of a living context of love. Ultimately, God is this generative context of all love; but on earth, grandparents participate in creating and making visible this context of love for the nuclear family.

As parents see children taking on fatherhood and motherhood, they have to decide on what message they will live by in order to reaffirm the prerequisite for a life of complete love. Pope Benedict expressed this to us two years ago in Valencia, when he called grandparents "guarantors of . . . affection and tenderness" and encouraged them in being the "memory and richness of families" that offer youth "the perspective of time," and for "bearing witness to their faith at the approach of death."[313] Grandparents can offer the wisdom of age in better understanding the theological virtues of faith, hope, and love (charity) not only to their grandchildren but also to their adult children. These virtures make life truly human as we experience the challenges presented throughout our life. This is a message no generation can ignore or fail to pass on without consequences.

The American Context: Love

To some degree, it is impossible to discuss parenthood and grand-parenthood without considering love. Unfortunately, it is impossible to discuss *American* parenthood and grandparenthood without also considering divorce. This includes not just legal dissolutions of marriage, but the separations brought by incarceration, by single-parenting, by immigration, by workaholism, or the constraints of poverty. Statistically, we know that many of these are linked; demographically, we know these burdens fall heavily upon ethnic minorities. For example, 1 in 100 people in the United States is either in jail or in prison; half of these are parents. But among black men between ages twenty and thirty-four—in other words, the prime age for marrying and fathering—one in nine are behind bars. *One in nine!* This presents an enormously burdensome situation on women and their children—not to mention on the men themselves.

As the nuclear family itself is pulled apart in this way, the presence of grandparents is crucial to the survival of not just the general concept of family to these children, but of the specifics of stability, human dignity, and love itself. Thankfully, in a growing number of these cases, grandparents are answering to this need in an intimate way by living with their grandchildren. And although this is still the minority of cases, so significant has this become that it has gained recognition outside of private research, and, for the first time in 2000, the U.S. census gathered information on co-resident grandparenting. What it found was that since 1970, the percent of children age eighteen living in the same house as their grandparents has more than doubled; in three out of four of these households, the grandparents are the primary caregivers to children. Considering that grandparents have no legal obligation, this is a truly remarkable testament to love.

But as the divorce generation ages, grandchildren are not just negotiating the divorces of their parents, but their grandparents as well. According to Merrill Silverstein, "nearly half of U.S. families with children have at least one set of grandparents who have been divorced."[314] This causes another new focus on grandparenting, as children might have more grandparent figures than is natural.

To these children, family can seem like the mythic Hydra of Hercules' labors, when in the place of every severed marriage, two more can take its place, and to a child, it can seem impossible. Although relatively little research has been done on the effects of divorcing grandparents, what has been done has important implications for the lives of the grandchildren. One study by Paul Amato and John Cheadle studied the effects on education, and found that even "after taking grandparent education into account, grandparent divorce was associated with an average nine-month reduction in education for each grandchild."[315] The authors of the study considered the educational deficit even more remarkable considering that only one-in-ten of these grandchildren had been born when the divorce took place. In other words, even when the grandchildren did not experience their grandparents' divorce, there were still dramatic effects. It is not only the divisive act of divorce that leaves a mark, but simply having a grandparent who took part in a divorce, and having a parent who is a child of divorce.

To you gathered here today, thankfully I do not have to repeat the enormity of the consequences of divorce. Speaking of the American grandparenting experience only as it fills in the gaps of deconstructed families is perhaps unfair, and defining it this way it is rather like framing the negatives of your wedding photos. These situations, after all, are by no means the majority. Yet as these trends continue to grow, their continued prevalence requires renewed and redoubled efforts to give a positive message of life, marriage and family.

The American Context: Wisdom in Age

Grandparents contribute to giving a positive message of life by speaking from their experience to convey the worth of life and the dignity of age. Humans are the only animals who live a third of their lifetimes after the age of childbearing. Yet in popular culture, this "agefullness" is often rejected within the family. These are two strange and seemingly contrary set of trends taking place in the United States now, often simultaneously. On one hand, the presence and visibility of grandparents is increasing. On the other hand, age is being rejected as the mature life is forced into a reversion to a life of unattached youth. The multi-billion dollar industry of cosmetics, surgery, overflowing old-age homes, often out of sight and out of mind from families, even the interest in cloning to perpetuate personal traits—these try to push aging from our experience. These attempts to avoid the signs of age from life convey an unhealthy relationship with temporality. It is a rejection of temporality as part of our human experience. It sets us apart from God and rejects as well life's finality and ultimately life's dignity. It gives a fragmented view of the human experience.

For the 1994 World Day of Peace, Pope John Paul II said, "You grandparents, who with the other family members represent unique and precious links between the generations, make a generous contribution of your experience and your witness in order to link the past to the future in a peaceful present."[316] Grandparents are, in a very real sense, the guardians not only of temporality, but also continuity.

In the U.S., how grandparents respond to this responsibility will have a tremendous impact as the American population ages; paralleling the trends you are familiar with in Europe, by 2030, an estimated 70 million Americans will be over the age of sixty-five, double what it is now.[317] Right now, this means that grandchildren have many years of exposure to old age through the long lives of their grandparents. However, this unique time will soon change. As marriage and childbearing continues to be delayed, this relationship will shift. In a generation or two, while the lifespan will remain long, the spacing between generations will increase, partially undoing the current trend. In the past thirty years, the average age of the mother at first birth rose from twenty years old to twenty-four; among women of higher education and career expectations, that age rises an additional five years, for a total of nine years difference from the 1970s. And this is only one generation—unless something changes, and a grandchild of a highly educated women can lose ten to twenty years of knowing their grandparent. Their grandparents, on average, will be older than grandparents are now. And that generation of grandparents—who right now are in their youth—are in danger of hearing and accepting the message that old age has little dignity and less worth. Certainly, this is the extreme case, but this is a societal trend that grandparents now can work to prepare for. It is important during this window of long grandparenting, of younger grandparents, to decide what message they will give their grandchildren.

The Faith, in the Lives of Grandparents

Before his election to the papacy, Cardinal Ratzinger wrote an article for *Communio* "On Hope," in which he cautioned about the temptation to "spend one's whole life missing the point, falling into alienation, drowning in the secondary."[318] While this is sometimes more associated with youth, this applies just as much to the elderly. Grandparents are, in a way, a mirror in which their children and grandchildren see their own possible future. If a young person is going through a difficult time, they often ask "is this all there is to life" and might look to their grandparents for an answer. Grandparents are expected to have found some meaning in life. Actually, with suicide being the leading cause of death among ten- through nineteen-year-olds, grandparents are *begged* to have found the meaning of life.[319] Grandparents are begged to give witness to a life that is not "missing the point, falling into alienation, [or] drowning in the secondary." In infirmity, they must be able to express a hope that "consists in the human need for something that goes beyond all human ability."[320] After a life of experience, they must not only say "Nothing under the sun is new,"[321] but also to speak of one who makes all things new.[322]

Perhaps the American population can find inspiration from the early Christian church in Saint Basil the Great. Brought up in a family situation not unlike many Americans, much of his youth was spent being raised by his mother and his paternal grandmother. In his case, all of his paternal figures had died—of age, hardship, or execution under the emperor Diocletian. In a letter, he gives an image of the wisdom he found as a youth:

> What clearer evidence can there be of my faith, than that I was brought up by my grandmother, blessed woman . . . the celebrated Macrina who taught me the words of the blessed Gregory; which, as far as memory had preserved down to her day, she cherished herself, while she fashioned and formed me, while yet a child, upon the doctrines of piety.[323]

Aside from the spiritual nature of Macrina's message, we see in Saint Basil a reverence for her use of her experience. When an older person affirms the worth of experiences in youth, it should not simply be considered reminiscence, but rather an affirmation that life is not simply comprised of experiences, but that life is enriched by experiences.

Conclusion

This brings us to an important place with regard to grandparenting, in which both generations share the same message, but receive it differently from each other. It is important, because this commonality reaffirms the human experience, human dignity, and the enduring nature of love. Perhaps this message was best said on this day forty years ago by the Reverend Martin Luther King. In a powerful speech of charity and hope, he recalled the good reformations of the nation, and he said

> I don't know what will happen now. We've got some difficult days ahead. But it doesn't matter with me now. Because I've been to the mountaintop. And I don't mind. Like anybody, I would like to live a long life. Longevity has its place. But I'm not concerned about that now. I just want to do God's will.[324]

Dr. King was a man in his forties then. What Martin Luther King did not know as he spoke these words of hope and longevity, was that the very next day he would be assassinated. But his messages of hope and charity, and the fundamental goodness of life, and the trust in good triumphing over evil, have resonated with Americans for decades—for a reason. Because, regardless of the youth's uncertain future, or written past, this message does not change. It is the message that grandparents are in the unique place of being able to give strongest, because they speak it not out of motives for change, but from the context of love. More than anything, through this, by living and exemplifying this message, American grandparents—and all grandparents—are called not to be just a supportive background, but to be a context in the truest sense of the word, to be *contextus*, to be "joined together" with and for the family.

Conclusion

*"For, the idea of a nation is not what it thinks of itself in time,
but instead what God thinks of it in eternity."*

—VALDIMIR SERGEYEVICH SOLOVYEV, 1888

This book begins by quoting an American president and asking, "What should America be?" It concludes with this quote from a Russian mystic and the suggestion that as a nation, we have not seen Solovyev's insight as an either-or proposition. Our history is better considered in terms of both time and eternity. Most Americans readily agree that we are "one nation under God." Asked what that means, many will likely reply that the phrase affirms the Declaration of Independence and its rejection of absolutist government—or, as John F. Kennedy put it, our rights come not from the generosity of the state but from that of our creator.

Rather than a religious reduction, this claim about the origin of rights rests on the reality that, as David Schinder writes, "Love is the basic act and order of all things because all things are created by God," and from this it follows that the fundamental *truth* of all things is rooted in the generosity of God.[325] Love is thus an ontological and theological reality. This presents a special responsibility for everyone, not only for Christians. Pope John Paul II sought to elevate our thinking by proposing the idea of "a civilization of love."[326] Indeed, as Pope Benedict XVI states in his first encyclical, *God is Love,* the revelation of a God who loves is made first to Israel, who is chosen among all the nations. He writes, "The love-relationship between God and Israel consists at the deepest level, in the fact that he gives her the *Torah,* thereby opening Israel's eyes to man's true nature and showing her the path leading to true humanism."[327] Jesus summarizes this history in the great commandment to love the Lord with all one's heart and to love one's neighbor as one's self (Matt. 22:37–39).

Thus, Tolstoy's crucial observation in *War and Peace,* "Everything that I understand, I understand only because I love,"[328] still requires seeing what is so necessary today—understanding reality as a gift of the God who loves. Love is more than affection or a moral imperative. It both opens our eyes and lets us see that love itself is the basic God-given order of things.

America today is deeply divided, and many of our fellow citizens fear the nation's center is no longer capable of holding. What role do faith communities have in building for the future? This brings us again to a civilization of love as the response to the God who loves and to the person whose destiny and meaning is to be found in love. Dr. King's challenge still rings true today: do we have the courage to "cut off the chain of hate . . . by projecting the ethics of love to the center of our lives"?[329] If people of faith have that courage, then their witness will be powerful and radiate a new spirit of social friendship in both our culture and our politics and bring us all closer to the promise of America. This witness depends upon the robust exercise of our liberties, and that is why we have always rightfully regarded them as sacred.

Endnotes

Acknowledgments

1. John Paul II, *Arise, Let Us Be on Our Way* (New York: Warner Books, 2004), 55.

SECTION 1

2. Charles Péguy, *Temporal and Eternal*. Translated by Alexander Dru. (New York: Harper and Brothers, 1958), 131. Quoted in Luigi Giussani et al. *Generating Traces in the History of the World: New Traces of the Christian Experience* (Montréal: McGill-Queen's University Press, 2010).

3. Beyond the supreme knights' respective records of service, the Order's incorporators and members of the first council showed a dedicated and diverse record of engagement in the civic, political, and municipal life of the city, state, and country. This included a member of the General Assembly of Connecticut and future New Haven mayor, a fire commissioner, a constable, an alderman, and a councilman, as well as others involved in local politics and elections. Alfred Downes, for whom Father McGivney stepped up as guardian, went on to take a pivotal PR role In New York politics as a *New York Times* political reporter. His brother, Edward Downes, served as city clerk and later became Consul for the United States stationed in Amsterdam.

4. As Daniel Colwell, the long-serving National Secretary and original incorporating member, would recall: "It was designed to unify American Catholic citizens of every national and racial origin in a social and fraternal organization, giving scope and purpose to their aims as Catholics and as Americans, whether in developing the social and fraternal spirit that should exist among those who are sons of the same Church and citizens of the same republic, or in furthering great educational and religious enterprises undertaken by the Church in America."

5. As reported: 180 in 2015, 250 in 2016, 275 in 2018.

6. Jonathan Luxmoore, "Religious rights group deplores 'anti-Christian hostility' in France," *Catholic Philly*, Feb. 15, 2019. http://catholicphilly.com/2019/02/news/world-news/religious-rights-group-deplores-anti-christian-hostility-in-france/

Chapter 1

7. Pope Benedict XVI, "Address to the Bishops of the United States of America on their '*Ad Limina*' Visit" (Consistory Hall, Vatican City, January 19, 2012).

8. Thomas Paine, "Rights of Man," in *Rights of Man; Common sense; and other political writings* (New York: Oxford University Press, 1998), 137.

9. Steven Waldman, *Founding Faith: How Our Founding Fathers Forged a Radical New Approach to Religious Liberty* (New York: Random House, 2008), 114–115.

10. James Madison, "Memorial and Remonstrance against Religious Assessments" (1785), in *Writings*, edited by Jack N. Rakove (New York: Library of America, 1999), 30.

11. Ibid.

12. Rev. Martin Luther King, "Letter from a Birmingham Jail" (University of Pennsylvania, African Studies Center <http://www.africa.upenn.edu/Articles_Gen/Letter_Birmingham. htm>l)

13. James Madison or Alexander Hamilton. "Federalist No. 51: The Structure of the Government Must Furnish the Proper Checks and Balances Between the Different Departments" (from the New York Packet, February 8, 1788), *The Federalist Papers*. (Library of Congress, "The Federalist Papers" <http://thomas.loc.gov/home/histdox/fed_51.html>)

14. Benedict XVI, "Address to the Bishops of the United States on their *'Ad Limina'* Visit," (January 19, 2012).

15. Paul Ricoeur, *Freud and Philosophy: An Essay on Interpretation* (New Haven: Yale University Press, 1970), 33.

16. Pope Benedict XVI, "Address to the Bishops of the United States."

17. Stephen L. Carter, *The Culture of Disbelief: How American Law and Politics Trivializes Religious Devotion* (New York: Basic Books, 1993), 122–123.

18. Ibid., 123.

19. Ibid., 273.

20. Ibid., 273–274.

21. Clarence H. Miller, in Thomas More, *The Yale Edition of the Complete Works of St. Thomas More*, vol.14, *De Tristitia Christi* (New Haven: Yale University Press, 1976), 775.

22. G.K. Chesterton, *The Fame of Blessed Thomas More* (London: Sheed and Ward, 1929), 63.

23. Vatican II, *Gaudium et Spes* ('Pastoral Constitution on the Church in the Modern World'), no. 16: http://www.vatican.va/archive/hist_councils/ii_vatican_council/documents/vat-ii_cons_1965127_gaudium-et-spes_en.html

24. Pope Benedict XVI, "Address to the Bishops of the United States."

25. Joseph Ratzinger, "Conscience and Truth" (keynote address of the Tenth Bishops' Workshop of The National Catholic Bioethics Center, February 1991), in Joseph Ratzinger, *On Conscience* (San Francisco: Ignatius Press, 2007), 11–41.

26. Ibid., 16.

27. John Paul II, *Evangelium Vitae* (March 25, 1995).

28. Ibid, no. 95.

29. John Paul II, *Centesimus Annus* (May 1, 1991), no. 13.

30. Ibid., no. 52.

31. Ratzinger, "Conscience and Truth."

32. Newman to the Duke of Norfolk, December 27, 1874, quoted in Ratzinger, *On Conscience*, 23.

33. Ratzinger, *On Conscience*, 25.

34. Ibid., 32.

35. Ibid., 36.

36. Thomas Jefferson, letter to Sr. Marie Theresa Farjon de St. Xavier, May 15, 1804, available at the RJ&L Religious Liberty Archive, <http://www.churchstate law.com/historicalmaterials/images/thomas_jefferson_letter_1804.pdf>

37. James C. Capretta, "Health Care with a Conscience," *New Atlantis* 22 (Fall 2008): 69.

38. Jacques Maritain, *Christianity and Democracy* (San Francisco: Ignatius Press, 2011), see generally ch. 2.

39. Anne Hendershott, "How Support for Abortion Became a Kennedy Dogma", *Wall Street Journal*, January 1, 2009, http://online.wsj.com/article/SB123086375678148323.html

40. Albert R. Jonsen, *The Birth of Bioethics* (New York: Oxford University Press, 2003), 290.

41. Hendershott, "How Support for Abortion Became a Kennedy Dogma."

42. John Courtney Murray, *We Hold These Truths* (Lanham, MD: Rowman & Littlefield, 1960), 150–151.

43. Ibid.

44. Michael Novak, "The Achievement of Jacques Maritain," *First Things* (Dec. 1990).

45. Maritain, *Christianity and Democracy*, 28.

46. Benedict XVI, "Responses of His Holiness Benedict XVI to the Questions Posed by the Bishops" (National Shrine of the Immaculate Conception in Washington, D.C., Wednesday, 16 April 2008), Question 1.

47. Ibid.

48. Joseph Ratzinger, *What It Means to Be a Christian* (San Francisco: Ignatius, 2006), 24–25.

49. Thomas Jefferson, "Freedom of Religion at the University of Virginia," in Saul K. Padover, ed., *The Complete Jefferson* (New York: Duell, Sloan & Pierce, 1943), 958.

50. Ronald Reagan, "Remarks Announcing America's Economic Bill of Rights" (address at the Jefferson Memorial, July, 3, 1987). Available at The Ronald Reagan Presidential Library <http://www.reagan.utexas.edu/archives/speeches/1987/070387a.htm>

Chapter 2

51. John Tracy Ellis, *American Catholicism*, (Chicago: University of Chicago Press, 1956), 47.

52. http://www.archives.gov/nhprc/annotation/march-2002/religion-founding-fathers. html Accessed 2009.

53. Ronald Bayor and Timothy Meagher; *The New York Irish* (Johns Hopkins University Press, 1997), 14.

54. Joseph Ratzinger, *Principles of Catholic Theology: Building Stones for a Fundamental Theology* (San Francisco: Ignatius Press, 1982), 391.

55. Joseph Ratzinger, *Salt of the Earth* (San Francisco: Ignatius Press, 1997), 269.

56. Otto Von Bismarck, in conversation with Meyer Von Waldeck, Aug. 11, 1867. Quoted in *The Oxford Dictionary of Quotations*. Ed. Elizabeth Knowles. (Oxford: Oxford University Press, 1999), 116.

57. For example, *Christifideles Laici*, no. 41: "*Charity towards one's neighbor*, through contemporary forms of the traditional spiritual and corporal works of mercy, represent the most

immediate, ordinary and habitual ways that lead to the Christian animation of the temporal order, the specific duty of the lay faithful."

58. Benedict XVI, Address at the Welcoming Ceremony, Apostolic Journey to the United States, White House, Washington D. C., April 16, 2006. *https://w2.vatican.va/content/benedict-xvi/en/speeches/2008/april/documents/hf_ben-xvi_spe_20080416_welcome-washington.html*

59. Benedict XVI, Message to the Youth of the World on the Occasion of the 22nd World Youth Day, 2007. Vatican, January 27, 2007. *http://w2.vatican.va/content/benedict-xvi/en/messages/youth/documents/hf_ben-xvi_mes_20070127_youth.html*

Chapter 3

60. http://www.washingtonpost.com/wp-dyn/content/article/2011/02/18/AR2011021803251.html

61. Ratzinger, *Principles of Catholic Theology*, 391.

SECTION 2

Chapter 4

62. Francis, Address of the Holy Father, Meeting with the members of the General Assembly of the United Nations Organization, United Nations Headquarters, New York. September 2, 2015. http://w2.vatican.va/content/francesco/en/speeches/2015/september/documents/papa-francesco_20150925_onu-visita.html

63. Francis, Homily at Santa Marta, Vatican. Reported and quoted by Catholic News Agency, "Pope Francis urges Armenian Catholics to remember their martyrs," Vatican City, September 7, 2015. https://www.catholicnewsagency.com/news/pope-francis-urges -armenian-catholics-to-remember-their-martyrs-46104

64. Ibid.

65. United Nations, Convention on the Prevention and Punishment of the Crime of Genocide, Article II.

66. Philip Jenkins, *The Lost History of Christianity: the thousand-year golden age of the church in the Middle East, Africa, and Asia—and how it died.* (New York : HarperOne, 2008), 162.

67. Paul VI, Message for the Celebration of the World Day of Peace, January 1, 1972. http://w2.vatican.va/content/paul-vi/en/messages/peace/documents/hf_p-vi_mes_19711208_v-world-day-for-peace.html

68. https://www.reuters.com/article/us-pakistan-assassination/militants-say -killed-pakistani-minister-for-blasphemy-idUSTRE7211GH20110302

69. Daniel Philpott, "Neither Reformation nor Enlightenment: The Seeds of Religious Freedom Within Islam." *The Public Discourse.* January 31, 2017. https://www.thepublicdiscourse. com/2017/01/18471/; Quoting Quran 2.256. The ideas in the article received fuller treatment in Philpott's 2019 book, *Religious freedom in Islam : the fate of a universal human right in the Muslim world today.* (New York : Oxford University Press, 2019).

70. Vatican II, *Dignitatis Humanae*, ("Declaration on Religious Freedom"), no. 2.

71. Ibid., no. 3.

72. Ibid.

73. Ibid., no. 4.

74. Ibid., no. 7.

75. Samuel P. Huntington, *The Third Wave: Democratization in the Late Twentieth Century*. (Norman: University of Oklahoma Press, 1991).

76. Ibid., 77n.

77. Ratzinger, *Principles of Catholic Theology*, 381.

78. Ibid., 391.

Chapter 5

79. Pope Francis used the phrase a number of times, for example, on the centenary of the Armenian Genocide. (Francis, Message of His Holiness Pope Francis on the 100th Anniversary of "Metz Yeghern," April 12, 2015; https://m.vatican.va/content/francescomobile/en/messages/pont-messages/2015/documents/papa-francesco_20150412_messaggio-armeni.html The Message cites the "Common Declaration" of Pope John Paul II and Karekin II, at Holy Etchmiadzin, Armenia, September 2001.

80. Jay Winter, editor, America and the Armenian Genocide 195 (2003) at https://books.google.com/books?id=pnLSRXAXTfcC&lpg=PA198&dq=near%20east%20relief%2025%20million&pg=PP1#v=onepage&q&f=false

81. Joseph Naayem, Shall this Nation Die? xvi (1921) at https://books.google.com/books?id=hokGAQAAIAAJ&lpg=PR16&ots=1wrLicUlSu&dq=%22immediate%20and%20total%20destruction%22%20mesopotamia&pg=PR3#v=onepage&q=%22immediate%20and%20total%20destruction%22%20mesopotamia&f=false

82. Universal Declaration of Human Rights, G.A. Res. 217A, U.N. GAOR, 3rd Sess., 1st plen. Mtg., U.N. Doc A/810 (Dec.12, 1948).

83. International Religious Freedom Act of 1998, 22 USCS §§ 6401–6481 (2016).

Chapter 6

84. Inés San Martín, "Syrian Catholic leader challenges claims Islam is non-violent," Aug. 3, 2016. https://cruxnow.com/global-church/2016/08/03/syrian-catholic-leader-challenges-claims-islam-non-violent/

85. Ibid.

86. John M. Owen, IV, *Confronting Political Islam: Six Lessons from the West's Past* (Princeton: Princeton University Press, 2015), 45.

Chapter 7

87. H.Con.Res 75 in 2016 and HR 390 in 20 "Iraq and Syria Genocide Relief and Accountability Act of 2018."

Chapter 8

88. https://www.theguardian.com/world/2015/dec/24/martin-scorcese-film-silence-martyrdom-japan-hidden-christians

89. Shusaku Endo, *Silence: A Novel,* translated by William Johnston (New York: Picador Modern Classics, 2016), 157.

90. Ibid., 159.

91. This idea is more or less explicitly voiced by Fr. Rodrigues in this conversation: "Christianity and the Church are truths that transcend all countries and territories. If not, what meaning is there in our missionary work?" Endo, *Silence,* 161.

92. Mar Bechara Boutros Rai, "The Ministry of Social Charity," (Bkerke, March 25, 2017) https://sjmaronite.org/files/The-Ministry_of_Social_Charity.pdf

93. Benedict XVI. *Deus Caritas Est.* (December 25, 2005), no. 2.

94. Francis, Regina Caeli Address, May 8, 2016. https://w2.vatican.va/content/francesco/en/angelus/2016/documents/papa-francesco_regina-coeli_20160508.html

95. http://www.express.co.uk/news/world/671524/forgive-them-last-words-of-Christian-girl-burned-alive-by-ISIS-Mosul-Iraq

96. http://abcnews.go.com/International/young-iraqi-christian-refugee-forgives-isis-displacing-family/story?id=35764582

97. http://www.christianitytoday.com/news/2017/april/forgiveness-muslims-moved-coptic-christians-egypt-isis.html

98. http://www.asianews.it/news-en/Shia-leader-thanks-Iraqi-Christians-37645.html

99. Augustine, *City of God,* translated by Marcus Dods, *From Nicene and Post-Nicene Fathers,* First Series, vol. 2. edited by Philip Schaff. (Buffalo, NY: Christian Literature Publishing Co., 1887.) Revised and edited for New Advent by Kevin Knight. http://www.newadvent.org/fathers/120101.htm

Chapter 9

100. "Today we are dismayed to see how in the Middle East and elsewhere in the world many of our brothers and sisters are persecuted, tortured and killed for their faith in Jesus. This too needs to be denounced: in this third world war, waged piecemeal, which we are now experiencing, a form of genocide—I insist on the word— is taking place, and it must end." http://w2.vatican.va/content/francesco/en/speeches/2015/july/documents/papa-francesco_20150709_bolivia-movimenti-popolari.html

101. European Parliament, European Parliament resolution on the systematic mass murder of religious minorities by the so-called 'ISIS/Daesh' February 3, 2016 http://www.europarl.europa.eu/doceo/document/RC-8-2016-0149_EN.pdf?redirect

102. http://www.express.co.uk/news/world/671524/forgive-them-last-words-of-Christian-girl-burned-alive-by-ISIS-Mosul-Iraq

103. http://abcnews.go.com/International/young-iraqi-christian-refugee-forgives-isis-displacing-family/story?id=35764582

104. http://www.asianews.it/news-en/Shia-leader-thanks-Iraqi-Christians-37645.html

SECTION 3

Chapter 14

105. The CDC names heart disease "the leading cause of death for both men and women," taking about 610,000 lives each year in the United States and accounting for 1 in 4 deaths. https://www.cdc.gov/heartdisease/facts.htm. By contrast, as published on the CDC website, the report "Abortion Surveillance—United States 2015" records that 638,169 abortions were performed. Even this figure is an underestimate, since it does not count abortions from 3 out of 52 reporting areas. (Jatlaoui TC, Boutot ME, Mandel MG, et al. Abortion Surveillance—United States, 2015. MMWR Surveill Summ 2018;67(No. SS-13):1–45. DOI: http://dx.doi.org/10.15585/mmwr.ss6713a1)

106. In 2019, the total number of ultrasounds donated by the Knights of Columbus reached 1,000, placed in every state of the United States as well as in Canada, Latin America, and Africa. https://www.kofc.org/en/news/releases/1000-ultrasound-machine-dedicated.html

107. Quoted in the Westminster Collection of Christian Quotations, compiled by Martin H. Manser (Louisville: Westminster John Know Press, 2001).

108. Quoted in Frank M. Chapman's "Introduction" to Theodore Roosevelt, *The Works of Theodore Roosevelt, Vol. 5* (New York: Cosmo Classics, 2006), xvii.

Chapter 15

109. Benedict XVI, Address to participants in an International Congress Organized by the John Paul II Institute for Studies on Marriage and Family, April 5, 2008. http://w2.vatican.va/content/benedict-xvi/en/speeches/2008/april/documents/hf_ben-xvi_spe_20080405_istituto-gpii.html

110. Karol Wojtyla, *Love and Responsibility,* translated by H.T. Willetts (New York: Farrar, Straus and Giroux, 1981), 284–85.

111. John Paul II, *Evangelium Vitae* (1997), no. 99.

112. Ibid., no. 11.

113. Pew Research Center, "Public Takes Conservative Turn on Gun Control, Abortion: Americans Now Divided Over Both Issues," April 30, 2009.

Chapter 16

114. Barack Obama, Commencement Address at University of Notre Dame, May 17, 2009.

115. Oliver Wendell Holmes, Lecture 1 on "Early Forms of Liability" in Oliver Wendell Holmes, *The Common Law* (Boston: Little, Brown and Company, 1881), 1.

116. Henry Kissinger, *A World Restored: Metternich, Castlereagh and the Problems of Peace, 1812–1822* (New York: Mariner Books, 1973), 2–3.

117. Michael Novak, ed., *Democracy and Mediating Structures* (Washington, D.C.: American Enterprise Institute, 1980).

118. Sarah Mendelson, "Dark Days for Civil Society," Foreign Affairs, March 11, 2015.

119. https://www1.compareyourcountry.org/social-expenditure/en/0/547+548/default/2018

120. Robert Samuelson, "Our Giant Welfare State," *Washington Post*, November 25, 2014. https://www.washingtonpost.com/opinions/robert-samuelson-our-giant-welfare-state/2014/11/25/ 28f815bc-74c1-11e4-a755-e32227229e7b_story.html

121. Kissinger, *A World Restored*, 2–3.

122. Stephen Carter, *The Culture of Disbelief: How American Law and Politics Trivialize Religious Devotion* (New York: Basic Books, 1993), 38–39.

123. "Ethics and Culture," *Notre Dame Center for Ethics and Culture Newsletter*, 2013–2014, 3.

124. Francis, Address to the European Parliament, November 25, 2014.

125. Vatican II, *Gaudium et Spes*, no. 17.

126. Franklin D. Roosevelt, Address on Receiving an Honorary Degree from Notre Dame University, December 9, 1935.

Chapter 17

127. http://www.hfea.gov.uk/en/1581.html

128. http://news.bbc.co.uk/2/hi/health /6978384.stm

129. http://www.timesonline.co.uk/tol/news/uk/article2393704.ece

130. Ibid.

131. http://www.zenit.org/article-20429 ? l =english

132. Advanced Cell Technology, "Advanced Cell Technology Announces Use of Nuclear Transfer Technology for Successful Generation of Human Embryonic Stem Cells," press release, November 12, 1998, http://www.advancedcell.com/press-release

133. Paul Ramsey, *Fabricated Man: The Ethics of Genetic Control* (New Haven: Yale University Press, 1970), 151–52.

134. Ibid., 152.

135. *Roe v. Wade*, 410 U.S. 113 (1973).

136. 31 N.Y.2d 194; 286 N.E.2d 887 (1972).

137. John T. Noonan, Jr., *A Private Choice: Abortion in America in the Seventies* (New York: Free Press, 1979), 17.

138. John Paul II, *Roman Triptych Meditations* (Washington, DC: USCCB Publishing, 2003), 21.

139. Ibid., 39.

Chapter 18

140. From Janusz Rolicki, *Edward Gierek: przerwana dekada.* Quoted in John Koehler, *Spies in the Vatican: The Soviet Union's Cold War Against the Catholic Church* (New York: Pegasus Books, 2009) 65.

141. Benedict XVI, Homily for Epiphany, January 7, 2010. http://www.zenit.org/article-27979?l=english

142. Quoted in Jan Józef Lipski, *KOR: A History of the Worker's' Defense Committee in Poland, 1976–1981* (Berkeley: University of California Press, 1985), 334.

143. John Paul II, Angelus Address, February 8, 1998.

144. *Gal. 2:20.*

145. John Paul II, General Audience, October 19, 1988.

146. John Paul II, Angelus Address, May 17, 1981.

147. John Paul II, Angelus Address, May 23, 1981.

148. John Paul II, Address to Sick and Disabled, Fourth World Youth Day, August 19, 1989.

149. John Paul II, Angelus Address, May 29, 1994.

150. http://www.vatican.va/holy_father/john_paul_ii/angelus/1998/documents/hf_jp-ii_ang_08021998_en.html

151. Quoted in Adam Boniecki, *The Making of the Pope of the Millennium*, (Stockbridge, MA: Marian Press, 2000), 355.

152. Boniecki, *The Making of the Pope of the Millennium*, 46–47.

153. John Paul II, Address at a Meeting with the Faithful, Mission Dolores Basilica, San Francisco. September 17, 1987.

154. John Paul II, from his last Angelus address while he lived, delivered by Archbishop Leonardo Sandri to the youth gathered there.

SECTION 4

155. *Civilization of Love: What Every Catholic Can Do to Transform the World* (New York: Harper One, 2008); *Our Lady of Guadalupe: Mother of a Civilization of Love* (New York: Doubleday, 2009).

Chapter 19

156. Martin Luther King, Jr. *Where Do We Go from Here: Chaos or Community* (Boston: Beacon Press, 2010), 64–65.

157. King, *Where Do We Go from Here*, 65.

Chapter 20

158. Augustine, *City of God*, 35.

159. Robert Kennedy, "Statement on the Assassination of Martin Luther King, Jr." Indianapolis, Indiana, April 4, 1968. https://www.jfklibrary.org/learn/about-jfk/the-kennedy-family/robert-f-kennedy/robert-f-kennedy-speeches/statement-on-assassination-of-martin-luther-king-jr-indianapolis-indiana-april-4-1968

Chapter 22

160. Karol Wojtyła , Address to a Conference of Physicians, February 21, 1958 in Adam Boniecki ed., *The Making of the Pope of the Millennium*, 166.

161. Ibid.

162. Maria Faustina Kowalska, *Diary* (Stockbridge, MA: Congregation of Marians of the Immaculate Conception, 1987), 742.

163. John Paul II, *Evangelium Vitae*, no. 99.

164. Post by "Melody," for *The JPII Generation Says "Thank You,"* gathered by the Knights of Columbus for HeadlineBistro, http://www.headlinebistro.com/hb/en/specialtopic/jpII/thanksjpII.html

165. John Paul II, Message for the World Day of Peace 2002, January 1, 2002.

166. Ibid.

167. Ibid.

168. Ibid.

169. John Paul II, *Dives in Misericordia*, no. 15.

170. John Paul II, Message for the World Day of Peace 2002, January 1, 2002, no. 10.

171. Post by "Jeremy Boguslawski," for *The JPII Generation Says "Thank You,"* gathered by the Knights of Columbus for HeadlineBistro, http://www.headlinebistro.com/hb/en/special-topic/jpII/thanksjpII.html

172. John Paul II, Homily for the Beatification of Four Polish Saints, August 18, 2002.

173. Karol Wojtyła, Address to a Conference of Physicians, February 21, 1958. *The Making of the Pope of the Millennium*, 166.

174. John Paul II, Homily for the Beatification of Four Polish Saints .

SECTION 5

175. *John* 1:4.

176. *Matthew* 22:34–40.

177. John Paul II, Message for the World Day of Peace 24, no. 10, http://www.vatican.va/content/john-paul-ii/en/messages/peace/documents/hf_jp-ii_mes_20031216_xxxvii-world-day-for-peace.html

178. Benedict XVI, *Deus Caritas Est* (2005), no. 28b.

179. John Paul II, Homily, Pastoral Visit to Civitavecchia, March 19, 1987, no. 7; http://www.vatican.va/content/john-paul-ii/it/homilies/1987/documents/hf_jp-ii_hom_19870319_concelebrazione-civitavecchia.html

180. Vinko Puljic, at the XIII Ordinary General Assembly of the Synod of Bishops, October 2012, on the New Evangelization for the Transmission of the Christian Faith. Holy See Press Office, *Synodus Episcoporum Bulletin* http://w2.vatican.va/news_services/press/sinodo/documents/bollettino_25_xiii-ordinaria-2012/02_inglese/b09_02.html

181. Leo XIII, *Quod Apostolici Muneris*, no. 8. http://www.vatican.va/content/leo-xiii/en/encyclicals/documents/hf_l-xiii_enc_28121878_ quod-apostolici-muneris.html

182. According to the U.S. Census Bureau, in 2018, 65% of children ages 0–17 lived with two married parents, of which the vast majority—92%—were living with both of their biological/adoptive married parents. https://www.childstats.gov/americaschildren/family1.asp

Chapter 23

183. John Paul II (Karol Wojtyła), *Bellezza e Spiritualita dell'Amore Coniugale*, edited by Ludmiła Grygiel, Stanisław Gryiel, and Przemysław Kwiatkowski. (Siena, Italy: Editrice Cantagalli, 2009). Section "Necessità di uscire dal vicolo cieco" ("Need to get out of the dead end").

184. Vatican II, *Apostolicam Actuositatem* ('Decree on the Apostolate of the Laity'), no. 11.

185. John Paul II, *Familiaris Consortio*, no. 43.

186. Ibid., no. 86.

187. John Paul II (Karol Wojtyła), *Bellezza e Spiritualita dell'Amore Coniugale*, section "Necessità di uscire dal vicolo cieco" ("Need to get out of the dead end").

188. Ibid., section "La perfezione Cristiana nella vita di coppia" ("Christian perfection in a couple's life").

189. Ibid., *Bellezza e Spiritualita dell'Amore Coniugale*, section "La perfezione Cristiana nella vita di coppia" ("Christian perfection in a couple's life").

190. Ibid., *Bellezza e Spiritualita dell'Amore Coniugale*, section "La perfezione Cristiana nella vita di coppia" ("Christian perfection in a couple's life").

191. T.S. Eliot, *The Idea of a Christian Society* (New York: Harcourt, Brace and World, 1940.), 4.

192. John Paul II, *Familiaris Consortio*, no. 11.

193. Ibid.

194. Ibid., no. 15.

195. Ibid.

196. Ibid., no. 14.

197. Ibid., no. 18.

198. Idib., no. 21.

199. Ibid.

200. Ibid., no. 64.

201. Ibid., no. 43.

202. Ibid., no. 42.

203. Ayn Rand, "Faith and Force: Destroyers of the Modern World," Lecture delivered at Yale University, February 17, 1960, in *Philosophy: Who Needs It* (New York: Signet Books, 1984), 67.

204. Ibid., 60.

205. Ayn Rand, *The Virtue of Selfishness* (New York: Signet/New American Library, 1970), 18.

206. Ibid., 26.

207. Ayn Rand, *Philosophy: Who Needs It*, 61.

208. Ayn Rand, *The Virtue of Selfishness*, 39.

209. John Paul II, *Letter to Families*, no. 15.

210. Benedict XVI, *Caritas in Veritate*, no. 3.

211. John Paul II, *Familiaris Consortio*, no. 86.

212. Benedict XVI, Homily at the Beatification of Pope John Paul II, May 1, 2011.

213. Ibid.

214. John Paul II, *Letter to Families*, no. 11.

215. Benedict XVI, *Deus Caritas Est*, no. 28b.

216. Benedict XVI, Address to Participants in the Oil on the Wounds Conference on the Effects of Abortion and Divorce, April 5, 2008, in *Oil on the Wounds*, edited by Livio Melina and Carl A. Anderson (Garden City Park, NY: Square One Publishers, 2011), xii.

217. Benedict XVI, Ad Limina Address to the Irish Bishops, October 28, 2006.

218. John Paul II, *Address to the Assembly of CELAM* (March 9, 1983), quoted in John Paul II, *Ecclesia in America* (January 22, 1999), no. 66.

219. Paul VI, *Evangelii Nuntiandi* (Dec. 8, 1975), no. 41; cited by John Paul II in *The Letter to Families*, no. 23.

220. *The Making of the Pope of the Millennium*, 198.

221. Benedict XVI, *Deus Caritas Est*, no. 28b.

222. Testimony of "Kenneth," posted on *The JPII Generation Says "Thank You,"* at headlinebistro.com

223. Benedict XVI, Address to Catholic Educators, Catholic University of America, April 17, 2008.

224. John Paul II, *Letter to Families*, no. 13.

225. Benedict XVI, *Spe Salvi*, no. 28.

226. Ibid.

227. Benedict XVI, Address to Catholic Educators, Catholic University of America, April 17, 2008.

228. Benedict XVI, "Address at the Second Ecclesial Convention of Aquileia," Pastoral Visit to Aquileia and Venice, May 7, 2011.

229. Ibid.

230. Ibid.

Chapter 24

231. Benito Mussolini, Milan, October 28, 1925. Quoted in David Roberts, *The Totalitarian Experiment in Twentieth-Century Europe* (Abington, England: Routledge, 2006), 526.

232. Carl A. Anderson and William J. Gribbin, *Emblem of Freedom: The American Family in the 1980s* (Durham, N.C.: Carolina Academic Press, 1981), 24.

233. Allan Carlson, "The 'Proletarization' of the American Family," *Persuasion at Work*, (November, 1985), 2.

234. Friedrich Engels, *The Condition of the Working Class in England* (New York: Oxford University Press, 1993), 140.

235. Friedrich Engels, *The Origin of the Family, Private Property, and the State* (New York: Pathfinder, 1972), 94.

236. Ibid., 103.

237. Friedrich Engels, in *The Condition of the Working Class in England* (1845), stated that when

married women enter the industrial labor force, "family life is . . . destroyed and . . . its dissolution has the most demoralizing consequences both for parents and children."

238. Ibid.

239. Igor Shafarevich, *The Socialist Phenomenon* (New York: Harper & Row, 1975), 261.

240. John Stuart Mill, *The Subjection of Women* reprinted in *The Basic Writings of John Stuart Mill* (New York: The Modern Library, 2002), 123.

241. Ibid., 206.

242. Ibid., 222.

243. Ibid., 173–175.

244. Ibid., 209.

245. John Paul II, *L'Osservatore Romano* (English edition) February 13, 1982.

246. Paul Ramsey, *Ethics at the Edges of Life: Medical and Legal Intersections* (New Haven: Yale University Press, 1978), xiv.

247. John Paul II, *Centesimus Annus*, no. 17.

248. Ibid., 213.

249. Ibid., 47.

250. Ibid., 41.

251. Ibid., 46.

252. United Nations, *World Population Prospects: The 2002 Revision*, http://esa.un.org/unpp/p2k0data.asp

253. Laurence J. Kotlikoff and Scott Burns, *The Coming Generational Storm* (Cambridge: MIT Press, 2004), 18.

254. Homily on the Capitol Mall, October 7, 1979. See, John Paul II, *The Pope Speaks to the American Church* (New York: HarperCollins, 1992), 116.

Chapter 25

255. Salvador Minuchin, *Families and Family Therapy* (Cambridge : Harvard University Press, 1974).

256. Eric Erikson, *Childhood and Society* (New York: W.W. Norton and Co., 1963), 247.

257. Talcot Parsons and Robert Bales, *The Family, Socialization and Interaction Process* (Glencoe, IL: Free Press, 1955).

258. William Nichols, and Craig Everett, *Systematic Family Therapy* (New York: Gilford Press, 1986), 92.

259. Ibid., 69.

260. Ibid., 131.

261. Ibid., 104.

262. Judith Wallerstein and Joan Kelley, *Surviving the Breakup: How Children and Parents Cope with Divorce* (New York: Basic Books, 1980); see also, Judith Wallerstein and Sandra Blakeslee,

Second Chances: Men, Women and Children a Decade After Divorce (New York: Ticknor and Fields, 1989).

263. Wallerstein and Kelley, *Surviving the Breakup*, 35.

264. Ibid., 46.

265. Ibid., 73.

266. Ibid., 88.

267. Ibid., 68.

268. Ibid., 94.

269. Ibid., 306.

270. Ibid., 10–11.

271. National Center for Health Statistics, *Advance report of final divorce statistics, 1988*. Monthly Vital Statistics Report, vol. 39, no. 12, suppl. 2. (Hyattsville, MD: Public Health Service, 1991).

272. Henry Biller, *Fathers and Families: Paternal Factors in Child Development* (Westport, CT: Auburn House, 1993), 70–71.

273. Ibid., 71.

274. Ibid., 87; see also, Robert Coles, *The Moral Life of Children* (Boston: Atlantic Monthly Press, 1986).

275. Biller, *Fathers and Families*, 87–88.

276. Ibid., 115.

277. Armand Nicholi, "The Impact of Family Dissolution on the Emotional Health of Children and Adolescents," in *When Families Fail . . . The Social Costs*, edited by Bryce Christiansen (Lanham, MD: University Press of America, 1991), 31.

278. Ibid., 36.

279. Joseph Guttmann, *Divorce in Psychosocial Perspective: Theory and Research* (Hillsdale, NJ: Lawrence Erlbaum Associates, 1993), 175.

280. Ibid.

281. Ibid., 176.

282. "Study finds great risks in single-parent families," *Washington Times*, July 10, 1993 .

283. Urie Bronfenbrenner, "Discovering What Families Do," in *Rebuilding the Nest: A New Commitment to the American Family*, edited by David Blankenhorn, Steven Bayme, Jean Elshtain (Milwaukee, WI: Family Service America, 1990), 34.

284. Guttmann, *Divorce in Psychosocial Perspective*, 186.

285. Ibid., 187.

286. Ibid., 188–189.

287. Nicholas Zill and Charlotte Schoenborn, "Developmental, Learning, and Emotional Problems, Health of Our Nation's Children," National Center for Health Statistics, *Advance Data*, No. 190, Nov. 16, 1990, Tables 1–5.

288. Deborah Dawson, "Family Structure and Children's Health and Well-Being: Data from

the 1988 national Health Interview Survey on Child Health," *Journal of Marriage and the Family,* vol. 53 (August 1991), 573.

289. Ibid., 580.

290. Ibid., see specifically: Nicholas Zill, "Behavior, achievement, and health problems among children in stepfamilies: Findings from a national survey of child health," in E. Mavis Hetherington and Josephine D. Arasteh, editors, *Impact of Divorce, Single Parenting, and Stepparenting on Children* (Hillsdale, NJ: Lawrence Erlbaum Associates, 1988).

291. See, for example: Robert Emery, E. Mavis Hetherington, and L.F. DiLalla, "Divorce children, and social policy," in H.W. Stevenson and A.E. Siegel eds. *Child Development Research and Social Policy* (Chicago: University of Chicago Press, 1985); E. Mavis Hetherington, Martha Cox, and Roger Cox, "Effects of divorce on parents and young children," in M. Lamb ed. *Nontraditional Families: Parenting and Child Development* (Hillsdale, NJ: Lawrence Erlbaum Associates, 1982); and James Peterson and Nicholas Zill, "Marital disruption, parent-child relationships, and behavior problems in children," *Journal of Marriage and the Family,* vol. 48, 295 (1986).

292. Dawson, op. cit., 581.

293. Ibid.

294. Arnold Gesell, Frances Ilg, Louise Ames and Janet Rodell, *Infant and Child in the Culture of Today: The Guidance of Development in Home and Nursery School* (New York: Harper and Row, 1943), 7.

295. Ibid., 40.

296. Ibid., 10.

297. Wallerstein and Kelly, *Surviving the Breakup,* 308.

298. Ibid., 368.

299. Ibid.

300. Walter Weyrauch and Sanford Katz, *American Family Law in Transition* (Washington, DC: Bureau of National Affairs, 1983), 1.

301. *A Growing Crisis,* op. cit., p. 12.

302. United States Bureau of the Census, *Current Population Reports: Consumer Income* (Series P-60, No. 145, 1984), 4.

303. William May, *Sex, Marriage, and Chastity* (Chicago: Franciscan Herald Press, 1981), 77–79.

304. The text of the Convention on the Rights of the Child was adopted by the United Nations General Assembly on November 20, 1989.

305. See generally, Lenore Weitzman, *The Divorce Revolution: The Unexpected Social and Economic Consequences for Women and Children in America* (New York: Free Press, 1985).

306. See, David Popenoe, "Family Decline in America" in *Rebuilding the Nest,* 45.

307. J.D. Zizioulas, "Human Capacity and Human Incapacity: A Theological Exploration of Personhood," *Scottish Journal of Theology,* vol. 28, p. 410 (1973).

308. Ibid., 408.

Chapter 26

309. Catholic Encyclopedia. http://www.newadvent.org/cathen/01538a.htm Encyclopedia Britannica. https://edit.britannica.com/getEditableToc?tocId=69520

310. U.S. Government Center for Disease Control and Prevention, "Unmarried Childbearing" http://www.cdc.gov/nchs/fastats/unmarry.htm

311. Peter Damian, Homily III, for the Birth of the Blessed Virgin Mary.

312. *Gen. 2:24.*

313. Benedict XVI. Vigil of Prayer, at the world Meeting for Families, in Valencia. *July 8, 2006.* http://www.vatican.va/holy_father/benedict_xvi/speeches/2006/july/documents/hf_ben-xvi_spe_20060708_incontro-festivo_en.html

314. http://www.divorcereform.org/all.html

315. http://www.divorcereform.org/all.html#anchor1037643

316. John Paul II, Message for the World Day of Peace, 1994.

317. U.S. Department of Health and Human Services, Administration on Aging. http://www.aoa.gov/press/fact/pdf/ss_stat_profile.pdf

318. Joseph Ratzinger, "On Hope," *Communio.* 1985.

319. U.S. Government Center for Disease Control and Prevention. http://www.cdc.gov/ncipc/osp/data.htm

320. Ratzinger, "On Hope."

321. *Ecc. 1:10.*

322. *Rev. 21:5.*

323. St. Basil. *Basil: Letters and Selected Works.* Letter 203, "Letter to the Neocaesareans," Section 6. Translated by Philip Schaff / Blomfield Jackson. Grand Rapids, Michigan: Eerdmans Publishing Company. Christian Classics Ethereal Library Online. http://www.ccel.org/ccel/schaff/npnf208.ix.ccv.html

324. Martin Luther King, Jr., "I've Been to the Mountaintop" Speech. http://www.american-rhetoric.com/speeches/mlkivebeentothemountaintop.htm

Conclusion

325. David L. Schindler, *Ordering Love: Liberal Societies and the Memory of God* (Grand Rapids, MI: William B. Eerdmans Publishing Co., 2011), 5.

326. Pope John Paul II, "Message for the Celebration of the World Day of Peace: Dialogue Between Cultures for a Civilization of Love and Peace," January 1, 2001.

327. Pope Benedict XVI, *Deus Caritas Est,* (2006) no. 9.

328. Leo Tolstoy, *War and Peace,* translated by Louise and Aylmer Maude (London: Everyman's Library, 1911), vol. 3, 216.

329. Martin Luther King, Jr., "Nonviolence and Racial Justice," *Christian Century,* February 6, 1957.

Credits

Page 105. "The Next Big Threat to Iraq's Christians: Iran-backed militias are keeping minority groups from returning home post-ISIS." Op-ed, *Wall Street Journal*, April 12, 2019.

Page 108. "ISIS Crimes Against Christians Amount to Genocide: Canada should lead on the question of genocide by ISIS, rather than following a UN commission's misguided exclusion of Christians from such a designation." Op-ed co-authored with Archbishop Bashar Warda (Chaldean Catholic Archbishop of Erbil, Iraq). *Vancouver Sun Times*, August 5, 2015.

Page 111. "A Year Ago We Declared ISIS Genocidal. Why Are Its Victims Still Waiting for Aid?: Time is running out to preserve these historic communities." Op-ed, *Washington Post*, March 21, 2017.

Page 115. "A Mass Christian Exodus from the Middle East Would Be a Catastrophe." Op-ed, *New York Post*, November 15, 2019. Reprinted with permission.

Page 180. "MLK's Example Holds the Answers to Both Racism and Political Violence." Op-ed co-authored with Rev. Eugene F. Rivers, III. *Time Magazine*, October 18, 2017.

Page 195. "After Today, the 'Catholic Vote' Should Matter More, Not Less." Op-ed, *Crux*, November 8, 2016. Reprinted with permission.

About the Author

Carl Anderson holds degrees in philosophy and law. During the Reagan Administration, Anderson served in various positions of the Executive Office of the President of the United States, including as special assistant to the president and acting director of the White House Office of Public Liaison, as well as serving on the U.S. Commission on Civil Rights. Since 2000, Anderson has served as the Chief Executive Office and Chairman of the Board of the world's largest fraternal service organization, the Knights of Columbus. As Supreme Knight, he has initiated life-saving programs worldwide and led the Knights to record-breaking levels of annual giving, including 77 million volunteer hours and $187 million in charity to address needs at every level, from local communities to international natural disasters. A sought-out advisor and popular speaker, he has extensive experience as a member of many Vatican commissions, and has appeared on numerous national radio and television shows. He is also the author and co-author of five books, including the bestseller *A Civilization of Love*. All proceeds from the sale of this book will go to support Knights of Columbus charities. For more information on the work of the Knights of Columbus, please visit: KofC.org.